The Excellent Mind

The Excellent Mind

Intellectual Virtues for Everyday Life

NATHAN L. KING

OXFORD

UNIVERSITY PRESS

OXFORD
UNIVERSITY PRESS

Oxford University Press is a department of the University of Oxford. It furthers
the University's objective of excellence in research, scholarship, and education
by publishing worldwide. Oxford is a registered trade mark of Oxford University
Press in the UK and certain other countries.

Published in the United States of America by Oxford University Press
198 Madison Avenue, New York, NY 10016, United States of America.

Library of Congress Cataloging-in-Publication Data
Names: King, Nathan L., 1976– author.
Title: The excellent mind : intellectual virtues for everyday life / Nathan L. King.
Description: New York, NY, United States of America : Oxford University Press, 2021. |
Includes bibliographical references and index.
Identifiers: LCCN 2020032332 (print) | LCCN 2020032333 (ebook) |
ISBN 9780190096250 (hbk) | ISBN 9780190096267 (paperback) |
ISBN 9780190096281 (epub)
Subjects: LCSH: Virtue epistemology. | Virtues. | Character. |
Education—Philosophy.
Classification: LCC BD176 .K56 2021 (print) |
LCC BD176 (ebook) | DDC 128/.3—dc23
LC record available at https://lccn.loc.gov/2020032332
LC ebook record available at https://lccn.loc.gov/2020032333

DOI: 10.1093/oso/9780190096250.001.0001

Paperback printed in Canada by Marquis Book Printing
Hardback printed by Bridgeport National Bindery, Inc., United States of America

For my parents, Jim and Dede King,
with love and gratitude

Contents

PART III: PUTTING ON VIRTUE

Preface

My thinking about the topic of this book began while I was looking for a job. The signatures on my doctoral diploma were barely dry, and there I was, writing purpose statements in application for professorships. As I started writing, I began thinking about what I wanted for my students. How did I want the educational process to pan out for them? What makes for a complete education? I knew that someday soon, a student would look toward the front of the classroom, lock eyes with me, and ask, "Why are we here? What is college *for*?" I wanted to have a good answer.

Writing those purpose statements led me to ask more general questions—questions relevant not just for my students, but for everyone. *What is it, really, to be educated? What are the qualities of a good thinker? What is it to have an excellent mind?*

Perhaps, I thought, a lot of knowledge is required. There are certain things an educated person should know. The basic elements of theories in the hard sciences. Some lines from Shakespeare or Dostoyevsky. Maybe some political thought and a bit of economics. And so on. But after a little reflection, I realized that knowledge was not enough. For starters, given human limitations, my students were sure to forget much of what they learned in my classes. Further, even if they retained much of their knowledge, this wouldn't ensure that they grasped how it fit together. They could know a lot, but fail to see the logical connections between their beliefs. This might leave them without a coherent view of the world. Still further, merely knowing a lot wouldn't necessarily keep my students from faulty reasoning.

So, in addition to knowledge, my students would need *skills* in logic and critical thinking. That addition made for a more complete educational package, at least to my mind. But eventually it became clear that even taken together, knowledge and skills were not enough. Knowledgeable, skilled thinkers can use their acumen to intimidate others, to mask poor arguments with slick rhetoric, or to seek the appearance of cleverness for its own sake. Moreover, thinkers who focus only on knowledge and skills might learn only what they must learn in order to "get by"—to pass a test, get a good grade, or receive a credential. As valuable as these things might be, I didn't want my classes to produce a bunch of academic mercenaries.

I wanted my students to care deeply about truth, knowledge, and understanding—and to care about these for more than just their practical benefits. I wanted students to become engaged in a life-long effort to get, keep, and share knowledge. And I wanted them to be the kinds of people who do these things consistently, as an expression of who they *are*. I became convinced that if my students were to be successfully educated, they would need to grow in traits like curiosity, intellectual carefulness, intellectual humility, intellectual courage, and open-mindedness.

These character traits are called *intellectual virtues*, and they are important for far more than education. They are central to our general flourishing, both individually and collectively. Once I began to think seriously about them, I came to see that the language of "intellectual virtue" gave me a kind of vocabulary that helped me to articulate goals, and to diagnose problems, in many areas of life. My supervisor was good at running meetings because she was both *open-minded* and *intellectually firm*. The rise in uncivil discourse between the political Right and Left was marked with arrogance—a failure of *intellectual humility*. Some people seemed to apply stricter standards to the views of those on the other side of the political aisle than they did to their own views—a failure of *fair-mindedness*. You get the idea. And I'm sure you can think of your own examples.

Life is complicated. So the pursuit of things we care about—including personal success, loving relationships, and responsible citizenship—requires good thinking. Failures in these areas often result from failures to think with intellectual virtue. By contrast, virtuous thinking fosters purposeful living, attentive listening, and informed action. Thus, the intellectual virtues are far from merely academic.

I did not invent the term *intellectual virtues*. Intellectual character has been a prominent topic of scholarly discussion for over three decades. I am excited to invite readers into this conversation, and to introduce some of its key participants. While I hope that professional philosophers and other academics will learn something from this book, I have written it mainly for students and general readers. I have tried to make the book as accurate as possible without sacrificing readability, and as readable as possible without sacrificing accuracy. To encourage the study of the intellectual virtues beyond this book, I have provided suggestions for further reading at the end of each chapter.

In my own thinking about intellectual character, I am indebted to Lorraine Code, James Montmarquet, Linda Zagzebski, Robert Roberts, Jay Wood, Jason Baehr, Heather Battaly, and Ron Ritchhart, among many others. These thinkers have pioneered a new approach to thinking about knowledge and education that gives virtues of intellectual character a fundamental role. They have produced a wealth of insightful work addressing the question I asked on behalf of my students all those years ago: *what is it to have an excellent mind?* The main goal of this book is to address this question by exploring the intellectual virtues—to consider what they are, why they matter, and how we can grow in them.

Initial Exercise

Take an inventory of your own vocabulary as far as good thinking is concerned. Take out a sheet of paper and, in your own words, answer the following questions. What is it to have an excellent mind? What traits must an excellent thinker possess? What are the traits of a really bad thinker? List as many traits as you can.

PART I

WHAT ARE INTELLECTUAL VIRTUES AND WHY DO THEY MATTER?

1

Why Good Thinking Matters

It's day three of my Western Thought course—Aristotle day. I greet the students as they settle in. They ready their notepads and silence their cell phones. I feign a sullen look. "I have some bad news," I announce. I wonder what they're thinking. Is there an impending pop quiz? Are they in for an awkward "ice-breaking" exercise? I snap the cap off the dry-erase marker and deliver the news: "You're all going to die." They sit silently, stunned and confused. I try to break the tension with a wry smile. There's giggling—some genuine and some manufactured. I walk over to the board. "Let's talk about what you want in your obituary."

The exercise is a bit clichéd, but the students are eager to participate. They start to volunteer how they'd like to be remembered: she was honest; he was humble; she loved her friends and family; he was kind to strangers; she was brave; he overcame obstacles; she was compassionate; and so on. I've conducted this exercise many times. Except jokingly, no one has ever listed wealth, fame, fashion sense, good looks, or good grades. Without fail, the discussion always reaches the same conclusion: in the end, character matters—a lot.[1]

I feel a twinge of guilt for forcing this activity on my students. I wouldn't blame them for resenting me. The exercise is a little grim. As a society, we pay doctors handsomely to keep illness and death away from us. We pay athletes and actors even more to help us forget about death altogether. And here I am, the philosopher, forcing my students to think about their own demise. Little wonder my paychecks pale in comparison to those of doctors, athletes, and actors.[2]

The Excellent Mind. Nathan L. King, Oxford University Press (2021). © Oxford University Press.
DOI: 10.1093/oso/9780190096250.003.0001

Why the painful exercise? Because the prospect of death helps us to see clearly what matters in life. The moment they're primed to focus on what really matters, my students start to grasp that having a good character is central to living a good life, a point Aristotle made over 2,000 years ago.

This is a book about character—*intellectual* character. We're all familiar with moral virtues—traits like justice, courage, and moderation. Virtues like these make up the character of the morally good person. They make the difference between someone who is morally excellent and someone who is morally mediocre. But here's a point that's easy to miss: each of us has not just a moral character, but also an intellectual character. When it comes to our thinking, we can be intellectually courageous or cowardly. We can be intellectually humble or arrogant. We can be curious or indifferent toward learning. We can be intellectually careful or careless. And so on.

Our focus from here on out will be the *intellectual* virtues. These are the character traits of excellent thinkers, where such thinking extends not just to our *getting* truth, knowledge, and understanding, but also to our *keeping* and *sharing* them. As important as moral virtues are, they won't occupy the center of our attention. Rather, our aim is to discover what it is to have an excellent mind—a mind that is curious, careful, self-reliant, humble, confident, honest, persevering, courageous, open, firm, fair, and charitable. In the chapters that follow, we'll consider what these virtues are like, why they are important, and how we might acquire them.

Here is a crucial point. Despite their label, intellectual virtues are not just for scholars, academics, or other highbrows. It's not as though the practically minded among us could sensibly decide to focus on moral virtues, and leave the intellectual ones to the bookworms. At least in practice, the intellectual virtues are hard to separate from the moral ones (but see chapter 2 for more on the distinction). Our intellectual character affects what we believe, and what we believe affects how we act. As David Hume notes, "Many of those qualities, usually called intellectual virtues, such as prudence, penetration, discernment, [and] discretion, [have] a considerable influence on conduct."[3] It works like this. Our intellectual character guides how we think and what we believe. Our beliefs in turn guide our actions. So, indirectly, our intellectual character guides our actions. Because these actions are of crucial importance, our intellectual character is, too. At some level, everyone is—or should be—an intellectual. Intellectual virtues are for everyday life.

At least in a backhanded way, most of us acknowledge that these virtues are valuable. We turn on the news or surf the Net, and come across people speaking with arrogance or dogmatism. And we hate these vices—at least when we see them in others. This should impel us to seek the corresponding virtues—traits like intellectual humility and open-mindedness. Thus, the Roman poet Horace:

> First step in virtue is vice to flee;
> First step in wisdom is to be folly-free.[4]

So far, so good. But the point of seeking virtue isn't just to avoid vice. Rather, the pursuit of intellectual virtues is central to several things we care about. These virtues are for anyone who wants to seek and find success, to act lovingly, to enjoy better relationships, to be well educated, and—not least—to find good answers to important questions. Achieving all these things requires good thinking. And to think well consistently, we need good minds.

Intellectual Virtues in Everyday Life

To appreciate the practical importance of the intellectual virtues, it will help to consider the importance of good thinking in several different areas, including general "success" in life, relationships, citizenship, and education. Let's take these in turn.

Success

Every year, millions of us awake some morning in January and commit to doing better than we did last year. We promise ourselves that we'll work harder and smarter to, well, you fill in the blank.

Everyone wants to be a success in life. But what does that amount to? What is it to live a good life? And how do we go about living one? These are hard questions. We need help to answer them. So maybe we log on to Amazon.com and click our way to the "Self-Help" section. We're overwhelmed with hundreds of titles to pick from, titles like

- *Anyone Can Be Cool, but Awesome Takes Practice*
- *Shut Up, Stop Whining, and Get a Life: A Kick-Butt Approach to a Better Life*
- *Divorcing a Real Witch*

In case you were wondering, yes, these titles are real. But how are we supposed to know which books will aid our success? Some of the books are surely helpful; others are stuffed with ancient platitudes dressed up as innovative lifehacks. One volume touts the importance of "getting in the zone." Another says we need to stick to a daily schedule. $23.99 for *that*? No sale. Another book talks about overcoming life's obstacles. It looks interesting, but the wealthy author on the cover doesn't look like he's had to overcome much. Even after an hour of browsing, it's hard to tell whether any of these books will be helpful. Defeated, we click over to social media.

Figuring out what it is to be successful, and discerning how to achieve success, are serious mental exercises. To protect ourselves against aimlessness and failure, we'll want to think well about these things. We'll need to figure out our goals. We'll need to consider which habits and strategies will help us achieve those goals and which will hinder. We'll need to plan the steps that are necessary for success, and then we'll need to execute them. This means that we'll need to think *wisely* about what's worth wanting, and *carefully* about how to achieve it. Along the way, we'll encounter obstacles to achievement. To figure out how to solve our problems and overcome these obstacles, we'll need to think with *perseverance*. To be consistently, reliably, and purposefully (as opposed to luckily) successful, we must think well. And if we want to think well consistently, we should seek to develop intellectually virtuous character.

Loving Relationships

Recall my students' fake obituaries. These often feature the refrain that a good life involves having loved others well—especially one's family and friends. At least at first, it's tempting to think that such love is just an emotion, a kind of warm feeling toward those we love. But warm feelings don't count for much unless they result in loving actions—and loving actions often require careful thought. So, when we consider what it is to love others well, we can't avoid the topic of good thinking. Try placing yourself in the following scenes:

> *Scene 1*: You've been dating Bobby for a year now. You enjoy the relationship. But he's often unreliable, sometimes inconsiderate, and unable to hold down a steady job. Your parents like him, and they're rooting for him. However, they worry that if you marry him, he'll constantly disappoint you, sap your strength, and drain your financial resources. You think they are probably right. Despite this, you still love him. After a romantic dinner, he pops the question. How will you know what's best to say next?

> *Scene 2*: Your best friend Brittany is an alcoholic. She's destroying her once-promising life. It started with partying, which she enjoyed in excess during her college years. Now she's 32, and her drinking can no longer be chalked up to youthful exploration. Alcohol is leading Brittany to neglect her children

and to show up late for work. She seems depressed. She turns to the bottle for help, but its help is fleeting. You decide it's time to intervene. You know that Brittany trusts you. But she can be defensive and combative. How will you help her see the error of her ways?

Scene 3: Your father lies in the ICU after a terrible car accident. He is on life support, with massive brain injuries. The doctors can perform a surgery that stands a good chance of saving his life. However, there's a fifty-fifty chance that even if the surgery succeeds, your father will emerge a shadow of his former self. He may not be able to speak, walk, or even feed himself. He has told you that he would never want to live like this. Before you ask for life support to be unplugged, the doctor reminds you there's a chance that the surgery will enable your father to live normally. How will you decide what you should do?

Sadly, many of us will find ourselves in such situations at some point. What kinds of thinking habits do we want at our disposal when we arrive? (Please close the book for a moment to think about how you would answer this question for each of the three scenarios.)

Clearly enough, to make loving decisions in such cases, we'll want good thinking habits. To decide well about complicated matters while under duress, we'll need to be *careful* and *thorough*; loving decisions can't be made in careless haste.[5] Further, we'll need to be *humble* enough to know when our own cognitive resources aren't up to the task of making the decision—a good thinker knows when to seek advice from others. If we lack these virtues, we may not be able to make the decisions that are best for our loved ones. For we can no more "turn on" good thinking patterns that we haven't ingrained than a ballplayer can expect to hit home runs without taking batting practice. To make loving decisions in trying conditions requires good thinking.

And to think well consistently, we must practice virtuous habits of mind.

Note, though, that intellectual virtues are relevant to more than just momentous life decisions. They're crucial to acting lovingly in the midst of our daily routines. This is because loving action contains an intellectual component; and unloving actions often involve intellectual failures. To put myself on the hook for a moment, I might consider some questions. Earlier today, was I *attentive* to the fact that my wife had a migraine and needed an extra cup of coffee? Was I *careful* to remember which clothes go in the laundry machine and which are hand-wash only? Was I *fair* in responding to my younger daughter's reasons for wanting another scoop of ice cream? Did I *persevere* in seeking a creative idea for my older daughter's birthday invitations? Have I been *courageous* in addressing my friend's tendency to misrepresent the views of his political opponents? Have I been *humble* enough to admit that, when it comes to parenting, I am often just making things up as I go? I won't confess my own answers here—that could get embarrassing. But by asking yourself similar questions, you can start to see the importance of intellectual virtues in everyday life. Intentional, loving action requires good thinking; and consistently good thinking requires virtuous habits of thought.

Responsible Citizenship

The point about loving actions extends beyond our families and friends to society as a whole. We want (or *should* want) to be responsible citizens—and this requires good thinking. At the founding of the United States, Thomas Jefferson observed, "The basis of our government is the opinion of the people."[6] Our beliefs or opinions influence our voting behavior, along with the rest of our civic activity. To form such beliefs carelessly is to shirk a duty to our fellow citizens. W. K. Clifford puts the point like this:

No real belief, however trifling and fragmentary it may seem, is ever truly insignificant; it prepares us to receive more of its like, confirms those which resembled it before, and weakens others; and so gradually it lays a stealthy train in our inmost thoughts, which may someday explode into overt action, and leave its stamp upon our character forever. And no one man's belief is in any case a private matter which concerns him alone. . . . Our words, our phrases, our forms and processes and modes of thought, are common property.[7]

When Clifford says that our beliefs aren't private, and that our modes of thought are "common property," he means that these things have consequences for those around us. The social consequences of our beliefs, Clifford says, create an obligation for us to seek reasons for what we believe. We owe this to one another. Intellectual carefulness is a requirement for responsible citizenship.

Consider the number and magnitude of problems today's nations must address. In the United States alone, there are many: racial injustice, a deadly pandemic, climate change, poverty, terrorism, pollution, blue-collar crime, white-collar crime, the nuclear threat (check the Doomsday Clock), dwindling Social Security funds, religious bigotry, anti-religious bigotry, immigration debates, healthcare woes, declining education rankings, and corrupt politicians—just to name a few. If we want to solve any of these problems, we'll need to think well. We'll need thinking that is careful, creative, and courageous. Further, as we seek to solve our society's problems, our conversations will inevitably yield controversy. To ensure that discussions of controversial topics produce more insight than inflammation, we'll need our thinking to be open-minded, fair, charitable, and—perhaps surprisingly—firm. In short, we'll need our thinking to be *virtuous*. Such thinking is far from a *merely* academic exercise—though it is central to academic success, as we'll see next.[8]

Education

It's the first day of the fall semester. A gaggle of nervous teenagers shuffles in for the premiere of my first-year seminar. Today's question: *Why did you decide to attend college?* Most students begin by saying they're here because they want to become doctors or lawyers. A few admit that, really, they just want to earn a bunch of money. Most agree that they want to make lifelong friends. Many say they're here to get good grades. After a few moments of silence, a junior transfer student says she's here to gain knowledge about her chosen field because she finds it interesting—the most thoughtful response yet. But it soon becomes clear that knowledge can't be the whole story. We've all known people with a lot of knowledge who are arrogant or dogmatic. We signal their lack of virtue with the derisive label "know-it-all." Finally, a pair of thoughtful students come out with it: they're here because they want to become *better thinkers*. I curb my enthusiasm so the other students don't feel left out. The discussion is moving in the right direction.

Over the course of a career, most college grads will change jobs several times, and many will change fields altogether. A recent LinkedIn study reports that "job-hopping" has almost doubled in the past 20 years.[9] So, it can be shortsighted for students to attend college just to prepare for a single, specific job. And though in some fields (say, math and music) the requisite knowledge base is fairly stable, in other fields (business, technology, economics, sociology, political science, psychology, and the hard sciences) the needed stock of knowledge is constantly changing. Today's knowledge may be obsolete tomorrow; and we might forget it in the meantime. So, though knowledge is a vital part of an education, the purpose of attending college can't be just to gain it.

Skills—particularly transferrable skills like critical thinking and clear communication—are an important supplement. They, at least, can transfer across fields. But without a certain sort of character, graduates might apply their skills unwisely, or not at all. They might use critical thinking skills just to look clever, or to disguise poor arguments with slippery phrasing. Indeed, they might be especially dangerous to society if they do this in ways that are both knowledgeable and skilled. For then they might know just which words will manipulate their hearers *and* have the skill to carry out the ruse. George Orwell remarks:

> In our time, political speech and writing are largely the defence of the indefensible. [Indefensible acts] can indeed be defended, but only by arguments which are too brutal for most people to face, and which do not square with the professed aims of political parties. Thus political language has to consist largely of euphemism, question-begging and sheer cloudy vagueness. . . . Political language—and with variations this is true of all political parties . . . —is designed to make lies sound truthful and murder respectable, and to give an appearance of solidity to pure wind.[10]

None of this befits a proper education.

What graduates need, in addition to knowledge and skills, are the virtues that will help them put their knowledge and skills to good use—for their own good, for the good of others, and out of reverence for truth itself.

In his award-winning book, *College: What It Was, Is, and Should Be*, Columbia University professor Andrew Delbanco develops several arguments for attending college. His central argument focuses on the well-being of the college graduate. You should go to college, he says, because it will help you flourish as a person. In stating the argument's key premise, Delbanco recalls a remark from his colleague Judith Shapiro: "You want the inside of your head to be an interesting place to spend the rest of your life."[11] To be such a place, a mind needs to take on certain characteristics. Delbanco identifies five:

1. A skeptical discontent with the present, informed by a sense of the past.

2. The ability to make connections among seemingly disparate phenomena.
3. Appreciation of the natural world, enhanced by knowledge of science and the arts.
4. A willingness to imagine experience from perspectives other than one's own.
5. A sense of ethical responsibility.[12]

Though Delbanco doesn't use the language of intellectual virtue, such language helps to clarify what he wants for his students. Consider his list. Item (1) seems well characterized as a kind of intellectual caution, along with a humble willingness to learn from our forebears. Item (2) is a matter of intellectual attentiveness and creativity. Item (3) suggests curiosity and the love of knowledge. Item (4) highlights the importance of open-mindedness and fair-mindedness. Item (5) surely includes the kind of intellectual responsibility that informs good ethical decisions. We can summarize Delbanco's argument for college like this: you should go to college because it can help develop your character, particularly your intellectual character. Those who grow in this way ensure that they continue learning beyond their college years—something all professors hope for their students. (We should add: growth in intellectual virtue is decidedly *not* reserved for those who have had a formal higher education. Plenty of formally educated people squander the gift of college. Plenty of people who miss college exhibit intellectual virtue nonetheless. The point is that a complete education—whether formal or not—should help pupils develop the character of a lifelong learner, a character that includes the intellectual virtues.)[13]

Truth and Knowledge

"All humans by nature desire to know."[14] So says Aristotle. And *he* would know, having made millennia-lasting contributions to several different fields, including logic, politics, ethics, and rhetoric. We have an innate desire for knowledge. As any parent knows, young children ask loads of questions. Adults have different questions, and may be reluctant to ask them in public. But the questions remain.

We have questions. We want answers. But not just any answer will do. We want our answers to be *true* (to describe things accurately). We want true answers based on *good reasons* instead of lucky guesses. And we want to understand *why* things are the way they are. We want *explanations*. At least some of the time, we want this kind of understanding not just for some practical purpose, but for its own sake. We naturally want—or *should* want—knowledge, not just because it helps us "get by," but because it's valuable in its own right.

When it comes to knowledge and understanding gained in the course of inquiry, the difference between ignorance and enlightenment often lies in intellectual virtue. This is because inquiry presents unexpected and daunting challenges—challenges that stretch us beyond our current knowledge and ability. We'll observe this point repeatedly in the chapters that follow. For now, consider the perseverance needed for Isaac Newton to invent the calculus central to his groundbreaking physics. (Students lament that calculus is hard to learn. Imagine *inventing* it!) Through a combination of genius and years of persistent inquiry, Newton gave us unprecedented insight into the natural world. His contemporary, Alexander Pope, put it like this:

> Nature and nature's laws lay hid in night.
> God said, "Let Newton be!" And all was light.[15]

Centuries later, Albert Einstein's theory of special relativity supplanted Newton's theory. Einstein reportedly saw perseverance as central to his success: "It's not that I'm so smart. I just stay at the problems longer."[16]

Of course, few of us can sensibly aspire to Newton-Einstein levels of achievement. These thinkers were geniuses, and they still had to outwork their peers in order to make their discoveries. But in a way, that's the point. If Newton and Einstein needed intellectual perseverance in their quest for knowledge, we should expect to need some, too.[17]

Intellectual Virtues Are for Everyone

In this chapter, we have considered why intellectual virtues are important. The pursuit of these traits isn't just for those who want a PhD, an MD, or some other set of letters behind their name. Intellectual virtues aren't just for academic professionals. They're for anyone who cares about flourishing relationships, responsible citizenship, quality education (whether formal or not), and the quest for knowledge. That is to say, intellectual virtues are for everyone. Now that we've established their importance, it's time to explore in greater detail what intellectual virtues *are*.

For Reflection and Discussion

1. Try the "obituary exercise" the author discusses in this chapter. What, if anything, does this exercise reveal about what is important to you? Does the notion of character play a role in your answer?
2. How might being intellectually virtuous (fair-minded, humble, etc.) help your relationships? How might it help you be a more responsible citizen? See if you can support your answers with specific examples.
3. What do you think is needed for a good education? Do intellectual virtues play a role in your answer? If so, why so? If not, why not?
4. Do you value truth, knowledge, and understanding? If not, why not? If so, why do you value them?

Further Reading

A central source for thinking about the nature and importance of the virtues is Aristotle's *Nicomachean Ethics* (many editions available). For an insightful, accessible introduction to the topic of moral character, see Christian B. Miller, *The Character Gap: How Good Are We?* (New York: Oxford University Press, 2018). For detailed narratives exploring the role of character in the good life, see David Brooks, *The Road to Character* (New York: Random House, 2015). For a lively, sure-handed introduction to recent philosophical work on moral and intellectual virtues, see Heather Battaly's book *Virtue* (Malden, MA: Polity Press, 2015). Linda Zagzebski's *Virtues of the Mind* (New York: Cambridge University Press, 1996) was massively influential in drawing philosophers' attention to the study of intellectual virtue. For a discussion of the mind's role in responsible citizenship, see W. K. Clifford's classic essay, "The Ethics of Belief" (many editions). Readers interested in the role of intellectual virtue in education will find excellent resources in Jason Baehr's comprehensive manual for intellectual virtues education, *Cultivating Good Minds* (available online at intellectualvirtues.org). See also *Intellectual Virtues and Education*, ed. Jason Baehr (New York: Routledge, 2016), and Ron Ritchhart, *Intellectual Character: What It Is, Why It Matters, and How to Get It* (San Francisco: Jossey-Bass, 2002). In this chapter, I claim that intellectual virtues help us pursue truth, knowledge, and understanding. For a defense of the stronger claim that acts of intellectual virtue are required for knowledge, see Zagzebski's *Virtues of the Mind*.

Notes

1. In *The Road to Character* (New York: Random House, 2015), David Brooks helpfully distinguishes between "résumé virtues" and "eulogy virtues." The traits we'll study in this book are in the latter group.
2. For more on the cultural values that give rise to the relative neglect of philosophy, see Thomas Morris, *Making Sense of It All: Pascal and the Meaning of Life* (Grand Rapids: Eerdmans, 1992), chapter 3. I borrow the point about doctors, athletes, and actors, from Morris.
3. David Hume, *An Enquiry Concerning the Principles of Morals*, ed. L.A. Selby-Bigge and P. H. Nidditch (New York: Oxford University Press, 1975), 313.
4. Horace, *Epistles*, Epistle I (to Maecenas), in *The Complete Works of Horace*, ed. Casper J. Kraemer Jr. (New York: Random House Modern Library, 1963), 307.

5. I am indebted to Philip Dow here. Dow develops this point in *Virtuous Minds: Intellectual Character Development* (Downers Grove, IL: Intervarsity Press, 2013), chapter 11.

6. Quoted in Andrew Delbanco, *College: What It Was, Is, and Should Be* (Princeton: Princeton University Press, 2012), 28.

7. W. K. Clifford, *The Ethics of Belief and Other Essays* (Amherst, NY: Prometheus Books, 1999), 73.

8. For a detailed discussion about the link between intellectual responsibility and moral responsibility, see James A. Montmarquet, *Epistemic Virtue and Doxastic Responsibility* (Lanham, MD: Rowman & Littlefield Publishers, 1993).

9. Guy Berger, "Will This Year's College Grads Job-Hop More Than Previous Grads?," LinkedIn official blog, April 12, 2016, retrieved from https://blog.linkedin.com/2016/04/12/will-this-year_s-college-grads-job-hop-more-than-previous-grads.

10. George Orwell, "Politics and the English Language," in Orwell, *George Orwell: A Collection of Essays* (New York: Harcourt, 1981), 166–67, 171. I have omitted the specific political parties and the acts Orwell discusses here, in order to foster reflection by proponents of different political parties.

11. Delbanco, *College*, 33.

12. Delbanco, *College*, 3.

13. For a detailed defense of the claim that intellectual virtues are the key character traits of lifelong learners, see Jason Baehr, "Educating for Intellectual Virtues: From Theory to Practice," *Journal of Philosophy of Education* 47, no. 2 (2013), 248–62.

14. Aristotle, Metaphysics, Book I, line 1, trans. W. D. Ross, in *The Complete Works of Aristotle*, vol. 2, ed. Jonathan Barnes (Princeton: Princeton University Press, 1984), 1552. I have ungendered this quotation to prevent unnecessary distraction.

15. This poem was intended as an epitaph for Newton, who is buried at Westminster Abbey. Further information is available at the Abbey's website: http://www.westminster-abbey.org/our-history/people/sir-isaac-newton.

16. This quotation is attributed to Einstein in dozens of publications. I have not been able to find the original source.

17. On Newton, see James Gleick, *Isaac Newton* (New York: First Vintage Books, 2004). On Einstein see Walter Isaacson, *Einstein: His Life and Universe* (New York: Simon and Schuster, 2007).

2

The Intellectual Virtues

A Closer Look

There are at least three ways to improve our grasp of the intellectual virtues. First, we can list them. Intellectual virtues include traits like curiosity, intellectual carefulness, intellectual autonomy, intellectual humility, self-confidence, intellectual honesty, intellectual perseverance, intellectual courage, open-mindedness, intellectual firmness, fair-mindedness, and intellectual charity. Second, we can develop an account of what these virtues are. We began that task in chapter 1, where we saw that intellectual virtues are the character traits of excellent thinkers. We'll continue unpacking that account in this chapter. Before we do, let's consider a third way of getting to know the virtues of the mind: let's see how they look "in action."

Intellectual humility is the virtue that enables us to consider, assess, and own our mental limitations.[1] Limitations might concern our intellectual character, our abilities, our circumstances, or our having believed something false. We might be biased, incapable, dogmatic, or ignorant—or simply wrong. Owning any of these shortcomings takes humility. Richard Dawkins recalls a prominent zoologist who taught at Oxford during Dawkins' undergraduate days:

> For years he had passionately believed, and taught, that the Golgi Apparatus (a microscopic feature of the interior of cells) was not real: an artefact, an illusion. Every Monday afternoon it was the custom for the whole department to listen to a research talk by a visiting lecturer. One Monday, the visitor was an American cell

The Excellent Mind. Nathan L. King, Oxford University Press (2021). © Oxford University Press.
DOI: 10.1093/oso/9780190096250.003.0002

biologist who presented completely convincing evidence that the Golgi apparatus was real. At the end of the lecture, the old man strode to the front of the hall, shook the American by the hand and said—with passion—"my dear fellow, I wish to thank you. I have been wrong these fifteen years." We clapped our hands red. . . . The memory of the incident I have described still brings a lump to my throat.[2]

When we reflect on the kind of humility needed to admit a mistake of this magnitude, in front of one's colleagues, with one's hard-won reputation on the line, we rightly find ourselves, well, *humbled*.

Here's another example. *Intellectual perseverance* is the virtue that disposes us to continue in our intellectual tasks in the face of obstacles. This trait is often needed to pursue new knowledge (recall the examples of Newton and Einstein). But sometimes, we must exercise perseverance in order to keep knowledge we already have, or to share it with others. In medieval Irish monasteries, the descendants of an illiterate people did just this.[3] After the fall of Rome in the 5th century, much of Western European culture lay in ruins. Those with the means for academic learning departed for safety in the East, where they would remain for centuries. In the West, there were the monks. Tucked away in their monasteries, they took to reading and copying books, from the Bible to the works of the ancient Greeks and Romans. In an age before the printing press, they had to copy manuscripts by hand. (To get a feel for this task, spend ten minutes copying text from your own favorite book. To mimic the monks' working conditions, do this in the cold, by candlelight.) Given the difficulty of this labor, it is unsurprising that the margins of medieval texts are sometimes littered with complaints: "Oh, my hand"; "I am very cold"; "Now I've written the whole thing . . . give me a drink."[4] As if the work itself weren't hard enough, the monasteries were sometimes attacked, despite their remote locations. The monastery at Skellig Michael, a rock island eight miles off the Irish coast, was routinely attacked by Viking raiders. The monastic village at Glendalough was destroyed by fire at least nine times in 300 years. To keep their books safe from invaders' clutches, the monks often buried them, or sent them to more secure locations.[5] It is hard to overstate the importance of such efforts. In his bestselling book, *How the Irish Saved Civilization*, Thomas Cahill remarks,

> Without the Mission of the Irish Monks, who single-handedly re-founded European civilization throughout the continent in the bays and valleys of their exile, the world that came after them would have been an entirely different one. . . . And our own world would never have come to be.[6]

Faced with daunting challenges, the Irish monks preserved knowledge during a Dark Age—intellectual perseverance at work.

We could multiply examples. Doing so would and will help us understand the intellectual virtues in greater depth. Stay tuned. For now, let's pause and consider the nature of the intellectual virtues. That is, let's unpack our account of intellectual virtues as the character traits of excellent thinkers. This will sharpen our vision of the virtues and prepare us for the chapters ahead.

Three Features of an Intellectual Virtue

Intellectual virtues are intellectually excellent features of persons. But not all intellectually excellent features of persons are virtues in the sense relevant to our study. In particular, intellectual virtues are different from excellent *faculties* (e.g., good eyesight), *talents* (say, being naturally smart), and *skills* (e.g., computer coding). What sets intellectual virtues apart is that they are good *character traits*. Specifically, they are good dispositions involving our thoughts, motives, and actions in relation to truth, knowledge, and understanding.[7]

To sort out the differences between faculties, talents, skills, and intellectual virtues, it will help to imagine an excellent thinker at work. Suppose she's a physicist trying to apply a difficult math equation, or a city planner puzzling over crime statistics. How will she use good judgment in order to apply the right problem-solving techniques? What will motivate her? What will she do as she sets out to solve the problem? The details will depend on the specific case. But we might expect her intellectual virtue to be expressed in ways like these: She will think well by selecting strategies that have worked on similar problems. She will desire to find knowledge and understanding. She will want to avoid false solutions, and will shun sloppy thinking. She will feel excited at the prospect of discovery. She will persist in working at the problem longer than a mediocre thinker would.

As our example illustrates, intellectual virtues generally have three components—one each for thought, motivation, and action. In typical virtuous thinkers, these components look something like this:

- *Thinking component*: virtuous thinkers believe that knowledge is valuable. They think it's unfortunate for a person to have false or unreasonable beliefs, or to be ignorant. They use good judgment in choosing their intellectual projects. They seek knowledge about what they rightly consider important. They wisely determine when to pursue their projects. When they seek knowledge, they use appropriate means and methods (say, reliable reasoning instead of guesswork). They believe that knowledge—along with truth and understanding—is worth keeping and sharing.
- *Motivational component*: virtuous thinkers desire true beliefs, knowledge, and understanding. They want to avoid falsehood and ignorance. They want their beliefs to be reasonable. They feel joy at the prospect of gaining knowledge, and feel an aversion to falsehood and ignorance. They value and care deeply

about truth and knowledge for their own sakes, and not just for the sake of, say, money or praise.[8]

- *Action (behavioral) component*: virtuous thinkers act according to patterns of thought and motivation like those just mentioned. They do this in order to gain, keep, and share truth, knowledge, and understanding. They act in these ways consistently, across time, and in different settings.

The details of these components will become clearer in due course. But even this description should help us see that intellectual virtues differ from excellent faculties, talents, and skills. Let's spell this out a bit.

Intellectual virtues require excellence in thought, motivation, and action in relation to knowledge. Not so for faculties, talents, or skills. Someone might have the faculty of excellent eyesight, but this is not a virtue in the sense at issue here. Joe Bloggs can have 20/20 vision but be completely bereft of intellectual virtue. He might be arrogant, dogmatic, and so on.

It's similar with talent. We can easily imagine a genius-level talent—say, someone with an IQ of 190—who cares nothing for knowledge, and doesn't think it is valuable. By way of her talent, she might display a kind of intellectual excellence. But she lacks intellectual virtue because she isn't motivated to get knowledge or to keep or share it. Raw intelligence isn't enough to ensure a virtuous mind.

Finally, we can imagine a person who is intellectually skilled, but who is lazy and so never uses those skills for the sake of knowledge—or who puts them to use in the service of intellectually bad ends (recall Orwell's deceptive politicians from chapter 1). It is possible to be highly skilled but wholly lacking in intellectual virtue.

We can sum up the point of the last few paragraphs like this. Unlike our faculties, talents, and skills, our intellectual character expresses a lot about who we are *as persons*. For instance, it reveals whether or not we think knowledge is valuable. It shows whether or not we care about truth and understanding. It makes clear whether we desire these goods or are indifferent to them. If we don't exhibit excellence along these dimensions, we don't have a virtuous intellectual character—even if our faculties, talents, and skills are top-notch.

Locating the Intellectual Virtues

As soon as we identify intellectual virtues as character traits, we face questions. What's the difference between moral and intellectual virtues? And what distinguishes intellectual virtues from intellectual vices? Let's take these questions in turn.

First: how do intellectual virtues differ from moral virtues? There's much to say here. But given our purposes, we can leave it at this: the difference between the two lies in their aims. Intellectual virtues aim at things like truth, knowledge, and understanding. Moral virtues need not have this focus. Rather, they aim at things like justice, kindness, and the reduction of pain. Thinkers who are intellectually curious, humble, fair-minded, and so on, *must* care about knowledge. That's part of what it is to be intellectually virtuous. By contrast, a morally compassionate person—Mother Teresa, say—can exercise her compassion without aiming to get, keep, or share knowledge. Her aim—her main motivation—is to alleviate the suffering of those in her care. As we saw in chapter 1, the two kinds of virtue often overlap in the real world. But again, our main focus will be the intellectual virtues.[9]

Second: what distinguishes intellectual virtues from intellectual vices? We can find help in answering this question by borrowing an image from Aristotle: the image of the mean.[10] In distinguishing *moral* virtues from moral vices, Aristotle argues that many virtues may be found in a mean between extremes of deficiency and excess. These extremes are *vices*. Consider the virtue of courage. Aristotle understands this as a mean between cowardice and rashness. On the deficiency side, we might imagine an otherwise normal grown-up cowering under a blanket for fear of the dark. That's cowardly. On the excess side, we might imagine a soldier who needlessly runs into enemy fire, oblivious to danger. That's rash. The courageous person, says Aristotle, finds the mean between the two.

We can use Aristotle's understanding of moral virtues to improve our grasp of *intellectual* virtues.[11] Like the moral virtues, many intellectual virtues exist as a mean between vices. There are deficiencies and excesses of intellectual character; the virtues stand between them. We can depict the traits as in table 2.1.

All intellectual virtues involve a positive orientation toward truth, knowledge, and understanding. This is what unifies the intellectual

Table 2.1   Intellectual Virtue as a Mean between Vices

Sphere of activity	Vice (deficiency)	Virtue (mean)	Vice (excess)
Managing our intellectual appetite	Indifference	Curiosity	Gluttony
Reasoning from evidence	Carelessness	Carefulness	Scrupulousness
Independent thinking	Servility	Autonomy	Isolation
Assessing our weaknesses	Arrogance	Humility	Self-deprecation
Assessing our strengths	Self-deprecation	Self-confidence	Arrogance
Overcoming obstacles	Irresolution	Perseverance	Intransigence
Persisting despite threats	Cowardice	Courage	Rashness
Transcending our perspective	Closed-mindedness	Open-mindedness	Indiscriminateness
Maintaining our perspective	Spinelessness	Firmness	Rigidity

virtues. But as table 2.1 suggests, each intellectual virtue also concerns a different area of activity. This helps distinguish intellectual virtues from each other. For instance, intellectual *autonomy* is the virtue most relevant when it comes to thinking for ourselves. The autonomous thinker avoids the deficiency of servility. She doesn't *just* rely on others when considering what she should think. She doesn't farm out her intellectual life. Rather, she takes responsibility for her own beliefs. But she also avoids the excess of isolation. She doesn't ignore others' valuable insights or expert advice. She doesn't live on an intellectual island. In determining when and how to think for herself, she finds the mean.

Another example: we often need to consider new ideas—even ideas contrary to our own. *Open-mindedness* is the virtue needed to take seriously the merits of those ideas. Now, it's easy to mistake this virtue for an uncritical willingness to listen to anything. But notice: not just any activity in this area will count as virtuously open-minded. A recent headline in *The Onion* clowns, "Open-Minded Man Grimly Realizes How Much Life He's Wasted Listening to Bullshit." The article goes on to describe Blake Richman, a 38-year-old man who has squandered his life listening to others' inane blathering, half-formed thoughts, and asinine suggestions.[12] Despite the article's headline, however, *that* is not open-mindedness. It's the excess of indiscriminateness. The genuinely open-minded person avoids this vice, along with its opposite, closed-mindedness—an unwillingness to take seriously even new ideas that have merit.

As table 2.1 shows, many other intellectual virtues similarly lie in a mean between extremes.*

The image of the mean gives us a good start in identifying several intellectual virtues and distinguishing them from their corresponding

---

* Perhaps not all intellectual virtues will fit into this framework. For instance, it is not clear that honesty (chapter 7) has an intellectual excess. Further, it is not clear that in all cases, exceeding a virtue is vicious. In chapter 11, I'll suggest that intellectual charity goes beyond fair-mindedness, but is virtuous nonetheless. Despite its limitations, this vice-virtue-vice picture will prove helpful as we seek to understand several intellectual virtues.

vices. However, taken alone, it's not as informative as we might like. Just learning that virtues stand between vices does not tell us why virtues are excellent. After all, sometimes, to be in the middle is to be *mediocre*. Nor does our vice-virtue-vice picture register the many ways we can fail to be virtuous. (As we'll see, there's more to it than "too little" and "too much.") Further, the simple image of the mean doesn't reveal how virtues and vices express our character—how they show what motivates us. To illuminate these issues, we need another image from Aristotle: the image of the archer.[13]

Acting with moral virtue, says Aristotle, is like hitting a target with an arrow: there are many ways to miss, but only one bullseye. An excellent archer hits the center of the target, shooting neither left nor right, high nor low. Similarly, Aristotle says, the morally virtuous person does the right thing, at the right time, in the right way, and for the right reason. In other words, a virtuous act requires the right object, occasion, means, and motivation. This is Aristotle's true, nuanced doctrine of the mean.[14] We can envision it as shown in figure 2.1.

This image promises to enrich our understanding of virtues.[15] It helps us see why the virtues are excellent. They are excellent

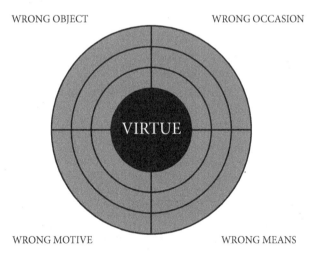

WRONG OBJECT   WRONG OCCASION

VIRTUE

WRONG MOTIVE   WRONG MEANS

Figure 2.1 Virtue as Hitting the Target

because they involve our acting in relation to the right things, at the right times, in the right ways, and for the right reasons. It takes excellence to "get it right" along all those dimensions, and to be disposed to do so consistently. Further, because the target image emphasizes the importance of our motives, it helps reveal how virtues express excellence of character. Virtuous people do the right thing for the right reasons, as an expression of what they value.

Let's apply all of this to our understanding of an *intellectual* virtue. Consider someone with intellectually virtuous perseverance—the virtue needed to overcome obstacles to getting, keeping, or sharing knowledge. She'll be the kind of person who continues in her intellectual projects, even when they're tough sledding. She'll keep going even though she wants to quit. She'll fight through distraction and discouragement. But she won't persevere in just *any* project. She might persist for years in cancer research, or spend a whole week trying to figure out what's wrong with her car engine. But she won't persist in memorizing random phone numbers. Her activity will take the right *objects*. She'll also be attentive to the *occasions* of her intellectual pursuits. For example, if she's a student, she won't set aside today's important writing assignment in order to continue a trivial task that could be done any time. In addition, she'll use good *means* as she continues her projects. If she's struggling to predict tomorrow's weather, she won't read tea leaves in order to solve her problem. She'll use a barometer or a modeling computer instead. Finally, she'll continue in her projects because she values knowledge, and not just (say) because she wants to earn praise. She'll act with right *motives*.

Plan of the Book

In the coming chapters, we will sketch "portraits" of several different intellectual virtues. Each portrait will include narratives of people—famous, non-famous, and infamous—who exhibit the intellectual virtues or their corresponding vices. We'll encounter heroes and villains, success stories and tragedies. As the mean and target images suggest, the virtuous characters will appear at the center of our portraits. Those with the vices will appear toward the edges. But their presence will be important nonetheless. It will set the virtuous characters in stark relief, thereby enabling us to see them clearly.

There is no official, comprehensive list of intellectual virtues.* Nor is there a standard taxonomy that shows exactly how these virtues relate to each other. This book does not aim to provide either of these things. Our goals are more modest. We'll simply aim to gain a better grasp of several important virtues, to trace some interesting connections between them, and to take some first steps toward growing in these traits.

Even so, it will help to have some rough-and-ready categories for sorting different virtues—some natural groupings that will give us a sense of how things fit together. (The categories that follow aren't mutually exclusive. They overlap and interlock in all kinds of interesting ways. A given virtue might fit into more than one category. But to get into all this here would be to get ahead of ourselves. For now, we'll keep it simple.)

We'll begin with three *virtues that help us get our inquiries off to a good start*: curiosity, carefulness, and autonomy. Beginning with these virtues helps us to clarify our intellectual goals, and to take responsibility for seeking them. Curiosity is the virtue that impels us toward the goals of truth, knowledge, and understanding—intellectual "goodies." Carefulness motivates us to avoid falsehoods and irrational beliefs—intellectual "baddies." Autonomy enables us to think for ourselves, to engage the quest for knowledge as a participant and not just as a spectator.

---

* Moving forward, sometimes we'll drop the "intellectual" in front of our virtue terms. Unless otherwise noted, all virtues discussed will be intellectual.

Of course, even if our thinking gets off to a virtuous start, there's no guarantee that it will continue in the right direction. We're bound to encounter challenges and pitfalls. We might underestimate our intellectual weaknesses, or overestimate our strengths. We may be tempted toward dishonest thinking. We may tend toward distraction or be beset by discouragement. We may be afraid to stand up for our beliefs. To stay on the right path in the face of these challenges, we'll want to pursue *virtues of self-regulation*—traits like humility, proper self-confidence, honesty, perseverance, and courage.[16]

That there are virtues of self-regulation does not imply that the pursuit of virtue is self*ish*. Rather, there are specific intellectual *virtues that help us to function well in communities*. We'll focus in particular on open-mindedness, firmness, fair-mindedness, and charity. These virtues help us to take seriously the merits of new ideas, to have productive conversations about controversial topics, and to guard our central beliefs even as we reexamine them. They help us to learn from others without thereby losing ourselves.

We'll close by considering some ways to foster growth in intellectual virtue. Such growth is the ultimate purpose of our study. As Aristotle notes, "We are inquiring not [just] in order to know what excellence is, but in order to become good, since otherwise our inquiry would have been of no use."[17] As we pursue intellectual virtue, we'll enlist the help of time-honored philosophical wisdom and cutting-edge research in empirical psychology. Through a combination of direct instruction, the study of narratives, and practice, meaningful growth in intellectual virtue is within our grasp.

For Reflection and Discussion

1. In this chapter, we explored two real-life examples of intellectual virtue in action (Dawkins's mentor and the Irish

monks). Try to think of one to two more examples of your own. Explain how these examples show what intellectual excellence looks like.

2. How are intellectual virtues different from good mental faculties, skills, and talents?

3. How can we use Aristotle's view of moral virtue as a mean between extremes to understand intellectual virtues? How does Aristotle's archery image provide still deeper understanding?

4. The archery image suggests that correct means, occasions, objects, and motives are all components of virtue. Can you think of any other important components? See if you can think of a different image or model that captures the notion of virtue better than the archery image does.

5. Look at the traits listed in table 2.1. Which intellectual virtues do you think are the most important? Which vices do you think are the most dangerous? Give reasons for your answers.

Further Reading

For more on the distinction between virtues of intellectual character (on the one hand) and faculties, talents, and skills (on the other) see Jason Baehr, *The Inquiring Mind: Intellectual Virtues & Virtue Epistemology* (New York: Oxford University Press, 2011), chapter 2. For an introduction to the idea that excellent faculties (like good eyesight) can be a kind of virtue, see Heather Battaly, *Virtue* (Malden, MA: Polity, 2015), and the sources cited in note 7 to this chapter. See also the entry "Virtue Epistemology" by John Turri, Mark Alfano, and John Greco in *The Stanford Encyclopedia of Philosophy* (available online for free). Linda Zagzebski's *Virtues of the Mind* (New York: Cambridge University Press, 1996) is largely responsible for drawing philosophers' attention to virtues of intellectual character. For a rich discussion of several intellectual virtues see Robert C. Roberts and W. Jay Wood, *Intellectual Virtues: An Essay in Regulative Epistemology* (Oxford: Oxford University Press, 2007). See also Baehr, *The Inquiring Mind*, chapters 8 and 9. For a scholarly but accessible discussion of intellectual vices, see Quassim Cassam, *Vices of the Mind: From the Intellectual to the Political* (New York: Oxford University Press, 2019). For a wide-ranging collection of essays on various aspects of intellectual virtue, see *The Routledge Handbook of Virtue Epistemology*, ed. Heather Battaly (New York: Routledge,

2019). For detailed treatments of several moral, intellectual, and theological virtues, see *Virtues and Their Vices*, ed. Kevin Timpe and Craig Boyd (New York: Oxford University Press, 2014).

Notes

1. For more on this claim, see chapter 6. There I am indebted to Dennis Whitcomb, Heather Battaly, Jason Baehr, and Daniel Howard-Snyder, "Intellectual Humility: Owning Our Limitations," *Philosophy and Phenomenological Research* 94, no. 3 (2017), 509–39.
2. Richard Dawkins, *The God Delusion* (New York: Houghton-Mifflin, 2006), 283–84.
3. For more on the Irish monks, see Thomas Cahill, *How the Irish Saved Civilization* (New York: Nan A. Talese, 1995). My account is indebted to Cahill's.
4. Colin Dickey, "Living in the Margins: The Odd and Amusing World of Medieval Marginalia," *Lapham's Quarterly*, March 22, 2012, retrieved from http://www.laphamsquarterly.org/roundtable/living-margins.
5. For further details see Cahill, *How the Irish Saved Civilization*, 211.
6. Cahill, *How The Irish Saved Civilization*, 4.
7. In focusing on virtues of intellectual character, I do not hereby dismiss the idea that other features of thinkers—especially excellent faculties— are worthy of the label "virtues." Some philosophers think of intellectual virtues as reliable faculties such as good vision, good reasoning, and accurate memory. By no means do I wish to dismiss this idea. Rather, I explicitly endorse virtue pluralism, the idea that there are different ways of understanding the nature of intellectual virtues, and different understandings of virtue are suitable for different purposes. All virtues display *excellence*. People can display intellectual excellence both in their faculties and in their character. Thus, there's more than one kind of intellectual virtue. My focus on intellectual virtues as character traits is a matter of emphasis, not of theoretical entrenchment. For more on intellectual virtues as reliable faculties, see Ernest Sosa, *A Virtue Epistemology: Apt Belief and Reflective Knowledge*, vol. 1 (Oxford: Oxford University Press, 2007). See also Sosa, *Reflective Knowledge: Apt Belief and Reflective Knowledge*, vol. 2 (Oxford: Oxford University Press, 2009); and John Greco, *Achieving Knowledge: A Virtue-Theoretic Account of Epistemic Normativity* (New York: Cambridge University Press, 2010). See also John

Turri, Mark Alfano, and John Greco, "Virtue Epistemology," *Stanford Encyclopedia of Philosophy*, ed. Edward N. Zalta, Fall 2019 ed., retrieved from https://plato.stanford.edu/entries/epistemology-virtue/.

8. For simplicity's sake, I include emotions and feelings as part of the motivational component of an intellectual virtue. Some theorists separate the two, opting for distinct affective and motivational components. See Jason Baehr, "The Four Dimensions of an Intellectual Virtue," in *Moral and Intellectual Virtues in Western and Chinese Philosophy: The Turn toward Virtue*, ed. Chienkuo Mi, Michael Slote, and Ernest Sosa (New York: Routledge, 2016), 86–98.

9. The question of what distinguishes moral and intellectual virtues is disputed among virtue theorists. For a helpful treatment see Alan Wilson, "Avoiding the Conflation of Moral and Intellectual Virtues," *Ethical Theory and Moral Practice* 20 (2017), 1037–50. See also Jason Baehr, *The Inquiring Mind: Intellectual Virtues & Virtue Epistemology* (New York: Oxford University Press, 2011), appendix.

10. See Aristotle, *Nicomachean Ethics*, Book II, especially part 6, trans. W. D. Ross and revised by J. O. Urmson, in *The Complete Works of Aristotle*, vol. 2, ed. Jonathan Barnes (Princeton: Princeton University Press, 1984).

11. This approach follows that of, among others, Linda Zagzebski, Robert C. Roberts and W. Jay Wood, and Jason Baehr. See Zagzebski, *Virtues of the Mind: An Inquiry into the Nature of Virtue and the Ethical Foundations of Knowledge* (New York: Cambridge University Press, 1996); Roberts and Wood, *Intellectual Virtues: An Essay in Regulative Epistemology* (Oxford: Oxford University Press, 2007), and Baehr, *The Inquiring Mind*.

12. *The Onion*, February 26, 2011, retrieved from http://www.theonion.com/article/open-minded-man-grimly-realizes-how-much-life-hes—19273.

13. Thanks to Daniel Russell for encouraging me to supplement the vice-virtue-vice scheme with the image of the archer, and for helpful discussion, including a pointer to Rosalind Hursthouse, "A False Doctrine of the Mean," *Proceedings of the Aristotelian Society* 81 (1981), 57–72. Thanks to Robin Henager for discussion of the mediocrity objection.

14. *Nicomachean Ethics*, Book II, part 6.

15. Here is a potential limitation of the target model. Because the four quadrants of the target (objects, occasions, means, and motives) don't overlap, the model apparently supplies no way to represent what happens when an action goes wrong in all four ways at once. For there is no point on the target that corresponds to this. To overcome this limitation, we might think of each act as analogous to the firing of four arrows at a time,

with one arrow each representing the actor's objects, occasions, means, and motives. An action with a wrong object, occasion, means, and motive would be analogous to all four arrows missing the mark. A virtuous action would be analogous to all four arrows finding the bullseye. An alternative to this four-arrow addendum would be to supplement the target model with a different model. Perhaps no model captures the notion of virtue perfectly. If so, we might achieve a more complete understanding of virtue by combining models that aren't fully adequate on their own. Thanks to an anonymous referee for helpful discussion here.

16. Autonomy—literally "self-rule"—is plausibly classed both as a virtue important for starting inquiry and as a virtue of self-regulation. Again: these categories aren't mutually exclusive.

17. Aristotle, *Nicomachean Ethics*, Book II, part 2, 1743.

PART II

INTELLECTUAL VIRTUES

3

Curiosity

A Healthy Appetite for Knowledge

A cat lies dead under suspicious circumstances. The main suspect is in custody. It looks like an open-and-shut case. But as we will see, the real culprits remain at large. Curiosity has been framed.[1]

Here is an account of the cat's demise as recorded in the *Washington Post* on March 4, 1916 (page 6):

CURIOSITY KILLED THE CAT.
Four Departments of New York City Government Summoned to Rescue Feline.
Curiosity, as you may recall—
On the fifth floor of the apartment house at 203 West 130th street lives Miss Mable Godfrey. When she came to the house about seven months ago she brought Blackie, a cat of several years' experience of life.

The cat seldom left the apartment. He was a hearth cat, not a fence cat, and did not dearly love to sing. In other respects he was normal and hence curious.

Last Tuesday afternoon when Miss Godfrey was out Blackie skipped into the grate fireplace in a rear room. He had done this many times before. But he had not climbed up the flue to the chimney. This he did Tuesday. Blackie there remained, perched on the top of the screen separating the apartment flue from the main chimney, crying for assistance. Miss Godfrey, returning, tried to induce her pet to come down. If you are experienced in felinity, you know that Blackie didn't come down.

The Excellent Mind. Nathan L. King, Oxford University Press (2021). © Oxford University Press.
DOI: 10.1093/oso/9780190096250.003.0003

On Wednesday the cat, curiosity unsatisfied, tried to climb higher—and fell to the first floor. His cries could still be heard by Miss Godfrey; who, to effect Blackie's rescue, communicated with the following departments:

1. Police department.
2. Fire department.
3. Health department.
4. Building department.
5. Washington Heights court.

Among them they lowered a rope to Blackie. But it availed neither the cat nor them anything.

Thursday morning, just before noon, a plumber opened the rear wall back of the chimney. Blackie was taken out. His fall had injured his back. Ten minutes later Blackie died.

The preceding article is real. It's also biased. Before all the facts are even in view, the author assumes that curiosity is Blackie's killer. But in the interest of due process, we'll carry out a more thorough investigation. We'll consider testimony both for and against curiosity. Some thinkers consider the trait a deadly vice, while others regard it as an important virtue. To resolve this dispute, we'll consider at length what curiosity *is*, and how the word "curiosity" has been used. Having clarified our terms, we'll locate curiosity in relation to its rivals: intellectual indifference and intellectual gluttony. As we'll see, the evidence points an accusatory finger toward these vices. But it exonerates curiosity as a virtue—the centrally motivating intellectual virtue.[2]

Curiosity's Checkered Past

Let's start with the testimony for the prosecution. Plutarch (AD 45–120) condemns curiosity in a chapter of his *Moralia* entitled "On Not Being a Busybody." He labels several varieties of curiosity "unhealthy and injurious," and calls the trait "a disease which is thought to be free from neither envy nor malice."[3] Curiosity, Plutarch says, leads to unhealthy interest in everything from the downfalls of great leaders to the dubious delights of the peeping Tom. Augustine (AD 354–430) denounces curiosity (Latin: *curiositas*) as "a vain inquisitiveness dignified with the title of knowledge and science."[4] He warns that *curiositas* leads people to gawk at mangled corpses, to become obsessed with gladiator games, and to absorb gossip. In short, it leads us to want knowledge about the wrong things.[5] Following Augustine, Thomas Aquinas (1225–1274) includes *curiositas* in his catalog of the vices as a variety of intemperance.[6] Finally, Blaise Pascal (1623–1662) remarks, "Mankind's chief malady is its uneasy curiosity about things it cannot know."[7]

Contrary to this testimony, other thinkers have come to curiosity's defense. They see it not as a vice, but as an intellectual virtue. Samuel Johnson (1709–1784) affirms, "Curiosity is one of the permanent and certain characteristics of a vigorous intellect."[8] Albert Einstein (1879–1955) counsels,

> The important thing is not to stop questioning. Curiosity has its own reason for existing. One cannot help but be in awe when he contemplates the mysteries of eternity, of life, of the marvelous structure of reality. It is enough if one tries merely to comprehend a little of this mystery every day. Never lose a holy curiosity.[9]

Likewise, theoretical physicist and bestselling author Michio Kaku (b. 1947) advises budding scientists: "Keep the flame of curiosity and wonderment alive, even when studying for boring exams. That is the well from which we scientists draw our nourishment and energy."[10] Finally, Eleanor Roosevelt (1884–1962) praises curiosity as a trait central to living a good life: "I think, at a child's birth, if a mother could ask a fairy godmother to endow it with the most useful gift, that gift would be curiosity."[11]

To sum up: some great minds think that curiosity is a dangerous vice, while others laud it as an intellectual virtue. What explains the apparent divergence? The answer, I suggest, is that we have a largely verbal dispute—in forensic terms, a case of mistaken identity.

The trait that draws the ire of Augustine and Aquinas, *curiositas*, comes into English as "curiosity." In condemning this trait, Aquinas considers several ways our desire for knowledge can go awry. We can want knowledge:

- about things that are in principle beyond our grasp;
- about things that are none of our business;
- to the detriment of our other obligations;
- through inappropriate means; and
- in order to revel in our own accomplishments.[12]

These are defective expressions of intellectual appetite. They involve wanting knowledge about the wrong things, at the wrong times, by the wrong means, or for the wrong reasons.

But note: the thinkers who condemn *curiositas* never condemn desiring knowledge as such. Nor do they condemn the question asking that often accompanies this desire. On the contrary, Aquinas affirms, "The desire or study in pursuing the knowledge of truth may be right or wrong."[13] He uses "studiousness" (*studiositas*) to label the virtuous desire for knowledge. Similarly, Augustine does not shun knowledge. He has a sophisticated theory about its nature and sources.[14] As for question asking, a careful reading of Augustine's *Confessions* turns up over 700 questions.[15] For Augustine and Aquinas, the corruption of the intellectual appetite is a vice. The appetite's legitimate satisfaction is human—and gloriously so.[16] For his part, Pascal gnashes his teeth at those who don't care to know the truth about important matters: "This indifference . . . annoys me more than it fills me with pity. It amazes and appalls me: it strikes me as wholly monstrous."[17]

On the other side of the discussion, the champions of curiosity don't embrace the unbridled fulfillment of our intellectual desires. We find no hint of that in Johnson or Roosevelt or Kaku. Einstein urges us never to lose a *holy* curiosity—the modifier indicating the possibility of unholy intellectual hunger. Despite their enthusiasm for curiosity, these thinkers never suggest that our quest for knowledge should become the intellectual equivalent of a trip to Paunch Burger. The curiosity they laud is not *curiositas*.

All parties agree that we have an intellectual appetite. All agree that this appetite can be satisfied in both virtuous and vicious ways. *Our* task is to clarify the difference between the two.[18]

Before we do, let's prevent further terminological confusion. Hereafter, we'll use "curiosity" to label the virtuous appetite for knowledge. This choice is in keeping with a fairly common usage. Moreover, the main alternative, "studiousness," gives the unfortunate impression that the desire for knowledge is only for academics—an impression we'll resist throughout this book.

Curiosity and Its Rivals

To be virtuously curious, we need to maintain a healthy intellectual appetite—a healthy desire for truth, knowledge, and understanding. This sort of curiosity is a mean between two extremes, the deficiency of indifference and the excess of gluttony. *Intellectual indifference* involves a lack of desire or motivation to fulfill our intellectual appetite. Indifference is not simple ignorance (not knowing). Indifference is a matter of not *wanting* to know. A professor once asked her student, "What's the difference between ignorance and indifference?" The student replied, "I don't know and I don't care"— which is exactly right.[19] Just as we can lack a healthy desire for food, so we can lack a desire for nourishment from truth, knowledge, and understanding. If in our settled dispositions we don't value knowledge, if we don't care about truth or understanding,

Table 3.1 Curiosity as a Mean between Extremes

Sphere of activity	Vice (deficiency)	Virtue (mean)	Vice (excess)
Managing our intellectual appetite	Indifference	Curiosity	Gluttony

we lack curiosity—and slouch toward the deficiency of intellectual indifference.

Starvation and malnutrition aren't the only potential problems with our relationship to food. Physical hunger can become greedy, acquisitive, obsessive, or gluttonous. Thus, comedian Jim Gaffigan: "I think I'm lactose intolerant. Last night I had four milkshakes and I felt like crap."[20] We sometimes want too much food, or want unhealthy food. Or perhaps we want it at the wrong times, or use it in the wrong ways, or want it for the wrong reasons. Something similar holds with truth, knowledge, and understanding—the objects of our intellectual appetite. We can want knowledge about the wrong things. We can want it at the wrong times or in the wrong ways. We can want it for the wrong reasons. Such expressions of intellectual appetite aren't virtuous. They bespeak *intellectual gluttony*, a disposition to fulfill our appetite for knowledge unfittingly. As table 3.1 suggests, this vice of excess also opposes virtuous curiosity.

The Structure of Curiosity

Locating curiosity as a virtue between vices gives us a good start. To go further, it will help to recall that finding the true mean—hitting the target—requires our doing the right thing, at the right time, in the right way, and for the right reason. In other words, virtuous curiosity requires right objects, occasions, means, and motives (figure 3.1).

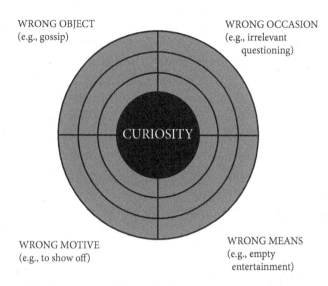

WRONG OBJECT
(e.g., gossip)

WRONG OCCASION
(e.g., irrelevant
questioning)

CURIOSITY

WRONG MOTIVE
(e.g., to show off)

WRONG MEANS
(e.g., empty
entertainment)

Figure 3.1 Curiosity as Hitting the Target

To improve our grasp of curiosity, let's think more about each of these dimensions of the virtue.

Objects

The desire for knowledge must be a desire *about* something. It must have an object or topic of concern. But we aren't virtuously curious if we want knowledge about just *any* old topic. If we strongly desire to know exactly how many numbers are in the local phonebook, we don't thereby count as *virtuously* curious. Our desire for knowledge is gluttonous because it is directed at a trivial truth. Likewise, if we gulp down casual celebrity gossip, we'll learn a few new facts about Hollywood stars and has-beens. But we won't thereby exercise virtuous curiosity, because our new knowledge won't be about anything worthwhile. *Virtuous* curiosity requires motivation for *important* knowledge.

Here come the obvious questions: Who's to say what's important? And what makes some knowledge more important than other knowledge? Let's take these questions in turn.

When it comes to what's important, it's *our* responsibility to decide. It's not like there's some International Committee on Knowledge Importance to do this for us. We must make our own judgments. Fortunately, it's often clear when knowledge is important and when it is not. To see this, we might consider which kinds of questions the virtuously curious questioner—the *inquisitive* thinker—will ask.[21] Contrast the lists in table 3.2.

The questions on the right are more important than those on the left. We grasp this intuitively. We don't need to understand *why* the

Table 3.2 Questions and Their Relative Importance

Are my favorite Hollywood stars having an affair together?	What kinds of entertainment can help me become a better person?
Do most of the cows in Texas have more than three spots on their hide?	How can we ensure that our animal-keeping practices are humane?
Which NFL quarterback said "hut" the most times in Super Bowl history?	Is the NFL doing enough to protect its athletes from head injuries?
My neighbor was just talking with the guy down the street. Were they flirting?	What skills are needed to develop healthy relationships?
What are my odds of winning the lottery two weeks in a row?	What math skills do I need to make better retirement investments?
What are the religious views of the *Star Wars* character Jar-Jar Binks?	Is there truth in any of the world's religions?
What is Bill Gates's net worth?	What is it to live a good life?
Do most scientists prefer wearing glasses or contact lenses?	What are the main claims made in disciplines like physics and biology?
Is the number of electrons in the universe odd or even?	Are unobservable entities (like quarks) mentioned in scientific theories actually real? Or are they just useful for guiding our predictions?

questions on the right are more important in order to know *that* they are.

Still, some observations can help explain the differences between the two lists. First, some of the questions on the right address "big picture" issues whose answers are central to our worldview—our beliefs about what's real, what we can know, and what's valuable. Our beliefs about such matters inform our beliefs and decisions about more specific issues. For example, our beliefs about what it is to live a good life influence what we think about how we should spend our time and money. Our beliefs about the good life, relationships, religion, and science tend to have far-reaching effects on the rest of our belief system. They can bring coherence (or the lack of it) to the rest of that system. So, it is important that we desire knowledge and understanding about such matters. By contrast, beliefs about celebrity dating, football trivia, and hypothetical lotteries rarely bear on the rest of what we believe. They aren't at the core of our belief system. From an intellectual standpoint, they're peripheral.

Second, many of the questions on the right side of the list are deeply related to what it is to live a meaningful human life, and to make sense of our place in the world. Our answers to questions about things like the nature of the good life, religion, the treatment of animals, and retirement investments can have obvious effects on the quality of our lives—and those of others. Indifference here is unwise. By contrast, unless we play Trivial Pursuit for a living, not much rides on our knowing the answers to arcane questions about (say) Super Bowl history. Thus, these questions deserve relatively little attention.

None of this implies that we should never play trivia games, watch television, or check our Facebook feed. The virtuously curious person needn't be a snob. We all have different interests, abilities, and vocations. Many combinations of these are consistent with being a curious person. We all need to "blow off steam" by seeking fun and entertainment—at least once in a while. (I write this as someone who owns two fantasy football teams and likes binge-watching a good show as much as the next person.) But if most of the knowledge we want is trivial or unworthy instead of important, we don't deserve a merit badge labeled "curious." There's something sadly incomplete about a life so stuffed with entertainment that it leaves no room for reflection on more important matters. It's like a stomach so full of Sweet-Tarts and frosting that it has no room for nutritious food. To lay hold of curiosity—and to satisfy our intellectual appetite—we must make room in our lives for knowledge of the things that matter most.

Occasions

Our target image suggests that for virtuous curiosity, timing matters. So, *when* should we express our desire for knowledge? An obvious answer: when we're aware that we lack it.[22] After all, it would be odd to express a desire to gain knowledge we already have!

So far, so good. But we can't stop here. As we saw earlier, not all knowledge is valuable. To want a lot of worthless knowledge is to veer toward the vice of intellectual gluttony—no matter the timing.

Suppose, then, that we limit ourselves to worthwhile topics—worthwhile objects of knowledge. The virtuously curious thinker won't express the desire for such knowledge at the wrong times. And she *will* express that desire at the right times. For instance, she won't ask penetrating questions about the intricacies of quantum physics during a lecture on the civil rights movement. However, if she desires further knowledge about the movement and thinks that asking her question will help her gain that knowledge, she'll probably ask away.

As this example illustrates, when it comes to finding the right occasions for wanting and seeking knowledge, much depends on our circumstances. Thus, it may help to keep a mental checklist that includes questions like these:

- Is there some cue or reason that tells me I should want knowledge of X right now? Has someone asked a good question about X? Do I have a burning question of my own about it? Am I interested in X?
- Am I capable of learning about X right now? Or is such learning beyond me—at least at the moment?
- Does seeking knowledge about X fit well with my current vocation? Does it fit with my social and family obligations?

When we can answer questions like these with a firm yes, we might move on to others:

- Will seeking knowledge about X cost me the opportunity to seek knowledge about some more important topic, Y?
- Will inquiring into X prevent me from fulfilling my other intellectual obligations (say, meeting a deadline for my essay on Y)?

If we can answer these questions with a firm no, that's a sign that the time is right to exercise our intellectual appetite.

Of course, this checklist doesn't give us an infallible decision procedure. Perhaps there are other factors that help determine when to exercise our desire for knowledge. The point for now is that asking questions like these can help us fit our inquiries into the rest of our lives—including our intellectual lives. To think and act wisely in response to such questions is to help ourselves inquire when, and only when, the occasion demands.

Means

There are many ways to express our desire for knowledge. We might sign up for classes, order books, attend lectures, listen to podcasts, and—not least, ask questions. These activities are means of trying to satisfy our intellectual appetite.[23]

There are good and bad ways of doing all of these things. Recall the quantum physics example from a little earlier. Asking questions about quantum physics is a particularly bad way to exercise a desire for knowledge about the civil rights movement. It won't help us get what we want. Likewise, ordering a statistics textbook would be a bad way to quench a thirst for knowledge about dolphins. The point: we need to choose ways of expressing our desire for knowledge that are suited to the knowledge we actually want. That's a good step toward managing our intellectual appetite well.

But perhaps the most important means of managing that appetite is to feed it properly. Managing our desire for knowledge is much like managing our desire for food. If we want to keep a healthy appetite, we should eat nutrient-dense fare. And we should avoid empty calories. If we fill up on donuts at breakfast, we shouldn't be surprised to find the vegetables on our lunch plates unappealing. Similarly, if we gorge ourselves on intellectually frivolous fritters, we're likely to find ourselves saying, "I'm already full" when someone passes a plate full of important knowledge. Conversely, if we get into the habit of seeking important knowledge, we'll be more likely to pass when someone serves us trivialities.

How, practically speaking, can we hone better habits in order to maintain a healthy intellectual appetite? By mimicking dieters' tricks.

Suppose I've packed on a few extra pounds because I've consumed too many empty calories. Here are two practices that can get me back on track. First, I can limit my access to junk food. Let's be honest: if I'm a little hungry and my cupboard presents me with a choice between Twinkies and unsalted almonds, the Twinkies are going to win six days a week. Like most sugary foods, Twinkies are engineered to be addictive. The only way those poor almonds stand a chance is if the Twinkies don't enter my home in the first place. The surest way to resist them is to leave them on the supermarket shelf.

Here's a second strategy for curbing bad eating habits: I can pay attention to what I do when I'm bored. During such times, I often find myself mindlessly, effortlessly reaching for unhealthy food—just to quell the boredom. I'll catch myself and say, "I don't want this food. I'm not even hungry! I just want something to do." It's an unhealthy habit. If I want to curtail it, I need to arrive at those moments of boredom with some better alternatives at hand. I need to retrain my default response so that instead of automatically reaching for junk food, I think to go for a walk or call a friend—or pick up an apple.

These strategies for controlling our bodily appetites have intellectual parallels—strategies we can use to maintain a healthy appetite for knowledge.

First, we can distance ourselves from sources of "empty" knowledge, and from low-value activities that fill the time we could otherwise use to consume valuable knowledge. For instance, we might delete distracting apps from our smartphones, or block mindless websites from our browsers. As it turns out, many of these products have been deliberately designed to be addictive.[24] They're *made* to be hard to resist. They suck us in and don't let go—which is all the more reason for us to use them sparingly and with caution. Too much of them can kill our appetite for good knowledge—just as an early dessert can spoil dinner. In this way, intellectual gluttony is the unlikely ally of indifference. By calling our attention to the flashy and trivial, it can make us indifferent to what's deep and important. (Some sobering numbers here: recent surveys suggest that today's college students spend an average of 13 hours per week studying for their classes, compared with over 16 hours on their phones looking at pictures, playing games, and using apps like Facebook, Twitter, Pinterest, Instagram, and YouTube. When all activities are added together, students average over 60 hours per week on cell phones. Even granting that many of those hours are well spent, it seems likely that a lot of learning opportunities are being lost.)[25] As healthy alternatives to our mind-numbing apps, we should keep sources of valuable knowledge—important books, informative podcasts, and so on—within easy reach.

Here's a second idea. In order to hone a healthy intellectual appetite, we can change our habits during moments of boredom. What do we reach for while waiting in line at the grocery store, or at the doctor's office, or for a friend to show up for coffee? Many of us reach for social media, or gaming apps, or the like. Now, these things aren't bad, especially in moderation. But we do have a choice here. I have a friend who chooses differently almost every time. She keeps a book or well-stocked e-reader constantly at the ready. During moments of waiting that might otherwise be wasted, she reads. During "downtime" alone, she reads dozens of books each year. As a result, she learns—a lot. And in her own winsome way, she often talks about what she is learning, and shares her knowledge with others. Admittedly, when she told me about her habit, I found myself a little annoyed (why hadn't I thought of it myself?). I also found myself instructed. My friend had found a good means of maintaining a healthy intellectual appetite and, in that way, of fostering a virtuous kind of curiosity.

Motives

Imagine that my friend—the one with the good reading habits—devoured all those books just to show off her knowledge or to feel superior to others. In that case, even if she also sought knowledge that was important, and sought it at the right times and through good means, she wouldn't be virtuously curious. *Virtuous* curiosity requires good motives, including a desire for knowledge in its own right. (Happily, my friend seems to have this.)

As a youth, I'm embarrassed to report, I didn't have such a desire—not much of it, anyway. My mother had to bribe me to read books during the summers. And I remember trying to negotiate with my parents what I might get paid for earning good grades in school.

Contrast my mercenary motivation with that of Mary Putnam Jacobi (1842–1906), whose efforts were influential in helping women gain access to higher education. From an early age, Jacobi was keenly interested in anatomy. As she recalls, "I began my medical studies when I was about nine years old."[26] Jacobi found a dead rat, and longed to dissect it in order to see its heart. She couldn't quite bring herself to start cutting. But her interest in biology was born, and would remain healthy from then on. She longed to become a doctor. The trouble was, during her time, women rarely achieved this feat. When she announced her plans to attend medical school, Jacobi's father balked. Rachel Swaby explains,

> Jacobi's father wasn't thrilled to hear that she'd decided to attend medical school. In response, he dangled the amount of her university tuition before her, a carrot that would be hers should she decide against higher education. Jacobi declined his offer, leaving for the Woman's Medical College of Pennsylvania, in the early 1860s, before continuing on to Paris for a second round of schooling.[27]

I've met—and been—the kind of student you have to pay to learn. Jacobi was the opposite. You couldn't pay her not to. In this, she displayed just the kind of motive that's characteristic of virtuous curiosity.

Solving a Murder

Return to the investigation with which we began. The suspects in Blackie's murder are curiosity, indifference, and gluttony. We can sum up our composite sketch of curiosity like this: *curiosity* is a healthy appetite for truth, knowledge, and understanding. It requires that we want valuable knowledge, and express that desire at the right times, in the right ways, and from the right motives.

This is not exactly the profile of a killer, feline or otherwise. Given this description, curiosity is unlikely to have been at the scene of Blackie's murder. It has a clean criminal record. It's not the sort of character likely to engage in gossip or excessive gaming, much less murder. Moreover, curiosity has a plausible alibi: at the time of Blackie's demise, it was probably off studying in the library. In sum, our evidence suggests that curiosity is innocent.

By contrast, both intellectual indifference and intellectual gluttony have vicious, even criminal, histories.

Indifference has a rap sheet including theft and conspiracy to commit murder. As for theft: apathy toward knowledge robs us of knowledge. Indifference pilfers learning opportunities. Because of this, indifference is a close friend to ignorance. This in turn makes indifference an accessory to murder—for ignorance is a known killer. Contrary to the popular saying, what we don't know *can* hurt us, even kill us. (Consider those who don't know the power of electricity or the properties of their medications. Their ignorance quickly turns lethal.) Indifference aids and abets such deadly ignorance.

Gluttony, too, is a suspect in multiple crimes. It is guilty of theft. (Recall those opportunities for deep understanding stolen by attention to unimportant topics.) It is also a key suspect in a murder. (Recall the ways in which a gluttonous feast on trivialities can kill our appetite for valuable knowledge.)

Curiosity, it seems, has been unjustly accused of killing the cat. But gluttony and indifference are dangerous characters, and each is associated with violent crimes. The two are known to work together on occasion, and suspects matching their descriptions were seen lurking near Blackie's chimney. Perhaps we should bring them in for questioning.

From Curiosity to Carefulness

We have established that, rightly understood, curiosity is not a vice. On the contrary, it is a central intellectual virtue. It is the starting point of inquiry and the cornerstone for anyone who wants to build an excellent mind. It impels us to seek truth, knowledge, and understanding.

To ensure that our seeking goes well, we'll need more intellectual virtues. Just as a desire for food does not guarantee that we will be fed, a desire for truth—however virtuous—does not guarantee that we will get it. We might fail to satisfy our intellectual appetite for any number of reasons. We might not take responsibility for our own search for knowledge, and so never begin the quest. We might fail to register our intellectual limitations and so veer off course. We might quit when the search becomes difficult or threatening. To avoid such pitfalls, we'll need intellectual virtues like autonomy, humility, perseverance, and courage. And crucially, we'll need to beware that the dangers of falsehood and irrationality lurk around every corner. To avoid these dangers and stay on the path to intellectual nourishment, we'll want to equip ourselves with intellectual carefulness, the virtue to which we now turn.

For Reflection and Discussion

1. Why is there an apparent debate about whether curiosity is a virtue or a vice? Do you agree with the way the author explains the "debate" as a merely verbal dispute? Why or why not?

2. We often express our curiosity by asking questions. In your view, what makes a question a good one? What makes an answer a good one?

3. In light of your answers to question 2, write down at least three good questions about a topic that interests you.

4. "Intellectual gluttony is the unlikely ally of indifference. By calling our attention to the flashy and trivial, it can make us indifferent to what's deep and important." Do you think these statements are true? If so, try to think of a specific example that illustrates them. If not, try to articulate the reasons for your answer.

5. Do you have any habits that put you in danger of intellectual indifference? Do you have any habits that put you in danger of intellectual gluttony? How might you change these habits? Do you *want* to change them?

6. Did curiosity kill the cat? Give reasons for your answer.

Further Reading

For insightful treatments of curiosity and inquisitiveness, see Lani Watson, "Curiosity and Inquisitiveness," in *The Routledge Handbook of Virtue Epistemology*, ed. Heather Battaly (New York: Routledge, 2019). See also Nenad Miscevic, "Curiosity—The Basic Epistemic Virtue," in *Moral and Intellectual Virtues in Western and Chinese Philosophy*, ed. Chienkuo Mi, Michael Slote, and Ernest Sosa (New York: Routledge, 2016). See also Lewis Ross, "The Virtue of Curiosity," *Episteme* (forthcoming). Unfortunately, I learned of Ross's paper too late in the writing process to incorporate its insights. For a rich discussion of the love of knowledge see Robert C. Roberts and W. Jay Wood, *Intellectual Virtues: An Essay in Regulative Epistemology* (Oxford: Oxford University Press, 2007), chapter 6. For a discussion of *curiositas* written from a theistic perspective see Paul J. Griffiths, *Intellectual Appetite: A Theological Grammar* (Washington, DC: Catholic University of America Press, 2009). For a discussion of curiosity within the Confucian tradition, see Ian James Kidd, "Confucianism, Curiosity, and Moral Self-Cultivation," in *The Moral Psychology of Curiosity*, ed. Ilhan Inan, Lani Watson, Dennis Whitcomb, and Safiye Yigit (Lanham, MD: Rowman & Littlefield, 2018), 97–116. For more on the addictive properties of smartphones and other technologies, see Adam

Alter, *Irresistible: The Rise of Addictive Technology and the Business of Keeping Us Hooked* (New York: Penguin, 2017).

Notes

1. I owe this hypothesis to the title of Dennis Whitcomb's paper "Curiosity Was Framed," *Philosophy and Phenomenological Research* 81, no. 3 (2010), 664–87.
2. I borrow this phrase from Nenad Miscevic. See Miscevic, "Curiosity— The Basic Epistemic Virtue," in *Moral and Intellectual Virtues in Western and Chinese Philosophy*, ed. Chienkuo Mi, Michael Slote, and Ernest Sosa (New York: Routledge, 2016), 160.
3. Plutarch, *Moralia*, trans. W. C. Helmbold, vol. 6 (Cambridge, MA: Harvard University Press, 1939), 473–75.
4. Augustine, *Confessions*, trans. Henry Chadwick (New York: Oxford University Press, 1992), Book X, xxxv (54), 211.
5. See especially *Confessions* Book X, xxxiv (53)–xxv (57). On gladiatorial games see Augustine's discussion in Book VI, viii (13) of his friend Alypius, who was addicted to watching such games.
6. *Summa Theologica*, Pt. II-II, Q 167, trans. Fathers of the Dominican Province, vol. 2 (New York: Benzinger Brothers, 1947), 1874–76.
7. Pascal, *Pensées*, trans. Honor Levi (New York: Oxford University Press, 2008), 136.
8. Samuel Johnson, *The Rambler* (no. 103) March 12, 1751, in *The Yale Edition of the Works of Samuel Johnson*, vol. 4: *The Rambler* (New Haven: Yale University Press, 1969), ed. W. J. Bate and Albrecht B. Strauss, 184–89.
9. Quoted in William Miller, "Death of a Genius," *Life*, May 2, 1955, 61–64.
10. Gus Lubin, "String Field Theory Genius Explains the Coming Breakthroughs That Will Change Life as We Know It," *Business Insider*, March 9, 2014, retrieved from http://www.businessinsider.com/michio-kaku-talks-about-coming-breakthroughs-2014-3.
11. Quoted in Susan L. Rattiner, *Women's Wit and Wisdom* (Mineola, NY: Dover Publications, 2000), 18.
12. *Summa Theologica*, Pt. II-II, Q 167–68.
13. *Summa Theologica*, Pt. II-II, Q 167.
14. For more on Augustine's theory of knowledge, see Eleonore Stump and Norman Kretzmann, eds., *The Cambridge Companion to Augustine* (New York: Cambridge University Press, 2001), chapters 2, 11, 12, and 13.

15. James J. O'Donnell, *Augustine Confessions*, vol. 2: *Commentary, Books 1–7* (Oxford: Oxford University Press, 2012), 20. Thanks to Aaron Cobb for pointing me to this source.

16. Though I lack the space to make the case here, there are good reasons for thinking that the Confucian tradition also lauds curiosity as an important virtue. See Ian James Kidd, "Confucianism, Curiosity, and Moral Self-Cultivation," in Inan et al., *Moral Psychology of Curiosity*, 97–116.

17. Pascal, *Pensées*, 159–60. For more on Pascal's disdain for indifference, see Thomas Morris, *Making Sense of It All* (Grand Rapids, MI: Eerdmans, 1991), chapter 2.

18. The parallel between physical and intellectual appetite has been around since at least the time of St. Augustine. For a thorough contemporary overview, see Frederick F. Schmitt and Reza Lahroodi, "The Epistemic Value of Curiosity," *Educational Theory* 58, no. 2 (2008), 125–48. For a detailed treatment of the vice of *curiositas* see Paul J. Griffiths, *Intellectual Appetite: A Theological Grammar* (Washington, DC: Catholic University of America Press, 2009).

19. I owe this anecdote to Morris, *Making Sense*, 15.

20. Jim Gaffigan, *Beyond the Pale* (Image Entertainment, 2006) (stand-up comedy set).

21. I am indebted to Lani Watson for helping me to see the relationship between curiosity and inquisitiveness. See Watson, "Curiosity and Inquisitiveness," in *The Routledge Handbook of Virtue Epistemology*, ed. Heather Battaly (New York: Routledge, 2019), 155–66. I follow Watson in thinking that curiosity is broader than inquisitiveness, but I cannot develop the point here.

22. See Watson, "Curiosity and Inquisitiveness," 158, for a development of this point.

23. See Watson, "Curiosity and Inquisitiveness" for further discussion of these means. Watson argues that the differences between these means help distinguish inquisitiveness from a broader kind of curiosity that needn't involve asking questions.

24. On the addictive properties of smartphones and gaming apps, see Adam Alter, *Irresistible: The Rise of Addictive Technology and the Business of Keeping Us Hooked* (New York: Penguin, 2017).

25. I glean the figure about time spent studying from Richard Arum and Josipa Roska, *Academically Adrift: Limited Learning on College Campuses* (Chicago: University of Chicago Press, 2011), 3. I glean the figures about cell phone time from James A. Roberts, Luc Honore Petnji Yaya, and Chris

Manolis, "The Invisible Addiction: Cell Phone Activities and Addiction among Male and Female College Students," *Journal of Behavioral Addictions* 3, no. 4 (2014), 254–65. I added the figures from each category listed (Facebook, Pinterest, etc.), which were reported in minutes per day. Please see table 1 in the article for additional figures.

26. Quoted in Rachel Swaby, *Headstrong: 52 Women Who Changed Science—and the World* (New York: Broadway Books, 2015), 5.

27. Swaby, *Headstrong*, 5. My account of Jacobi's curiosity follows Swaby's.

4

Carefulness

Mind Your Evidence

In the last chapter, we examined curiosity, a virtue that impels us toward truth and knowledge. In this chapter, we'll consider curiosity's mirror image: intellectual carefulness. This virtue repels us from falsehood and unreasonable belief. It supplies motivation to avoid these intellectual evils, and helps us succeed in doing so. If curiosity is the melody of the intellectual life, carefulness is a vital harmony.

Carefulness becomes relevant when falsehood and unreasonable belief are realistic threats. We're not likely to make mistakes about whether there's a book in front of us (when there is), or whether $2 + 2 = 4$. But in many areas, we're highly fallible. In these areas, it's easy for us to form beliefs that are false, or unreasonable, or both. To avoid such mistakes—and to raise our odds of getting things right—we'll want to mind our evidence. We'll want to avoid going where it doesn't lead, and to follow it where it does.

When it comes to doing this, we humans are a mixed bag. On the one hand, we know a lot. We've combined evidence from sense perception, memory, and rational insight to create modern science—a staggering display of intellectual prowess. On the other hand, credible research shows that we're prone to basic mistakes in thinking about probabilities, in weighing various bits of evidence, and in reasoning from small sample sizes.[1] As a way to explore this fallibility, try answering the following problems.

1. Linda is 31 years old, single, outspoken, and very bright. In college, she majored in philosophy. As a student, she was deeply

The Excellent Mind. Nathan L. King, Oxford University Press (2021). © Oxford University Press.
DOI: 10.1093/oso/9780190096250.003.0004

concerned with issues of discrimination and social justice, and also participated in antinuclear demonstrations. Which is more probable? (a) Linda is a bank teller; or (b) Linda is a bank teller and is active in the feminist movement.[2]

2. You are a doctor. Leonard comes to you for a blood test. When the results come in, you tell him that he has tested positive for HIV. Among those who are tested, the prevalence of HIV in Leonard's demographic is 1 in 10,000. When he presses for more information, you tell him that the test gives a false positive in only 1 out of 1,000 samples. That is, only 1 in 1,000 people without the disease will test positive anyway. Badly shaken, Leonard asks you for the odds that he really has HIV. Should you tell him: (a) there is a 999 in 1,000 chance that he has HIV; (b) he probably has HIV, though the chances are less than 999 in 1,000; (c) he probably does *not* have HIV; or (d) his odds of having HIV are around fifty-fifty?[3]

3. You're at a cocktail party for new employees at your company. You meet Andy, a new addition to your department. He seems nervous, and has difficulty keeping up the conversation. He brags about his education: "I went to Cornell. Maybe you've heard of it." He seems eager to advertise his accomplishments, and uninterested in yours. On the whole, the conversation leaves you with a poor first impression of Andy. He seems arrogant and cold. Because of this, you steer clear of him for six months. During this time, you retain your low opinion of him. How confident should you be that Andy is the jerk he seems to be?

The answers are below in the footnote.[*]

How did you do? If you're like most people, you probably missed at least one. There's no shame in this. (For what it's worth, I didn't

---

[*] The answers: 1. (a) is more likely than (b). 2. (c): the odds are only about 1 in 11 that Leonard has HIV. 3. Not very confident.

get all of them right on the first try, either.) Just missing these questions doesn't make you a careless thinker. The point is to see just how easy it is for us to make mistakes—and to begin to care about how to fix them. Let's dig into the problems and see what we can learn.

The Conjunction Fallacy (Question 1)

Most of those asked said that, given the description, it is more likely that Linda is a feminist and a bank teller than that she is a bank teller. But this is wrong. We can think of it this way: the claim that Linda is a feminist *and* a bank teller includes the idea that she's a bank teller *plus* the idea that she is a feminist. But adding to a claim can't make it more probable. In fact, it is a basic rule of probability theory that for any claims C1 and C2, the probability that both of them are true is less than or equal to the probability that one of them is true. Thus, the probability of (C1&C2) is less than or equal to the probability of C1 alone. To ignore this rule is to commit the *conjunction fallacy*. It can help to visualize the problem as in figure 4.1.

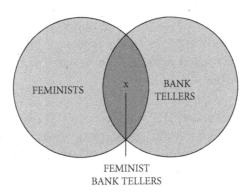

Figure 4.1 Specificity and Probability

The class of feminist bank tellers is already included in the class of bank tellers. So it can't be more likely that Linda is a feminist bank teller than that she's simply a bank teller.

If you missed this item, you're not alone. When asked the same question, 85% of students in the decision science program at Stanford Graduate School of Business ranked "feminist bank teller" as more likely than "bank teller"![4]

The Base Rate Fallacy (Question 2)

Recall the HIV test case. As it happens, this example is based on a true story. Former Caltech physicist and popular science writer Leonard Mlodinow describes it in his book *The Drunkard's Walk*. It all started when Mlodinow visited his doctor to take an HIV test in order to clear up some problems with his insurance company. When he tested positive for HIV, Mlodinow's doctor told him that there was a 999 out of 1,000 chance he actually had the disease, and would almost certainly die within ten years. On receiving the news one Friday afternoon, Mlodinow was stunned: "It is hard to describe or even remember how the weekend went for me, but let's just say I did not go to Disneyland."[5]

After a bit more thinking, Mlodinow figured out that the odds of his having HIV were actually quite low. Let's follow his reasoning. To solve the problem, we must remember *both* that the test has a very low false positive rate (1 in 1,000) *and* that HIV is rare in Mlodinow's demographic—male, heterosexual non-drug users who have taken the test. (The rate is 1 in 10,000.) The doctor's error was to ignore the latter figure. The prevalence of disease in Mlodinow's demographic is called the *base rate* for the disease in that group. And while base rates are crucial for judging the likelihood that a positive test is due to a disease, they are frequently ignored. To ignore the base rate is to commit the *base rate fallacy*.

To see why this is a mistake, let's suppose there are 10,000 people in Mlodinow's group. Assume a false negative rate near zero. Given the test's false positive rate of 1 in 1,000, about 10 people in the group will test positive despite *not* having the disease. Given the incidence of the disease in the group (1 in 10,000), one person will test positive due to the disease. That plus the 10 false positive tests adds up to 11 positive tests out of 10,000. The rest of the people in the group—9,989—will test negative. Now, because he tested positive, we know Mlodinow is not in that group. He's one of the 11 positive tests. But because there is only one *true* positive test in the 11 positives, this makes the odds of his having the disease given a positive test about 1 in 11. In other words, taking into account both the base rate and the false positive rate, the doctor should have concluded that Mlodinow's odds of actually having HIV were low—enough to justify a retest, but far from what had initially seemed like a death sentence. We can represent the situation as in figure 4.2 (one square represents 100 people).

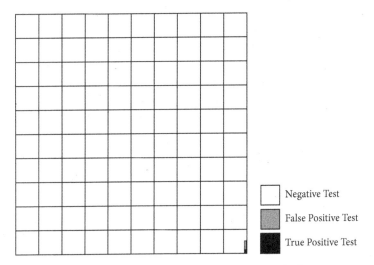

Negative Test

False Positive Test

True Positive Test

Figure 4.2 Probability of a True Positive, Accounting for Low Base Rate

One lesson here is that in order to avoid false diagnoses, doctors must remember to account for base rates. Another lesson is that patients must remind doctors to account for these rates. Recall: Mlodinow's example is not some abstract illustration of the base rate fallacy—it really happened. His careful assessment of the probability not only cleared up his insurance problems; it may have kept him from undertaking a harmful and unnecessary course of medicine.

Here's another reason to beware of the base rate fallacy: most people are inclined to commit it. Research by Amos Tversky and Daniel Kahneman shows that it's not just a mistake, it's one that we're prone to make.[6] Unfortunately, not even highly educated people (e.g., doctors) are immune to base rate neglect. Indeed, Mlodinow's doctor isn't an outlier; he's closer to the norm. The problem has become so widespread that there is a growing medical literature lamenting the frequency of misdiagnoses caused by cognitive mistakes, including the base rate fallacy.[7] To highlight these mistakes isn't to pick at intellectual nits. Such errors harm patients and undermine trust in doctors.

Unrepresentative Evidence (Question 3)

When Andy brags about having attended Cornell and then treats us coldly, it is natural to form a poor first impression of him. It's understandable that we'd want to avoid him, given that impression. The trouble is that if we avoid him for six months while retaining our low opinion of him, we base our view on a small and biased sample. Chances are, if we talked to Andy several times after the party, our interactions would be at least a bit better. And if we had dozens of moderately positive experiences with Andy, we'd have a larger and more representative sample from which to form beliefs about his character. Assuming Andy is at least a decent person (most people are—that's why the real jerks stand out), there is a lot of evidence "out there" that he's better than we initially thought. However, if we avoid him completely, we're blind to this evidence. Our good opinion once lost is lost forever.[8] But however rigid it becomes, this opinion is not likely to be true, based as it was on a small and tainted sample.

Careless Thinking Can Be Disastrous

Lots of us make mistakes in answering questions like the ones we considered above. Again: this doesn't mean that we're intellectually careless. Some of us just don't know the relevant rules of reasoning—or didn't know them until just now. The point is that as statistical reasoners, we humans are prone to error. As we seek to grow in intellectual carefulness, we'll want to learn more about how to avoid such mistakes. More on this in a bit.

For now, let's consider in more detail why careful thinking is important. Some of the cases we've discussed already suggest that it is. Medical misdiagnosis (Mlodinow's case) can be harmful, even deadly. And biased thinking about others (Andy's case) can hurt others and cost us friends. To thicken the mix, let's consider more examples. In his essay "The Ethics of Belief," W. K. Clifford (1845–1879) imagines a shipowner who is about to send an emigrant ship to sea:

> He knew that she was old, and not over-well built at the first; that she had seen many seas and climes, and often had needed repairs. Doubts had been suggested to him that possibly she was not seaworthy. These doubts preyed upon his mind and made him unhappy; he thought that perhaps he ought to have her thoroughly overhauled and refitted, even though this should put him to great expense. Before the ship sailed, however, he succeeded in overcoming these melancholy reflections. He said to himself that she had gone safely through so many voyages and weathered so

many storms that it was idle to suppose she would not come safely home from this trip also. He would put his trust in Providence, which could hardly fail to protect all these unhappy families that were leaving their fatherland to seek for better times elsewhere. He would dismiss from his mind all ungenerous suspicions about the honesty of builders and contractors. In such ways he acquired a sincere and comfortable conviction that his vessel was thoroughly safe and seaworthy; he watched her departure with a light heart, and benevolent wishes for the success of the exiles in their strange new home that was to be; and he got his insurance money when she went down in midocean and told no tales.[9]

Clifford's example, though vivid, is a fiction. Here are some real cases:

- In 1999, NASA's Mars Climate Orbiter was lost before entering into its scheduled orbit of Mars. The mission was a joint effort between aerospace company Lockheed Martin, which used English units in its computer files for the craft, and NASA's Jet Propulsion Laboratory, which used metric units in charting the craft's navigation. As the Orbiter approached Mars, the ground crew believed all was well. However, because no one converted the craft's flight instructions from English to metric units, the craft was left too close to the Martian surface to enter into orbit. The Orbiter crashed—a $125 million mistake.[10]
- The present author's wedding video was ruined when the videographer neglected a time zone difference and arrived an hour late—a $125 mistake.

In these examples, failures to heed evidence led to trouble because they led people into falsehood. But suppose that things had turned out differently. Suppose the shipowner's vessel had sailed safely and delivered the emigrants to kinder shores. Suppose the Mars Orbiter had somehow entered into a safe orbit. Suppose the wedding had been delayed by an hour. Would these happy reversals of fortune let everyone off the hook? Not at all. The relevant beliefs were formed carelessly. Had these beliefs turned out to be true, the people who formed them would not have been reasonable. They would have been *lucky*. In Clifford's words, they "would not be innocent. They would only be not found out."[11]

It matters a great deal whether our beliefs are true or false. So, it matters how we arrive at them. This point holds not just for those who lease ships or build spacecraft or film weddings. It holds for all of us. And it holds in daily life as well as on monumental occasions. If we want to avoid falsehood and its friend, irrationality, we'll want to grow in carefulness. With that, let's think some more about what carefulness *is*.

Intellectual Carefulness and Its Rivals

For starters, it will help to locate carefulness in relation to the vices that oppose it: the deficiency of carelessness and the excess of scrupulousness (see table 4.1).

We have already explored the deficiency end of the spectrum with the shipowner, Mars Orbiter, and wedding video cases. There we find people performing intellectually careless *acts*. These people form their beliefs as an intellectually careless person would. But this does not mean they have the vice of intellectual carelessness. To be careless *people*—to have the vice of carelessness—they would need to have a stable tendency to think carelessly as a matter of habit,

Table 4.1 Carefulness as a Mean between Extremes

Sphere of activity	Vice (deficiency)	Virtue (mean)	Vice (excess)
Reasoning from evidence	Carelessness	Carefulness	Scrupulousness

in many different situations. But they don't. Aerospace engineers aren't hired at NASA or Lockheed Martin for being careless.[12] And I hired my friend to record my wedding because I knew he was qualified and committed to doing a good job. In these cases, it seems likely that those involved acted uncharacteristically. Despite their usual carefulness, they committed careless acts on the given occasions. This does not excuse the acts. But one careless act does not make a careless character. (As for my wedding videographer, let's not be too hard on him. His mistake is not on the order of crashing the Mars Orbiter. And his mistake was uncharacteristic. He went on to produce Emmy-winning TV shows, no doubt executing production with great care.)

Intellectual carefulness is opposed not just to carelessness, but also to intellectual *scrupulousness*—an excessive obsession with avoiding intellectual mistakes. Consider these excessive acts:

- An otherwise normal office manager is writing an email to employees about an optional office party. In order to ensure that she has the party's date and time correct, she proofreads her message 35 times.
- A history student is weeks away from completing her doctoral dissertation. Her advisors assure her that the work is well argued. But she finds herself plagued with doubt over an unanswered objection to a relatively unimportant claim in the work's third chapter. Terrified of saying something false (even if insignificant), she lets this doubt overwhelm her view of the whole manuscript. She never submits the work, and never earns her degree.

The intellectually careful person won't be disposed toward such acts—at least not as a matter of habit. When it comes to seeking and evaluating evidence, the careful person will want and tend to avoid both the deficiency of carelessness and the excess of scrupulousness.

Table 4.2 Three Attitudes toward a Claim, C

Belief	Suspension of judgment	Disbelief
Thinking that C is true	Neither thinking that C is true nor thinking that C is false	Thinking that C is false

Once we recognize scrupulousness as a vice, we're in position to appreciate something that's easy to overlook: skepticism is not necessarily virtuous. To see the point, we can start by distinguishing three different attitudes we can take toward a claim. We can believe it (think it's true). We can disbelieve it (think it's false). Or we can suspend judgment about it—neither believing nor disbelieving, but instead offering an intellectual shrug of the shoulders. For example, in a typical kind of case, a theist believes in God, an atheist disbelieves, and an agnostic suspends judgment.[13] More generally, where C is a dummy letter that can stand for any claim we are considering, we can picture the situation as in table 4.2.

In the ancient world, some philosophers—the original Skeptics—argued that suspending judgment is always the reasonable attitude to take, because this is the attitude that our evidence always supports. According to this idea, suspending judgment is always justified—skepticism is a virtue.[14]

Now, there are lots of cases in which we *should* suspend judgment about a claim—say, cases where we haven't considered the relevant evidence at all, or where that evidence is divided. But suspending judgment isn't *always* sensible. If the forecast says there's a 95% chance of rain, suspending judgment would be silly; the evidence makes rain much more likely than not. Another case: my friend just told me that the New England Patriots won today's game against the Detroit Lions. I haven't yet checked the score online, but New England almost always beats Detroit. Further, my friend is an honest person, and I'm sure that he was in a position to know who won. In such a case, it is more reasonable to believe that New England won than it is to suspend judgment (or disbelieve, for that matter). Finally, if I buy a ticket for tonight's lotto drawing, it's far more reasonable for me to believe I'll lose than it is to suspend judgment about that claim.

There are innumerable cases like these, but the point is clear enough: suspending judgment doesn't get a free pass. It is just as subject to scrutiny as belief and disbelief are. Which attitude is most reasonable depends upon the details of a given case. It is no more careful to suspend judgment when the evidence strongly supports belief than it is to believe when the evidence supports suspending judgment. Further, if we perpetually suspend judgment in order to avoid falsehood, we're sure to find ourselves missing out on the truth. *Skepticism* in itself isn't a virtue. It can easily devolve into scrupulousness. *Carefulness* is the relevant virtue here.

Excellence in Minding Our Evidence

As we saw in chapters 2 and 3, just locating a virtue between two vices doesn't tell us all we want to know about it. We aren't simply seeking a happy medium, as if virtue were Goldilocks's porridge. We want to know what the mean consists in—for this will reveal why it is excellent. For that, again, the target image will help. In the case of carefulness, it might look something like figure 4.3.

To be virtuously careful, we need to focus on the right *objects*: we need to be careful in our thinking about the right claims and projects. We also need to exercise carefulness at the right *times* (on the right occasions). We need to use the right *means* and methods in assessing our evidence. And we need to be careful for the right reasons; our care must stem from the right *motives*. Gaining clarity on these matters will help us see why carefulness is excellent, and will show how it expresses the intellectual character of those who have it.

WRONG OBJECT
(e.g., easy topic)

WRONG OCCASION
(e.g., after double-
checking)

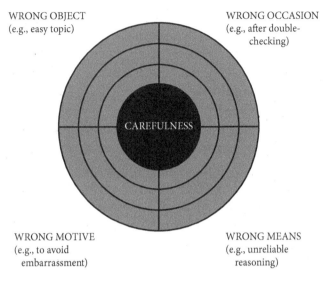

WRONG MOTIVE
(e.g., to avoid
embarrassment)

WRONG MEANS
(e.g., unreliable
reasoning)

Figure 4.3 Carefulness as Hitting the Target

Objects

Intellectually careful thinkers take the appropriate amount of care, given their objects or topics of study. There are at least three dimensions to this.

First, some topics seem to welcome precision while others stubbornly resist it. Some topics *allow* for more precision than others. It's our job to know the difference. As Aristotle says, "It is the mark of an educated person to look for precision in each class of things just so far as the nature of the subject admits."[15] In mathematics, for instance, we can reasonably expect that we'll be able achieve precise answers to our questions. But it would be absurd to expect mathematical precision in messy, humanistic fields like literary criticism and history—and virtue theory.

Second, some topics *demand* more precision than others do. Recall the dissertation author who became worried about a small detail. To be sure, it is important that she write carefully and seek to avoid error. But her chosen topic, history, does not call for absolute precision. She can submit genuinely excellent work even if her writing includes minor inaccuracies—especially if these don't affect the soundness of her argument. It might even be scrupulous for her to refrain from submitting the work and completing her degree on account of these inaccuracies. She may be well advised to follow the sage advice, "The best dissertation is a finished dissertation."

Contrast our dissertation author's project with that of chemist Jöns Jacob Berzelius (1779–1848). Berzelius's task was to measure the atomic weights of various elements. At the time, methods for doing so were shoddy and inaccurate, leaving the results of chemical experiments in doubt. A discontented Berzelius set out to do better. Rom Harré describes Berzelius's methods:

> The secret of his success was a kind of perfectionism, an obsession with accuracy. "My first attempts in this were not successful," he says. "I still had no experience regarding the great accuracy that was needed, nor how a greater accuracy could be obtained in the final results." The answer to these troubles lay in attention to detail. Equipment had to be designed so that there was as little loss of material as possible. In reactions which required pouring the vessels had to have lips that discharged the very last drop. Filter papers not only had to have a standard residue of ash, but it was advisable to wet them before they were to be used, to prevent some of the substances dissolved in the solute being dissolved by the fibres of the paper. But above all manipulative technique had to be precise. It consisted in "observing a large number of small details which, if overlooked, often spoil several weeks of careful work."[16]

This must have been maddeningly difficult labor. But because high-level chemistry is unfamiliar to many of us, it may be easier to appreciate Berzelius's work by analogy to cooking. Imagine making pancakes for an omniscient foodie. Indeed, imagine that this foodie is not only all-knowing, but also extremely *picky*, and so will chuck the whole batch if you omit a single drop of oil or grain of flour. *That* is the level of precision Berzelius's work demanded—for the slightest mistake would result in a ruined, unreliable data set. From 1810 to 1818, he further refined his techniques, so that by the end of the period Berzelius announced the atomic weights of 45 of the 49 elements then known. His painstaking methodology helped confirm the view that each element is made up of a different kind of atom—an advance that solidified the foundations of modern chemistry. Berzelius applied precisely the degree of carefulness for which his study called.

Here is a third point. As we saw in the last chapter, some topics are more important than others are. Indeed, some topics don't deserve our attention in the first place—so they certainly don't deserve our *careful* attention. If I'm already satisfying vain curiosity by counting the blades of grass on my lawn, it's not like I get extra credit for counting them carefully.

So: which objects deserve our careful thought? And of those objects that do deserve care, *how much* do they deserve? Unfortunately—but appropriately given our topic—these questions don't admit precise answers. There's no algorithm for intellectual carefulness. But a list of guidelines might include the following:

- When our beliefs about a topic X have logical implications for a large number of other beliefs, we should consider X carefully. Our beliefs about what's real, what can be known, and what it is to live well fit into this category.
- Other things being equal, topics central to human flourishing tend to deserve more care than those that are peripheral. Inquiries into medicine, the nature of justice, the ethics of war, the education of children, and the distribution of wealth will tend to deserve greater care than inquiries into celebrity fashion trends.

- Topics central to our vocation will tend to deserve careful thought. An auto mechanic will need to exercise care in engine diagnosis, a doctor in medical diagnosis, and so on.
- Topics about which we form policies that affect others will tend to deserve careful thought. For example, to vote responsibly, we must ensure that we are informed on the relevant issues and have arrived at our views by assessing relevant evidence carefully.

Virtuously careful thinkers seek to allocate their intellectual resources well by considering such factors.

Occasions

When should we be careful? Well, it's not like there's some specific time of day—say 9:00 a.m.—when carefulness becomes important. It's not like we could sensibly "clock in" to carefulness at nine, only to "clock out" at five in the afternoon. The "when" here is referring to our *circumstances*.

Not all circumstances call for carefulness. As we saw earlier, we needn't be careful when there's no realistic chance of our getting things wrong. We needn't exercise carefulness—or not much of it—when doing basic sums that we almost never miss. (So there is a close connection between the objects of our carefulness and the occasions for it.) Likewise, it's no failure of carefulness if, after double-checking a basic sum, we decline to triple-check it.

Nor do any circumstances demand our thinking about topics that don't matter. We shouldn't think about such topics at all, so we shouldn't bother thinking about them carefully. For nearly all of us, it would be a waste of time and intellectual energy to devote careful attention to discovering the thread-count of Justin Bieber's socks. There's no time at which we need to know that. Again, selecting the proper occasions for carefulness is partly a matter of selecting the proper objects.

Finally, we might have to "pass" on carefully considering important topic X in order to devote careful attention to some more pressing topic Y. After all, as finite beings, we don't have time to consider *everything* carefully. The cell biologist who declines to devote herself to the careful study of literature needn't thereby lack carefulness. Given her time constraints, scholarly responsibilities, and so on, it may be impossible for her to study both subjects with care.

If carefulness isn't called for all of the time, when *is* it called for? Here's a rule of thumb that should prove helpful. Whenever all three of the following conditions hold, it's an occasion for carefulness:

- there is a realistic possibility of our forming a false or unreasonable belief, so that we need to consider evidence in order to help ourselves avoid error;
- the topic at issue is important enough to merit our attention; and
- no more important or more pressing object of study presents itself at the time.

Fallibility. Importance. Timeliness. For many of us, these conditions will hold often, across a wide range of topics. At those times, we'll want to exercise carefulness. (Please take a moment to think of some topics on which these conditions hold for you, right now. Do you have them in mind? If so, the next step is to consider *how* to think carefully about them.)

Means

Once we realize we're in circumstances that call for carefulness—and thus for the evaluation of evidence—how should we proceed? What means can we employ in order to think more carefully?

A good answer: we can learn the key elements of logic, critical thinking, and statistical reasoning.

Of course, it can be hard to find time to do this. Here's a suggestion that may help in the meantime: we can learn a specific *thinking routine* that's easy to recall and use. We can learn to ask good questions about our evidence and the attitudes it supports. This should give us at least a puncher's chance in the fight against falsehood.

Harvard educational theorist Ron Ritchhart suggests such a routine: the CSQ (Claim, Support, Question) routine.[17] To use this routine, we identify the *claim* at issue (say, that Andy is a jerk or that Leonard has a disease). We then identify the *support* offered on behalf of that claim (that Andy said something arrogant or that Leonard tested positive). We then ask *questions* about the supporting link between the evidence and the claim. For example:

- Is my judgment based on a small or biased sample? (E.g., is it likely that I've ignored more flattering evidence about Andy?)
- If my topic is disputed, have I read arguments from different perspectives?
- Is my judgment based on *all* of the relevant evidence, or at least a representative sample?
- Am I ignoring part of my evidence? (E.g., am I ignoring my knowledge of the base rate for a disease?)
- What alternative conclusions are consistent with my evidence?
- Does my evidence *really* provide strong support for believing the claim at issue?
- Or does it support suspending judgment or even disbelief?

These are just a few of the many questions we might ask. Asking them won't always ensure that we avoid making mistakes— intellectual carefulness does not guarantee that we'll get the truth. But it does raise our odds. Asking questions like these can help us resist the temptation to make hasty judgments. It can signal that before we make a judgment about something that's not obvious, we need to brush up on the relevant rules of evidence, or to seek help from someone who knows them. Even modest progress in these areas can make a major difference for us. One fewer fallacy can mean one fewer false belief. One fewer mistake can mean one fewer disaster. And if we get in the habit of asking CSQ-style questions, over time, we're likely to get better at minding our evidence. In other words, we're likely to become more consistently careful thinkers.

Motives

As we've seen, virtuously careful thinkers exercise their care about the right things, at the right times, and in the right ways. They select good objects for carefulness, on appropriate occasions, and employ good means of reasoning.

So far, so good. But these factors alone don't ensure virtuous carefulness. Consider:

> *"Careful" Cal*: Cal works in the analytics department of a stock-trading firm. His job is to assess data about recent market trends for the traders who work alongside him. His work is complicated, so Cal is vigilant about avoiding errors. He's adept at figuring out precisely when his work calls for extra care. He uses reliable methods to avoid making false and unreasonable inferences from the data. Cal very much wants to avoid falsehoods and unreasonable beliefs. However, he only cares about these things because he wants to avoid being fired—or just embarrassed—for making a mistake.

In a way, Cal is careful. But his carefulness isn't virtuous because he lacks the right motive. To exercise virtuous carefulness, he must want to avoid making intellectual mistakes *because* these are intellectually bad. The same goes for us.

From Curiosity and Carefulness to Autonomy

In the last chapter, we explored curiosity—a virtue that motivates our quest for truth and knowledge. In this chapter, we considered carefulness—a virtue that motivates our efforts to avoid falsehood and unreasonable belief. At least in practice, we often pursue these goals in tandem. To arrive at the truth is to avoid falsehood. By carefully avoiding falsehood, we often get to the truth. Taken together, curiosity and carefulness get our thinking started, and send it in the right direction.

But the virtuous quest for knowledge is a little like a road trip—we shouldn't expect to get very far unless we're willing to do our share of the driving. As we pursue knowledge—and intellectual virtue—we must take responsibility for our own learning. No one will do this for us. With that in mind, let's turn our attention to intellectual autonomy, the virtue that leads us to think for ourselves.

For Reflection and Discussion

1. In this chapter, the author gives several examples in which careless thinking leads to disaster. See if you can develop an example of your own.
2. How is intellectual carefulness different from its vice counterparts?
3. Recall Berzelius's impeccable intellectual carefulness. Must we think of that carefulness as motivated by a desire to avoid error? Or could we sensibly think of Berzelius as motivated by a desire to get things *exactly right*? If the latter, how might the account of carefulness developed in this chapter need amendment?
4. Intellectual carefulness helps us avoid falsehood and unreasonable belief. But don't other intellectual virtues (say, humility and open-mindedness) do that, too? If so, what might

this suggest about how intellectual carefulness is related to these other virtues?

5. Take a moment to try Ritchhart's CSQ (Claim, Support, Question) routine. Do this with one of your own beliefs. Identify the claim. Identify your support for it. Then, make a list of questions about whether this support is adequate. Finally, answer these questions carefully.

Further Reading

For an introduction to logical reasoning skills, see Anthony Weston, *A Rulebook for Arguments*, (Indianapolis: Hackett, 2018). For a more thorough treatment, see Frances Howard-Snyder, Daniel Howard-Snyder, and Ryan Wasserman, *The Power of Logic* (New York: McGraw-Hill, 2020). Religiously oriented readers will appreciate T. Ryan Byerly's virtue-centered introduction to logic, *Introducing Logic and Critical Thinking: The Skills of Reasoning and the Virtues of Inquiry* (Grand Rapids, MI: Baker Academic, 2017). For an accessible discussion of reasoning about probability, see Leonard Mlodinow, *The Drunkard's Walk: How Randomness Rules Our Lives* (New York: Pantheon Books, 2008). For a more formal introduction, see Ian Hacking, *An Introduction to Probability and Inductive Logic* (New York: Cambridge University Press, 2001). For work in empirical psychology that treats a range of biases in human thinking, see Thomas Gilovich, *How We Know What Isn't So: The Fallibility of Human Reason in Everyday Life* (New York: The Free Press, 1991); also Daniel Kahneman, *Thinking, Fast and Slow* (New York: Farrar, Straus and Giroux, 2011); and Richard E. Nisbett, *Mindware: Tools for Smart Thinking* (New York: Farrar, Straus and Giroux, 2015).

Notes

1. For a helpful overview see Thomas Gilovich, *How We Know What Isn't So: The Fallibility of Human Reason in Everyday Life* (New York: The Free Press, 1991).

2. This example is drawn from the work of Amos Tversky and Daniel Kahneman. (The version stated here is slightly simplified.) For further discussion, along with a multifaceted, empirically based research program

addressing cognitive failures, see Kahneman's bestselling book, *Thinking, Fast and Slow* (New York: Farrar, Straus and Giroux, 2011). See chapter 15 for a discussion of the Linda problem.

3. This problem is gleaned from Leonard Mlodinow, *The Drunkard's Walk: How Randomness Rules Our Lives* (New York: Pantheon Books, 2008), 114ff. Thanks to Leonard Mlodinow and Martha Gady for helpful discussion of the problem. My explanation follows Mlodinow's closely.

4. Kahneman, *Thinking, Fast and Slow*, 158.

5. Mlodinow, *The Drunkard's Walk*, 114.

6. See, for instance, Amos Tversky and Daniel Kahneman, "Judgment under Uncertainty: Heuristics and Biases," *Science*, New Series, 185, no. 4157 (1974), 1124–31.

7. For discussion and references see Meredith Stark and Joseph J. Fins, "The Ethical Imperative to Think about Thinking: Diagnostics, Metacognition, and Medical Professionalism," *Cambridge Quarterly of Healthcare Ethics* 23, no. 4 (2014), 386–96; also Mark Graber and Bob Carlson, "Diagnostic Error: The Hidden Epidemic," *Physician Executive* 37, no. 6 (2011), 12–19.

8. I borrow this line from Jane Austen's Mr. Darcy. See Austen, *Pride and Prejudice* (Hertfordshire: Wordsworth, 1992), 54.

9. Clifford, *The Ethics of Belief and Other Essays* (Amherst, NY: Prometheus Books, 1999), 70.

10. Kathy Sawyer, "Mystery of Orbiter Crash Solved," *Washington Post*, October 1, 1999, A1.

11. Clifford, *The Ethics of Belief*, 72.

12. For this point, I am indebted to Philip Dow's treatment of the *Mariner 1* disaster in his *Virtuous Minds* (Downers Grove, IL: InterVarsity Press, 2013), chapter 2.

13. The qualifier, "in the typical case," is intended to cover cases of theists whose faith in God does not involve belief. For a helpful treatment of this kind of faith see Daniel Howard-Snyder, "Propositional Faith: What It Is, and What It Is Not," *American Philosophical Quarterly* 50, no. 4 (2013), 357–72. See also Daniel McKaughan, "Authentic Faith and Acknowledged Risk: Dissolving the Problem of Faith and Reason," *Religious Studies* 49, no. 1 (2013), 101–24.

14. For a detailed treatment see R. J. Hankinson, *The Sceptics* (New York: Routledge, 1995).

15. Aristotle, *Nicomachean Ethics*, Book I, part 3, trans. W. D. Ross with a revision by J. O. Urmson, in *The Complete Works of Aristotle*, vol. 2, ed.

Jonathan Barnes (Princeton: Princeton University Press, 1984), 1730. I have ungendered this quotation.

16. Rom Harré, *Great Scientific Experiments* (Oxford: Phaidon Press, 1981), 205.

17. See Ron Ritchhart, *Intellectual Character: What It Is, Why It Matters, and How to Get It* (San Francisco: Jossey-Bass, 2002), chapter 5.

5

Autonomy

Think for Yourself

In 19th-century America, many women labored outside the home.
They were paid far less for their work than men who did the same
jobs. A woman's wages could be confiscated and handed over to her
husband—even if he was a drunkard, and even if this left her desti-
tute. If she sought to divorce an abusive husband, she could count
on *his* being awarded custody of their children.[1] As for education,
the standard view was that women should be educated only to the
extent that it enabled them to make men happy.[2]

Women who sought to change these conditions were seen as
threats to the social order. Most men thought it unseemly for a
woman to contribute to public life. A widely circulated pastoral
letter warns any woman who would openly argue for her rights,
"When she assumes the place and tone of man as a public re-
former . . . she yields the power which God has given her for her
protection, and her character becomes unnatural."[3] When in
1836 Sarah and Angelina Grimké pioneered the practice of public
campaigning in front of mixed audiences, they were roundly
rebuked as agitators.

As if opposition from society weren't enough, women often faced
discouragement in their own homes. Elizabeth Cady Stanton was
born in November 1815. Her father, a judge, counseled women in
distress over laws that favored men. As a child, Elizabeth was ever-
present in her father's office. Repeatedly, she saw him provide assistance from his own pocket, but go on to explain that the women
had no legal recourse against their neglectful or abusive husbands.

The Excellent Mind. Nathan L. King, Oxford University Press (2021). © Oxford University Press.
DOI: 10.1093/oso/9780190096250.003.0005

Unfair laws impeded women's progress. Patriarchy prevailed. And the young Elizabeth was there to listen to it all.[4] Worse still, not even she could escape disregard on account of her gender. In a moving passage, she recalls,

> When I was eleven years old. . . . My only brother, who had just graduated from Union College, came home to die. A young man of great talent and promise, he was the pride of my father's heart. We early felt that this son filled a larger place in our father's affections and future plans than the five daughters together.[5]

After her brother's passing, Elizabeth found her father in the funeral parlor:

> As he took no notice of me, after standing a long while, I climbed upon his knee, when he mechanically put his arm about me and, with my head resting against his beating heart, we both sat in silence, he thinking of the wreck of all his hopes in the loss of a dear son, and I wondering what could be said or done to fill the void in his breast. At length he heaved a deep sigh and said: "Oh, my daughter, I wish you were a boy!" Throwing my arms about his neck, I replied: "I will try to be all my brother was."[6]

And so she did. Stanton went on to become a key organizer of the landmark Seneca Falls Convention for women's rights in 1848, and a central figure in the suffrage movement. In doing so, she stood autonomously against stale convention.

When she married Henry Stanton in 1840, Elizabeth refused to utter the traditional vow to obey her husband: "I obstinately refused to obey one with whom I supposed I was entering into an equal relation."[7] This she did with Henry's approval—a small win for women's dignity. But by then it had become clear that there would be no real change for women without the vote. To her dismay, when Elizabeth set out to work for suffrage, Henry resisted. In preparation for

Seneca Falls, Elizabeth drafted A Declaration of Sentiments. By design, the document paralleled the US Declaration of Independence, and argued that women were endowed with the same inalienable rights as men. When Elizabeth read aloud the Declaration's insistence on votes for women, Henry announced that he wanted no part of the convention—and left town. Elizabeth would have to present the document without her husband's support.[8]

The story of women in the 19th century is replete with similar scenes. Such stories illustrate intellectual autonomy in action. Suffragists pushed social boundaries forward in the face of overwhelming opposition. Stanton showed autonomy mainly through her revolutionary philosophizing about women's rights. Her most famous collaborator, Susan B. Anthony, showed it through her organization and advocacy. Anthony's groundbreaking use of the petition was a major factor in gaining a hearing for suffrage. She gave legs to Stanton's ideas, traveling and speaking on behalf of the cause with unprecedented fervor. During a women's rights event in Syracuse, New York, a mob of armed and angry men interrupted the lecture. The chief of police did nothing to help. Anthony stared down the rabble until the men reached the stage, while the other women in the hall were escorted out.[9]

People don't do such things without the willingness to think for themselves—without a willingness to take ultimate responsibility for the governance of their own minds, and to challenge stale thinking with fresh ideas. Such autonomy is important not just for suffragists, but for *everyone*. Parents want it for their children. They earnestly hope that their kids will grow up to think and live wisely once they're on their own. Bosses demand it of their employees— thus the business world cliché that good workers "think outside the box." Teachers want it for their students. I know progressive college professors who hope that their tutelage enables students to discard the orthodoxies of their conservative parents. And I know conservative professors who hope that their students have the autonomy needed to resist mindless political correctness. These hopes are at loggerheads. But they betray an underlying agreement: for students to have excellent minds, they must learn to think for themselves.

This kind of autonomy is arguably the star character of the 17th- and 18th-century Enlightenment. As standard history has it, ancient and medieval cultures overvalued authority in the economy of knowledge. The Enlightenment, by contrast, prized the solitary thinker, the scholar willing to buck trends and think autonomously in order to overturn outmoded doctrines. Immanuel Kant implores his reader: "Have courage to make use of your *own* understanding! is . . . the motto of enlightenment."[10]

As much as anyone, the scientific revolutionaries of the 16th and 17th centuries—Copernicus, Galileo, Brahe, Kepler, and Newton— embody this ideal.[11] They are the mentors of the Enlightenment thinkers who arrived a century later. Given their prominence in the history of autonomy, it is fitting for us to examine their story.

In 1543, Nicolaus Copernicus published *On the Revolutions of the Heavenly Spheres*. In this great work, he dared to oppose the Aristotelian-Ptolemaic astronomy that had reigned since ancient times. According to that view, the physics of the heavens are wholly different from those of Earth. The celestial bodies are perfect and unchanging, while things on Earth are in constant flux. The Earth sits still at the center of the universe: *geocentrism*. The Sun, Moon, and planets revolve around it in circular orbits. As they dance around the Earth, the planets pause mid-orbit for miniature loop-to-loops called *epicycles*. These explain why we observe retrograde motion: when viewed from Earth over several months, the planets appear to reverse their courses in the night sky. Figure 5.1 shows the movement of Mars, as seen from Earth. It appears to double back on itself and then continue forward. Figure 5.2 shows how the Ptolemaic view explains these observations: it affirms that the planets move backward before proceeding in their orbits.

It is hard for modern minds to appreciate how formidable the geocentric view was in its prime. A remarkable intellectual achievement, the system accurately predicted planetary orbits and eclipses.

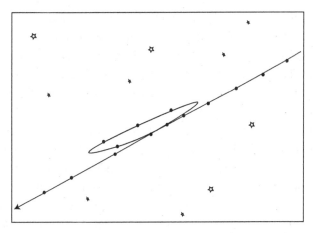

Figure 5.1 Retrograde Motion Viewed from Earth

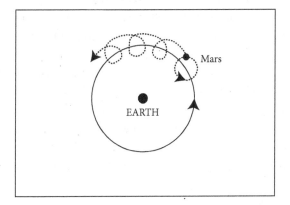

Figure 5.2 Epicycles Explain Retrograde Motion

It also enjoyed empirical support: if the Earth is rotating on its axis, why should our senses tell us that it is stationary? Surely a rotating planet would fling its inhabitants about like a merry-go-round does to unrestrained children. We see nothing of the sort, people thought, so the Earth must be still. The old view also had nearly two thousand years of tradition on its side. Thus, any model that would replace it had to overcome a lot of inertia. Finally, the Catholic Church's official position was that the Bible taught geocentrism. Given the weight of the evidence from these sources, at the time, the reasonable person could've been forgiven for sticking to the old view.[12]

The astronomers of the Scientific Revolution—including Copernicus (1473–1543), Tycho Brahe (1546–1601), Johannes Kepler (1571–1630), Galileo Galilei (1564–1642), and Isaac Newton (1643–1727)—would turn this view inside out. To do so, they would need to exhibit awe-inspiring independent thought. Copernicus struck first. His system swapped the Earth for the Sun as the center. Then, in 1572, from an observatory that he had designed himself, Tycho Brahe witnessed a supernova—the explosion of a star. Tycho's star appeared suddenly, and was brighter than other stars in the sky. Then, after just months on the celestial stage, it disappeared—visual proof that the heavens were subject to change.[13]

Brahe had to make his observations with the naked eye. Decades later, Galileo made his through a powerful new invention, the telescope. The device, which Galileo himself honed, revealed that the Moon was not pristine, as Aristotle had thought. It was pocked with craters. And the Sun had irregular dark features—sunspots— that laid bare its propensity to change. Venus showed phases in its perceived shape similar to those of our Moon. This in turn showed that Venus orbits the Sun, not the Earth.[14] The old system was showing its cracks.

However, at this point everyone—even the heliocentrists—still thought that planetary orbits *had* to be circular. For otherwise, how could they be perfect, as all heavenly things were supposed to be? Enter Kepler. In a feat of stunning ingenuity, he replaced circular orbits with elliptical ones. Once his system was worked out, it was extremely accurate at predicting planetary movements. And crucially, it had no need for epicycles. The new system was simpler. This, combined with its accuracy, made it preferable to the old. It explained away retrograde motion as an optical illusion. Given its smaller orbit, Earth regularly passes Mars, which makes it appear (from Earth) as if Mars is moving backward in its path. By positing sun-centered elliptical orbits, Kepler could explain why things look this way without the need for spirographic epicycles (figures 5.3 and 5.4).[15]

In the crowning achievement of the new science, Newton's theory of gravitation combined Copernican astronomy with a theory of motion that surpassed anything Aristotle could have imagined. His law of universal gravitation explained the motion of both little earthly bodies (apples) and large heavenly ones (planets). The physics of Earth and heaven became one. Further, Newton's laws predicted the elliptical orbits that Kepler's data suggested.[16] In the face of the mounting evidence, tradition would have to yield. And church officials would start to read their Bibles through a

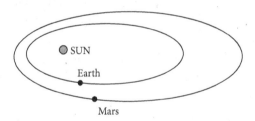

Figure 5.3 Positions of Earth and Mars at Time T₁

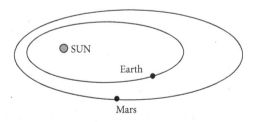

Figure 5.4 Positions of Earth and Mars at Time T₂

lesson Galileo learned from Cardinal Cesare Baronio: "The intention of the Holy Spirit is to teach us how one goes to heaven and not
how heaven goes."[17]

Dozens of science texts rehearse the preceding narrative in more detail than we have here. So what's the point of our doing it? It is this: intellectual autonomy played a major role in the invention of modern
science. In the face of tradition, experience, and authority, the scientific revolutionaries entertained the possibility that geocentrism was
wrong, and that physics and astronomy had to be remade. Without
their penchant for independent thought, our knowledge of the physical world would scarcely resemble what it is today. And—more to the
point—neither would our understanding of intellectual autonomy.

Getting Our Prepositions Right

These stories of suffrage and science are well known. Indeed, they
are so familiar that any reader who has had her morning coffee
might have predicted that they'd show up in a chapter on intellectual autonomy.

Here's something less obvious: as narratives of intellectual autonomy, the stories as told above are woefully incomplete. They
paint their protagonists as solitary rebels, and omit the ways in
which these thinkers relied on others' intellectual capital. But for
all its independence, intellectual autonomy is not a matter of going
it alone. As we'll see, no view of autonomy that neglects this point
can take the suffragists or scientists as its heroes. For *virtuous* independence, we have to rely on others, at least to some extent. We can
put it like this:

Autonomy requires thinking *for* ourselves, but not *by* ourselves.

A tendency toward independent thought is what sets intellectual
autonomy apart from other virtues; it's the central feature of the

trait. But this independence can't be absolute. To exercise *virtuous* autonomy, we need help. We need to borrow intellectual resources from others. To bring this point home, let's fill in some details from the stories already introduced.

The Suffragists

The 19th- and 20th-century suffragists refused to give in to a long-standing tradition of male dominance. They insisted on thinking for themselves in an effort to reimagine society. They developed novel arguments for their views—arguments renowned for their power and ingenuity. By all accounts, these suffragists were intellectually autonomous. But in no plausible sense were they *alone* in their thinking.

On the contrary, at its most successful, the early women's rights movement was collaborative. Stanton and Anthony are a case in point. They not only worked constantly, but constantly worked *together*. Further, as Eleanor Flexner argues in her momentous work *Century of Struggle*, "Without the work of countless others, even the Stanton-Anthony team could not have accomplished what they did."[18] Flexner goes on to call up an army of women crucial to the cause, including Lucy Stone, Lucretia Mott, Ernestine Rose, Abby Kelley Foster, and Paulina Wright Davis, along with African American abolitionist-suffragists such as Sojourner Truth, Frances E. W. Harper, and Sarah Remond.[19] In addition, before the Civil War, the suffragists gained support from powerful male abolitionists such as William Lloyd Garrison and Frederick Douglass.[20]

These women not only worked together; they called upon the intellectual heritage of those who had gone before them. They reached back to Mary Wollstonecraft's *Vindication of the Rights of Woman* (1792). They emulated the independence of Anne Hutchinson, a self-educated woman who advocated for women's rights and religious freedom in 17th-century America.[21] They relied on advances in women's education wrought by Emma Willard, who founded a school that Stanton herself attended, and Lucretia Mott, who served as Stanton's mentor.[22] In addition, they shrewdly implemented what they had learned from men. As we saw earlier, the young Stanton learned legal argumentation while sitting in her father's office. And her Declaration of Sentiments made ingenious use of the US Declaration of Independence.[23] We could multiply examples, but the point is clear enough: these women display autonomy through their exercise of independent thought. Their autonomy is *virtuous*, in part, because it does not neglect the contributions of other thinkers.

The Scientists

The scientific revolutionaries likewise got by with a little help from their friends. Without such help, their autonomous achievements would not have been possible, much less virtuous.

Copernicus might never have published *On the Revolutions* if not for the urging of his friends Nicholas Schönberg and Tiedemann Giese. In a letter to Pope Paul III, Copernicus recounts his agony over the decision: "When I contemplated the contempt I would face on account of the novelty and absurdity of my opinion, I almost gave up completely the work I had started."[24] But his friends would not let him quit. Of Giese, Copernicus writes, "Repeatedly he encouraged me, commanded me, sometimes sharply, to publish this book and let it see the light of day after lying buried and hidden not for nine years but going on four times nine."[25] While he was on his deathbed, his friends prepared Copernicus's work for publication, thereby giving the world access to his independent thought.

Kepler, too, had intellectual debts, not the least of which was due to Tycho Brahe. In over two decades of observation, Tycho had amassed the largest, most accurate set of astronomical data then available. More than anyone else, Tycho knew where the planets were supposed to be on any given night. When an ailing Tycho needed a mathematician to analyze his data, a mutual friend recommended Kepler, who joined Tycho and dutifully carried out the work his master required. The two worked uneasily, with Tycho holding back everything but the data Kepler needed for an appointed task.[26]

Then, a windfall. Upon Tycho's death, Kepler inherited all of his astronomical records. This enabled him to state and justify his famous laws of planetary motion, the first of which states that orbits are elliptical.[27] Kepler's egg-shaped orbits were shockingly innovative. Everyone before him was sure that planetary orbits were circular. But revolutionary as they were, Kepler's laws were founded on Tycho's observations. Even at his most independent, the elliptical astronomer needed outside help.

Galileo is explicit about his commitment to intellectual autonomy. In explaining his proclivity for disagreement with authorities, he is defiant:

> I say I do not wish to be counted as an ignoramus and an ingrate toward Nature and toward God; for if they have given me my senses and my reason, why should I defer such great gifts to the errors of some man? Why should I believe blindly and stupidly what I wish to believe, and subject the freedom of my intellect to someone else who is just as liable to error as I am?[28]

In asserting his independence, however, Galileo could not claim to work alone. He relied on Copernicus for inspiration. He enjoyed the sponsorship of the wealthy Medici family. And he owed his most famous invention—the telescope—to good old-fashioned luck. In the fall of 1608, two boys playing in a Dutch lens maker's shop noticed that when they looked through two lenses instead of one, the tower across the street looked larger. Before long, others caught on to the insight, and crude telescopes were selling at the summer fairs. When a friend came across the invention at a fair near Paris, he notified Galileo, who quickly used his knowledge of optics to build a better model. The scientist pointed the device heavenward, and quickly amassed evidence that allowed him to attack the old view of the universe. The telescope is often heralded as an instrument of independence—Galileo and his invention against the world. But it is equally a monument to his reliance on others. In the end, good fortune and friendship had underwritten Galileo's autonomous pursuit of truth.[29]

Let's return to the main thread of our discussion. In the feminist and scientific revolutionaries, we see virtuous autonomy at work.* We see people willing to think for themselves, even in the face of staunch and stale opposition. But we also see autonomous people who rely on help from others. This does not diminish their intellectual autonomy; it is, in part, what makes it virtuous.[30] Without the help they received, we would not know their names today. Nor would their independent efforts, undertaken without the aid of others, have been wise ventures. They were brave enough to think *for* themselves, but not so foolish as to think *by* themselves. As Newton himself famously put it, "If I have seen further it is by standing on the shoulders of Giants."[31]

Autonomy and Its Rivals

The "auto" in "autonomy" signals that ultimate responsibility—including intellectual responsibility—lies with the individual. We must stand on our own two feet. But as we have seen, this doesn't mean that we should stand alone. Virtuous autonomy is a mean between two extremes, as table 5.1 shows.

---

* Astute readers will notice that other virtues besides autonomy—perseverance, courage, and creativity—are also at work in the movements discussed in this chapter. This need not detract from the autonomy active in the movements—as if they were *really* examples of some other virtue and not of autonomy. Several different virtues may work together in a given inquiry. Stay tuned for more on this theme.

Table 5.1 Autonomy as a Mean between Extremes

Sphere of activity	Vice (deficiency)	Virtue (mean)	Vice (excess)
Independent thinking	Servility	Autonomy	Isolation

Thinking through these extremes can bring the mean into focus. Consider:

> *Servile Sara* doesn't want to think for herself. Seeking an intellectual proxy, she joins a cult and lets herself be brainwashed into believing everything her leader says. She never thinks twice about the leader's claims or asks for supporting evidence. When others question the leader, Sara berates them. Whenever she's thinking about a new issue, she refuses to form a belief about it without consulting the leader. She takes no responsibility for the contents or workings of her own mind.

When it comes to independent thinking, Sara is deficient. At the other extreme, we might imagine someone like this:

> *Isolated Isabel* is a young biologist who strives to be independent of outside influence. In her research, she casts aside vast bodies of knowledge, including knowledge her advisors have passed down to her. She ignores previous studies of her topic, thinking that she's more likely to get things right if she goes it alone. She rejects much of the relevant data that others have compiled, and tries to collect her own—even though she doesn't have access to a lab. She develops her own novel theories, even before uncovering problems with existing ones.

Isabel's isolation displays a vice of excess.[32] She opts to ignore evidence and expert opinion because she thinks her own mental resources outstrip the sum of everyone else's. In this way, she cuts herself off—isolates herself from—valuable information.

Most people are less extreme than Isabel and Sarah. They don't rely *completely* on others, nor do they rely *solely* on themselves. But many of us still lean too far in one direction or the other. Toward the deficiency end of the spectrum is the proverbial student who cannot write a paper without exhaustive, step-by-step instructions. Instead of taking a clear assignment and running with it, he repeatedly demands further guidance from his teacher: "Just tell me what I have to do to get an A." After a lot of haggling, he begrudgingly writes the paper, asking a classmate for help at several points. He's not as deficient as he could be, but he's deficient nonetheless. Toward the other extreme, there's the student who regularly asks his teacher's advice for term paper topics and sources, but then ignores most of this advice. He knows he should seek help, and listens intently to guidance. But in the end, he usually decides that relying on others is not for him. Most of the time, his work either "reinvents the wheel" or steers down blind alleys. He prides himself on his independence, mistaking isolation for virtue.

The student with virtuous autonomy avoids these extremes, relying on others neither too much nor too little. She reads the assignment carefully to ensure that she understands it. She completes any relevant reading, all the while looking for insights she can add to the discussion. She outlines her paper and writes a draft. Then, with her basic thoughts in hand, she meets with a professor to discuss a problem she came across in formulating her main argument. When the professor recommends a relevant article, she tracks it down, reads it carefully, and implements its best insights. She takes pains to ensure that her paper contributes something fresh and valuable.

Zeroing In on Autonomy
(on Our Own and Together)

We've seen that intellectual autonomy requires thinking for ourselves while relying on others appropriately—neither too much nor too little. Let's get more precise. What makes for "too much" or "too little"?

Here again, Aristotle's archer-and-target image will help. To improve our grasp of virtuous autonomy, we need to consider the proper objects, occasions, means, and motives for independent thinking. In other words: we must consider whether we're thinking independently about the right things, at the right times, in the right ways, and for the right reasons. (After this chapter, we won't refer to the target every time we discuss the mean. That could get tedious. But the point of the image will never be far from our view.)

Because this is a chapter on intellectual autonomy, it's fitting for us to do some independent thinking of our own. Choose a topic you would like to think about with greater autonomy. Maybe it's politics. Or literature. Or religion. Maybe it's art history or music. You decide. You needn't pick anything controversial, or on which "taking a stand" would put you up against a cultural consensus. Just pick something you'd like to think about with increasing independence. It will help to choose a topic about which you're neither a novice nor an expert. I'll do the exercise, too, and share my results below.

Have a topic? Here's your assignment. Consider what it would look like for you to think with virtuous autonomy about your topic. Jot down answers to the following questions:

Object: What have you chosen to think about? Is it wise for you to think independently about this topic, given your current training and ability?

Occasion: Is this the—or at least *a*—right time for you to think about the topic? When (if at all) should you stop thinking about it? When (if at all) should you pause your thinking and seek help from experts?

Means: What methods of thinking or research should you use? Are there patterns of reasoning you can learn and usefully apply?

Are there experts whose work you should consult? How should you use their work to inform your thinking?

Motive: Why do you want to think about this topic? Are your reasons purely pragmatic? Or do you also want to learn about the topic for the sake of learning?

Here's how the exercise went for me. For my topic (object), I chose women's suffrage. For a while, I'd wanted to learn more about the movement. I also wanted to improve my understanding of intellectual autonomy, and figured a study of suffrage would yield inspiring examples of the virtue. I knew a bit about the movement, and knew how I could find sources that would keep my inquiry from going off the rails.

As for the *occasion*, a study of suffrage fit well into my study of intellectual virtues. I knew just enough about suffrage that it was sensible for me to forge ahead. I also knew I'd have to do significant work on my own. To my knowledge, no one had done a detailed study of the relationship between suffrage and intellectual autonomy. I would have to draw some of my own connections between the two. No one would do the research for me. Nor would anyone write the vignettes of autonomy-in-action that I needed. It was time for me to get cracking.

What about my *means*? Well, I knew there was a lot of material available about the suffrage movement. However, not being an expert, I wasn't sure how to sort through it. I knew I could get into trouble if I just started googling terms like "suffrage" and "votes for women." I needed sources I could trust. So I wrote to my friend Kathryn Lee, who teaches courses on women's and gender studies at my college. She suggested I start with Eleanor Flexner's book *Century of Struggle*, a landmark study of the suffrage movement. Some additional reading from a vetted source (Blackwell's *Companion to American Women's History*) added some context while confirming the importance of Flexner's book. An additional book, *Elizabeth Cady Stanton: Feminist as Thinker*, provided insights into Stanton's philosophical views, while Stanton's own *Eighty Years and More* helped with personal details. Having read from those works, I felt confident enough in my grasp of the movement to write the vignettes that began this chapter.

My *motive* was to gain knowledge about suffrage—partly because I found the movement fascinating, and partly because I thought that learning about it would help me understand the nature of intellectual autonomy. Given that I had come close to the target in the other three areas—object, occasion, and means—my motivation to gain knowledge ensured that my inquiry was a step in the direction of virtuous autonomy. (I hasten to add: I'm not holding myself up as an exemplar of autonomy. Perhaps the exercise just caught me on a good day. Often enough, I have been as guilty of servility or isolation as the next person.)

How did the exercise go for you?

Notice that it helped us to zero in on virtuous autonomy by thinking about what makes for the *right* objects, occasions, means, and motives. This can be instructive all by itself. To supplement the exercise, we can think about what would be the *wrong* objects, occasions, means, and motives for exercising independent thought. This can help bring the target into tighter focus by showing us the many ways we might miss it.

Are there topics about which, given your current abilities, you shouldn't think independently? Are there inappropriate *objects* of independent thought, for you, right now? Are there *occasions* on which you shouldn't think about a given topic for yourself? What would be some bad ways or *means* of thinking independently? Are there inappropriate *motives* for independent thinking that tempt you? Think about these questions, and then fill in the archer's target in figure 5.5. (As before, I'll do this, too. I'll report my results below.)

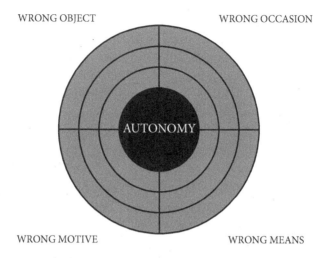

Figure 5.5 Blank Target Image for Intellectual Autonomy
(Reader: Fill In)

When I think about the upper-left quadrant of the target, it occurs to me that there are many topics about which I shouldn't think independently—at least for now. I know little about these topics. So if I strike out boldly on my own, I'll probably just strike out. Here's a partial list: quantum mechanics, the history of Central Asia, automobile exhaust systems (you lost me at "catalytic converter"), cricket (the game, not the bug), crickets (the bug, not the game), music theory, microbiology, and the causes of political revolutions. Beyond the most basic facts, I know so little about these topics that, if left to myself, I'd end up lost. At least for now, I need to rely on others who know more than I do.

In other areas, I'm suited to do at least some independent thinking. For example, I have a working knowledge of the history of science, basic automobile maintenance, American football, and the suffrage movement. On these topics, within modest boundaries, I can think for myself without risking intellectual disaster. But even here, I must take care not to overreach, and I must be open to changing my views in light of expert input. If a certified mechanic says the right pressure for my tires is 55 psi instead of 45, I should think 55 is right and inflate accordingly.

Finally, when it comes to some topics—say, morality, parenting, citizenship, and my own field (philosophy)—I would lurch toward deficiency if I *failed* to think independently. If I simply outsourced my thinking to others, I'd be exercising servility.[33]

There are various ways I might go awry when it comes to *occasions*. As we already saw, my independent thinking might take the wrong object. In that case, it would take the wrong occasion, too. Similarly, my independent thinking won't be well timed if I use bad means to execute it, or if I think with wrong motives. There are never good occasions to engage in *these* sorts of independent thinking. This much seems obvious. But notice: I might also err along the *occasions* dimension by *failing* to engage in independent thinking. For instance, when it came to my thinking about suffrage, the objects, means, and motives for my inquiry were all in good order. Given my other commitments, there would be no better time for me to start my study. If I had postponed, I would have missed the mark.

What about *means*? Here, the difference between hitting and missing the mark depends partly on the object. In other words: *how* we should think depends on *what* we're thinking about, and on how well equipped we are to think in discipline-specific ways. If I'm thinking about something new (how to replace my car's alternator and belt system), I'll need to defer to expert advice, and I'll need step-by-step instructions. If I go it alone, I'll end up forming all kinds of false beliefs. I'll probably break something, and I'll have to pay a large bill at the auto shop. Now, if you are an expert in the field (say an ASE-certified mechanic), it would be odd, and even inappropriate, for you to ask for expert advice in replacing the same part. For you would have replaced an alternator before, perhaps many times, and would already know the step-by-step instructions.

If you are somewhere between novice and expert, things are more complicated. To extend our example, if you're a mechanic-in-training, you might reasonably be expected to grasp the central features of alternator replacement. You should know what an alternator does (it recharges the car's battery), a bit about how it works, and you should know the basic procedures for replacing one. If asked about these matters, you should be able to answer without appealing to others. But amid a repair on a model you've never replaced, you might need to seek knowledge from a more senior mechanic, or to look at a manual. When you're basically competent but not an expert, you must rely on your own training while remaining attuned to your need for input from your superiors. To fail to do either of these would be a failure of intellectual autonomy. The upshot: when it comes to intellectual autonomy, which means are appropriate depends on our knowledge and abilities.

It is useful to think of a spectrum ranging from novice to expert status in using the methods appropriate to a given subject. As we progress along this spectrum, we're increasingly equipped to use the means experts use in thinking about the subject. In general, as we progress, it becomes more and more appropriate for us to exercise independent thinking.

Along with figure 5.6, the discussion just above reveals something important about intellectual virtues: to some extent,

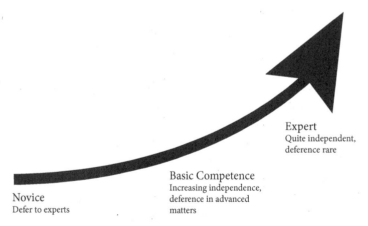

Expert
Quite independent,
deference rare

Basic Competence
Increasing independence,
deference in advanced
matters

Novice
Defer to experts

Figure 5.6 Independent Thinking Should Increase with Expertise

they are person-relative. This doesn't mean that when it comes to virtues, everything is "up for grabs." All virtues must display genuine excellence. However, what is needed for virtue is sensitive to individual knowledge bases, abilities, interests, circumstances, and vocations. What counts as excellence for us depends partly on the hands we're dealt and the roles we must play. The expert mechanic *should* exercise more independent thinking about engines than the rest of us should. Likewise, the meteorologist ought to use weather instruments and careful reasoning instead of consulting us for our best guess regarding tomorrow's weather. The astronomer should think more independently about planetary orbits than the rest of us do. And so on.

Finally, consider *motives*. As with other intellectual virtues, autonomy involves a desire to gain knowledge. But sometimes, the motives driving our independent thinking can oppose virtuous autonomy. If I decide to form my own opinions just for the sake of asserting my will, or to make a name for myself, I won't count as virtuously autonomous. If I defend some novel view of suffrage just to make a splash, I might gain attention, but I won't be acting virtuously. My inquiry will be poorly motivated.

Another point about motives: there are lots of scenarios in which my *not* thinking independently would be badly motivated. Suppose, for fear of making a mistake, for fear of believing a falsehood, or just out of sheer laziness, I decided to stop thinking about morality, or parenting, or citizenship. Or suppose that, given my desire to avoid rigorous thinking, I abdicated all of my thinking on these topics to others, despite my knowing enough to think independently to some degree. In these ways, too, I'd miss the mark. My desire to get the truth, and to understand things for myself, would be deficient. Maybe something similar is true in your case.

From Autonomy to Humility

One more exercise. Take a moment to consider how your own capacities for independent thinking depend on others. It will help to think of a specific topic. This time, pick something you know a lot about, and about which you're therefore well equipped to think on your own. What have others (parents, teachers, and friends) taught you about this topic? How would your thinking differ if they hadn't taught you anything? Would you be able to think about the topic at all? Would you be able to think well about it? What kinds of mistakes might you make if you didn't know what others have taught you? What opportunities might you have missed without help from your teachers? Reflecting on these questions might give you the sense that you owe debts of intellectual gratitude to others. It certainly did for me.[34] The exercise might also leave you with an increasing sense of your own intellectual smallness. If so, you're primed for the next chapter. It's time to think about intellectual humility—the virtue needed to recognize and own our intellectual limitations.

For Reflection and Discussion

1. In this chapter, the author argues that, surprisingly, virtuous autonomy requires us to rely on others. Do you agree with this? Why or why not?

2. Suppose virtuous autonomy does require relying on others. *How* could this be? How can a trait with independence as its key characteristic also require dependence?

3. Of the vices that surround autonomy—servility and isolation—do you tend toward one or the other? If so, how? If not, what have you done that has helped you avoid these vices?

4. What kinds of social or intellectual cultures make autonomy an especially important intellectual virtue? That is, what kinds of social or intellectual circumstances call for autonomy?

5. What value might there be in knowing about something "for yourself," as opposed to simply gleaning that knowledge from someone else?

Further Reading

For inspiring narratives that illustrate autonomy in action, see Eleanor Flexner, *Century of Struggle: The Woman's Rights Movement in the United States* (Cambridge, MA: Belknap Press of Harvard University Press, 1959). For a rich discussion of intellectual autonomy see Robert C. Roberts and W. Jay Wood, *Intellectual Virtues: An Essay in Regulative Epistemology* (Oxford: Oxford University Press, 2007), chapter 10. See also Heidi Grasswick, "Epistemic Autonomy in a Social World of Knowing," in *The Routledge Handbook of Virtue Epistemology*, ed. Heather Battaly (New York: Routledge, 2019), 196–208. For a helpful and measured treatment of autonomy as an educational value, see Kyla Ebels-Duggan, "Autonomy as an Intellectual Virtue," in *The Aims of Higher Education*, ed. Harry Brighouse and Michael McPherson (Chicago: University of Chicago Press, 2015), 74–90. For criticism of the idea of "thinking for yourself," see Alan Jacobs, *How to Think: A Survival Guide for a World at Odds* (New York: Currency, 2017), chapter 1. For discussion of deference as an intellectual virtue, see Kristoffer Ahlstrom-Vij, "The Epistemic Virtue of Deference," in Battaly, *The Routledge Handbook of Virtue Epistemology*, 209–20. For criticism of deference in moral matters, see Sarah McGrath, "The Puzzle of Pure Moral Deference," *Philosophical Perspectives* 23 (2009), 321–44. For a detailed treatment of intellectual authority in relation to autonomy, see Linda Zagzebski, *Epistemic Authority: A Theory of Trust, Authority, and Autonomy in Belief* (New York: Oxford University Press, 2012).

Notes

1. Much of the material about suffrage and women's rights in this chapter is drawn from Eleanor Flexner, *Century of Struggle: The Woman's Rights Movement in the United States* (Cambridge, MA: Belknap Press of Harvard University Press, 1959). See chapter 4 for discussion of the issues highlighted in this paragraph.
2. Thus, Rousseau, "The whole education of women ought to be relative to men. To please them, to be useful to them, to make themselves loved and honored by them, to educate them when young, to care for them when

grown, to counsel them, to console them, and to make life sweet and agreeable to them." Quoted in Flexner, *Century of Struggle*, 23–24.

3. Flexner, *Century of Struggle*, 46.
4. Flexner, *Century of Struggle*, 72–73.
5. Elizabeth Cady Stanton, *Eighty Years & More: Reminisces 1815–1897* (New York: Schocken Books, 1971), 20.
6. Stanton, *Eighty Years and More*, 20–21.
7. Stanton, *Eighty Years and More*, 72.
8. Flexner, *Century of Struggle*, 75.
9. Flexner, *Century of Struggle*, 108.
10. Kant, "An Answer to the Question, What Is Enlightenment?," in *Practical Philosophy*, trans. Mary J. Gregor, in *The Cambridge Edition of the Works of Immanuel Kant* (Cambridge: Cambridge University Press, 1996), 17.
11. In writing the material on the Scientific Revolution for this chapter, I benefited from John Gribbin, *The Scientists: A History of Science Told through the Lives of Its Greatest Inventors* (New York: Random House, 2002). I glean all dates from this text. Also crucial was Timothy McGrew, "The Scientific Revolution," in *Philosophy of Science: An Historical Anthology*, ed. Timothy McGrew, Marc Alspector-Kelly, and Fritz Allhoff (Malden, MA: Wiley-Blackwell, 2009), 95–107.
12. The account in this section leans heavily on McGrew, "The Scientific Revolution," 95–107.
13. Gribbin, *The Scientists*, 41ff., and McGrew, "The Scientific Revolution," 99.
14. See Gribbin, *The Scientists*, 89–90, and McGrew, "The Scientific Revolution," 101.
15. Gribbin, *The Scientists*, 61–62, and McGrew, "The Scientific Revolution," 100.
16. McGrew, "The Scientific Revolution," 105.
17. Quoted in *The Essential Galileo*, trans. and ed. Maurice A. Finocchiaro (Indianapolis: Hackett, 2008), 119.
18. Flexner, *Century of Struggle*, 89.
19. Flexner, *Century of Struggle*, 89–90.
20. Flexner, *Century of Struggle*, 76, 144, and 41–43. That she gained help from Douglass makes Stanton's well-known racism all the more lamentable. Let us learn from her autonomy while rejecting her prejudice.
21. See Flexner, *Century of Struggle*, chapter 1.
22. Flexner, *Century of Struggle*, 72.
23. Flexner, *Century of Struggle*, 74–75.

24. Copernicus, "The Motion of the Earth," in McGrew, Alspector-Kelly, and Allhoff, *Philosophy of Science*, 113.
25. Copernicus, "Motion of the Earth," 113.
26. See Gribbin, *The Scientists*, 58ff. for further details.
27. See Gribbin, *The Scientists*, 60–62, and McGrew, "The Scientific Revolution," 99–100.
28. Galileo, "Tradition and Experience" in McGrew, Alspector-Kelly, and Allhoff, *Philosophy of Science*, 137. In the text quoted, "for if they have given me my sense and reason" reads "for *it* they have given me my sense and reason." I have corrected this apparent typographical error.
29. McGrew, "The Scientific Revolution," 101. I follow McGrew's account of the telescope closely.
30. Thanks to Will Kynes for helpful discussion here.
31. Letter to Robert Hooke, February 5, 1676.
32. I am not certain I've chosen the best term for autonomy's excess vice. Reviewers suggested good alternatives, including "hyper-autonomy," "epistemic egoism," and "self-reliance." In the end, I settled on "isolation," because this term captures the way those who have this vice cut themselves off from others' knowledge and expertise. "Hyper-autonomy" doesn't quite capture this, and in any case seems less informative than "isolation." "Epistemic egoism" is a good term, but philosophers have already put it to use in other quarters. "Self-reliance" is the next-best term; however, at least to my ear, it carries a positive connotation. Perhaps my decision to depart from reviewers is evidence that I possess the vice in question.
33. For discussion of problems with outsourcing our moral beliefs see Sarah McGrath, "The Puzzle of Pure Moral Deference," *Philosophical Perspectives* 23 (2009), 321–44.
34. I would be remiss if I didn't acknowledge that my thinking about intellectual autonomy is indebted to the work of Robert C. Roberts and W. Jay Wood. Among other things, their work helped me to see that virtuous autonomy requires dependence on others. I first came across the quotation from Kant in their work *Intellectual Virtues: An Essay in Regulative Epistemology* (New York: Oxford University Press, 2007), 258.

6

Humility and Self-Confidence

Own Your Weaknesses—and Your Strengths

During the 2016 US presidential race, an MSNBC reporter asked candidate Donald Trump whom he consults about foreign policy. Trump replied, "I'm speaking with myself, number one, because I have a very good brain and I've said a lot of things . . . my primary consultant is myself and I have a good instinct for this stuff."[1] Trump took a beating from the press for his bluster. But months later, he doubled down. Claiming to hold the key to crushing the United States' enemies, he said, "I know more about ISIS than the generals do, believe me."[2] Shortly after the election, Trump continued the trend by ignoring regular intelligence briefings: "I'm, like, a smart person. I don't have to be told the same thing in the same words every single day."[3] Many who covered these stories lambasted the president-to-be for his arrogance. Good *instincts* for foreign policy? Whatever happened to the importance of experience? More knowledge in matters of national security than the *generals*? Not likely. How could someone with no elected experience and no military service so blatantly overestimate his knowledge of matters central to his new job? How, many wondered, could he be so oblivious to his limitations?

Arrogance, though, is a nonpartisan vice. Hardly any of his opponents or detractors thought Trump could be elected—until he was. When he announced his candidacy in July 2015, many were sure it was a joke. The Democrats thought so for most of

The Excellent Mind. Nathan L. King, Oxford University Press (2021). © Oxford University Press.
DOI: 10.1093/oso/9780190096250.003.0006

the election cycle. By November of 2016, Hillary Clinton stopped campaigning in several key states, thinking she had them won. The press and pollsters were sure Clinton would win in a land-slide. But just days after the election, Americans began reading egg-faced headlines like "The Democrats Screwed Up,"[4] "DNC Staff: Arrogance Cost Clinton the Election,"[5] and "Media Culpa? The Press and the Election Result."[6] The details differed. Some writers complained that the Democrats had badly underestimated voter turnout for Trump. Others claimed that the liberal press had irritated people into casting protest votes against Clinton. The common thread in such pieces was that arrogance led both Hillary Clinton and the press to think that a Clinton victory was a lock. They had underestimated their ignorance, and soon discovered humble pie on their plates. As I write this—some four years after the election—it is by no means clear that those on either side of America's political aisle have learned their lesson.

Of course, politics isn't the only venue in which arrogance rears its head. It appears in medicine whenever doctors ignore input from patients who are women, or ethnic minorities, or who are poor or elderly. It appears whenever CEOs overrate their ability to use an interview to predict a job candidate's success. And arrogance certainly shows its face in academic life. Their good qualities aside, professors are sadly known for their name-dropping, their smug tone, and their self-promotion. Once while attending a conference, I heard a talk by a brand-name academic. He was big-time, and he wanted everyone to know it. For years, he had lauded his own work in online forums as the best thing going—at least for his money. When the talk was over, I gathered my things and headed for the door. The room still full, the speaker basked in oratorical self-praise: "Wow. That was the best session I've ever seen!" I don't recall what happened after that, but I'm pretty sure I muttered some swear words as I slinked away.

Arrogance has two remarkable features. First, we hate it when we see it in others. Second, we often fail to see it in ourselves. But if it's arrogant to underestimate our weaknesses or overestimate our strengths, a lot of us are guilty. Consider the results from these psychological studies:

- In a survey of high school seniors, one million students were asked to rate their leadership abilities relative to those of their peers. 70% of students thought they were above average, while just 2% thought they were below average. When asked to rate their ability to get along with others, *all* of the students— remember there were one million—thought they were above average. 60% ranked themselves in the top 10%, and 25% placed themselves in the top 1%.[7]
- More than half of adults who drive automobiles rate themselves better than average drivers.[8]
- A large majority of people think they are more intelligent than the average person.[9]
- In a survey of university professors, 94% thought they were better at their jobs than an average colleague, and 68% rated themselves in the top quarter when it comes to teaching performance.[10]

Taken at face value, these studies suggest that many of us have inflated opinions of ourselves.[11] Indeed, many psychologists regard the phenomenon of overconfidence as so well established that they have a name for it: the "Lake Wobegon effect," in reference to an imaginary society where "the women are strong, the men are good-looking, and all the children are above average."[12] If we find the above figures concerning—and perhaps especially if we don't— we should want to learn more about humility and self-confidence. For these are the virtues needed to own our weaknesses and our strengths.

What Humility Is (and Isn't)

Let's start with humility. As we'll understand it here, intellectual humility has three key components:

1. An appropriate degree of attention to our intellectual weaknesses;
2. An accurate—or at least reasonable—assessment of our intellectual weaknesses (registering our weaknesses *as* weaknesses); and
3. An effort to *own* our intellectual weaknesses.[13]

A virtuously humble person displays each component consistently, as a matter of habit, and does so from good intellectual motives (say, to gain truth and avoid falsehood). Such humility repels several different vices: vanity, pride, neglect, arrogance, and self-deprecation.

Vanity and Pride

Consider the first component—the one about the degree to which we attend to our intellectual weaknesses. How much attention should we pay here? Obsession is unhealthy. But it's also unwise to ignore the matter altogether.

Perhaps we can back our way into thinking well about the appropriate amount of attention by considering clear excesses and deficiencies. On the excess side, we find *pride* and *vanity*. What's the difference? Jane Austen explains, "Vanity and pride are different things, though the words are often used synonymously. A person may be proud without being vain. Pride relates more to our opinion of ourselves, vanity to what we would have others think of us."[14] If this is right, then as far as intellectual weaknesses are concerned, prideful people are obsessed with their weaknesses, while vain people are obsessed with what others think about those weaknesses. (Proud and vain people might also be obsessed with their strengths, and with what others think about them. More on that later when we examine self-confidence—the virtue related to owning our strengths.)

When he considers his weaknesses, the prideful person is obsessed with them—perhaps with eliminating them or compensating for them. The vain person is obsessed with others' opinions about his weaknesses. He may not care about eliminating them, but he takes pains to ensure that others don't discover them or draw attention to them. Contrast these two individuals:

Proud Paul is a first-year student at Harvard. During the fall semester, he constantly compares himself to other students. He has a gifted mind, and he knows it. But he's obsessed with the fact that he's not *as* gifted at writing as some of his peers. And while his logical skills are good, his exams don't place him at the top of his logic class. As a result, he constantly berates himself for being stupid. When he corrects his weaknesses, he does so not for the sake of knowledge, but just to feel superior to others—less weak than them. He can't stand people who outperform him in the classroom. He doesn't care about learning; he wastes hour after hour fretting about how he'd like to be "less dumb." As a result, he sabotages his college experience, and learns much less than he should.

Vain Vince is a first-year student at a good private college. As he starts making friends in the dorms, he brags about his plans to transfer to Harvard next year: "I just think it would be a more intellectually vigorous environment." But Vince's commitment to excellence is all talk. He doesn't care about learning. His main focus is the embarrassment he feels over not getting into Harvard on his first try. What must his friends from back home—two of whom did get into Harvard—think of him? Worse, he sometimes frets about whether others think he even belongs at the college he is attending. Whenever a conversation moves away from his expertise, he clams up. A friend starts talking about Aldous Huxley's *Brave New World*, which Vince has never read. Despite his ignorance, Vince nods silently as if he understands. When that doesn't work, he changes the subject. During spring semester scheduling, he avoids classes that reveal his weaknesses.

Both pride and vanity involve excessive self-focus. But the vices are distinct because they're differently motivated. Prideful people are often vain, and vain people are often prideful, but things needn't go that way. Someone can be prideful in wanting to have fewer weaknesses than others, yet be aloof to what these others think. And someone can be vain in wanting others not to notice his weaknesses without caring about the weaknesses themselves.

As the examples of Paul and Vince make clear, intellectual pride and vanity are repellant. But why are these vices so bad? To make progress toward an answer, we might recall that all intellectual virtues involve a motivation to improve our cognitive lot. Virtuous thinkers want to gain knowledge while avoiding falsehood. But too much navel-gazing can distract us from these goals. Time spent thinking about how we compare with others, or about what others think of us, is time not spent thinking about algebra, or chemistry, or history. Excessive self-focus distracts us from learning. Pride and vanity take our eyes off the prize.

Bestselling author Anne Lamott conveys how vanity can derail a writer's work. Reflecting on the publication process, she bemoans,

I'm one of those people who feels beside herself the day after I've stuck the manuscript in the mail. It can't even have arrived [at the publisher] and already I'm feeling bitter and resentful about what cold, lazy, sadistic slime I'm surrounded by. There are other writers, and you may be one of them, who just push back their sleeves and get to work on the next piece. I could never be close to a person like this, but I know they exist. Anyway, if you are like me, you wait and wait and check your mail ten times each day, and feel devastated and rejected every hour that there is no response.[15]

Lamott goes on like this for pages in a frenzy of partly feigned self-obsession. By the time she has finished describing the process, her fretting has led her to consume whole pitchers of martinis and several pounds of chocolate. Of course, all of us have similar moments, and we can thank Lamott for putting such feelings into words. But no one who was habitually this vain would be likely to write much of consequence—which is how we know Lamott is not describing her daily routine. As she notes, after an episode of self-doubt, she finds a way to get back to work, getting at least something written on most days.

Neglect

The proud and the vain focus too much on their mental abilities. Theirs are vices of excess, and dangerous ones. But there's danger in the opposite direction as well. We can care *too little* about the state of our knowledge, or that of our intellectual skills or character. For example:

Neglectful Ned is a manager at the local auto parts store. His job is to balance the store's budget and supply numbers, to set the pay schedule for employees, and to organize inventory in the stockroom. Ned has poor math skills, and a barely passable knowledge of the software needed to track the store's budget and inventory. His frequent errors cost the company money. But Ned doesn't care. His father owns the store and would never fire him. It never occurs to Ned that taking a basic math refresher and a spreadsheets class at the local community college would drastically reduce his rate of error. Instead, Ned sluffs along, oblivious to his intellectual weaknesses.

Whereas Paul and Vince care too much about their intellectual weaknesses, Ned cares too little. The humble person, by contrast, cares about these things to an appropriate degree; that's our first component of humility.

Arrogance

The arrogance that opposes intellectual humility is the kind we show when we fail to register our own biases, blind spots, false beliefs, ineptitude, irrationality, ignorance, intellectual character flaws, or the like. We can exhibit this kind of arrogance by simply ignoring our weaknesses—by not attending to them enough.

But suppose we managed to focus on our intellectual weaknesses to the right degree. We could do this and still fail to be humble. We could pay the right *amount* of attention to our weaknesses but fail to be *accurate* (or even reasonable) in our assessments of them. We could underestimate our weaknesses. This, too, is a kind of arrogance. This is where the second component of humility comes in.

Recalling his past as a haughty teenager, Mark Twain is said to have quipped, "When I was a boy of 14, my father was so ignorant I could hardly stand to have the old man around. But when I got to be 21, I was astonished at how much the old man had learned in seven years."[16] The remark is probably apocryphal. But it nevertheless highlights the fact that underestimating one's ignorance is a trademark of the arrogant thinker. By contrast, the tendency to spot our weaknesses, and identify them *as* weaknesses, moves us closer to humility.

Consider the phenomenon of overreaching one's expertise. Because of its success, science has earned the esteem it enjoys. (If you doubt this, ask yourself how you'd get by without Novocain for your root canal, antibiotics for your bronchitis, or cross-country flights to see your favorite relatives.) We seek input from scientists whenever practically *anything* happens. If there's an earthquake in Los Angeles, you can expect to see a seismologist interviewed on the six-o'clock news. If there's an outbreak of bird flu in Thailand, expect an expert from the CDC. If we're having an unusually warm summer, it'll be a climatologist from the EPA. But strangely, scientists are also sought for their opinions on subjects outside their expertise. When this happens, a few intrepid scientists proceed as if they are experts in philosophy, ethics, theology, or public policy—a kind of intellectual trespassing.[17] As a result, they reveal their arrogant ignorance for all to see.

In the winter of 2016, Bill Nye ("The Science Guy") gave an interview for a popular website, *Big Think*. Asked why many scientists dismiss philosophy as irrelevant, Nye said,

> It gets back, it often, often gets back to this question, What is the nature of consciousness? Can we know that we know? Are we aware that we are aware? Are we not aware that we are aware? Is reality real or is reality not real and we are all living on a ping-pong ball that's part of a giant interplanetary ping-pong game that we cannot sense?[18]

Interplanetary ping-pong? What was this guy talking about? Just seconds after the interview began, it was clear that things were about to get loopy. Nye went on to accuse philosophers of believing that "reality isn't real," and to commit at least one logical fallacy that any beginning logic student knows to avoid. He closed the discussion by suggesting that the interviewer try dropping a hammer on his own foot to confirm that reality is real.

The exchange is painful to watch. Nye begins by running together the nature of consciousness (on the one hand) and the extent of our knowledge (on the other). He is unaware that these issues represent entirely distinct sub-disciplines of philosophy. Further, no philosopher who has ever lived has believed anything close to what Nye attributes, seemingly, to your friendly neighborhood Socrates. Sure, a few philosophers have denied that our senses deliver knowledge of ultimate reality. But to believe that *reality isn't real* would be a distinct level of lunacy, akin to believing that triangles have four sides. Finally, while some philosophers enjoy ping-pong, it isn't of the galactic variety. It is staggering that Nye would feel equipped to speak about philosophy without knowing these things.

Enough ranting. I haven't recounted Nye's travails in order to blow off curmudgeonly steam. Quite the opposite. I love happy endings. So I'm glad to report that Nye has repented of his arrogance. After his interview garnered backlash from philosophers, Nye came to see that his views of the field were ill-informed. Indeed, he began to see such value in the discipline that he said "everybody in the world" should be a kind of philosopher. He thanked Harvard philosophy BA Olivia Goldhill for writing an article critical of his previous views. The criticism, said Nye, "really led to something." He listened to philosophy lectures. He read and reread books about the history of philosophy. Over time, he came to acknowledge the role that philosophy has played in guiding scientists' choices between theories. He began to see "an intimate connection" between the two fields. Most importantly, he acknowledged his previous ignorance: "People allude to Socrates and Plato and Aristotle all the time, and I think many of us who make those references don't have solid grounding." By assessing his intellectual weaknesses accurately, Nye put himself in position to own those weaknesses. He put himself in position to exercise the admirable humility with which his story ended.[19]

Self-Deprecation

Humble people don't underestimate their weaknesses—they avoid arrogance. But humble people also avoid *over*estimating their weaknesses.

Some people seem to think that humility involves an unseemly kind of self-deprecation. (A colleague of mine once slipped and called it "self-defecation," which is somehow just about right.) On such a picture, humility demands that we exaggerate our weaknesses. Humility means *humiliation*. In rejecting this idea, G. K. Chesterton laments, we are at risk of "producing a race of men too mentally modest to believe in the multiplication table."[20]

This kind of "humility"—*false* humility—is no virtue at all. For one thing, it's dishonest, or at best self-deceiving. For another, it can keep us from learning. The middling student who feigns humility to get out of homework—"I can't do math *at all*"—is not likely to make much progress. Humble thinkers, by contrast, have an accurate picture of

Table 6.1 Humility as a Mean between Extremes

Sphere of activity	Vice (deficiency)	Virtue (mean)	Vice (excess)
Assessing our weaknesses	Arrogance	Humility	Self-deprecation

their cognitive weaknesses—a picture that helps them to see which weaknesses are most important for them to address. As table 6.1 suggests, humility is a mean between extremes. To underestimate our weaknesses is arrogant; to overestimate them is self-deprecating.

Owning It

Just hitting the mean with respect to attention and accuracy (our first two components of humility) is a considerable achievement. But even hitting both together isn't quite enough to make us humble. To see why, consider one more character:

Lazy Luke is a sophomore at State U. He hasn't yet chosen a major, but he pays careful attention to his intellectual abilities. He's not vain, proud, or neglectful. Though he regularly turns in his assignments, his work is sloppy. He ignores instructions. He makes basic mistakes in grammar and punctuation. He rarely writes a coherent paragraph. He doesn't distinguish between his claims and the evidence he offers for them. He hasn't earned a passing grade on a single assignment. Fortunately, Luke has a patient professor who gives meticulous feedback on students' work. Luke appreciates this, so he reads the feedback with care. As a result, he knows all his weaknesses. His view of them is totally accurate. He just doesn't care enough to fix them. He can't be bothered to correct even small mistakes, and has little desire to improve his skills in expressing what he knows. It's not that he's too busy or that he has other goals. Rather, Luke simply doesn't *care* enough to correct his weaknesses.

Unless he changes his ways, Lazy Luke won't amount to much. But even as things stand, he's good for at least this: he teaches us that intellectual humility requires a third component—*owning* our weaknesses.

Laziness is one way we might fail to own our weaknesses. There are others. We might deny that we have them, or try to cover them up, or get angry when others point them out, or simply put them out of our minds. Intellectually humble people don't do these things. They admit their mistakes. They confess when they don't have answers. They care about their weaknesses and do something about them.[21]

Owning our weaknesses can be difficult, especially when they're revealed in public. However, in the wake of Donald Trump's shocking victory over Hillary Clinton, some left-wing members of the press did just this. They realized that they'd made a mistake. They identified the cause of the mistake. They resolved to do better. Writing for CBS News, Will Rahn confesses that he and his fellow journalists underestimated their blindness to the political situation going into the election:

Journalists, at our worst, see ourselves as a priestly caste. We believe we not only have access to the indisputable facts, but also a greater truth, a system of beliefs divined from an advanced understanding of justice. . . . Journalists increasingly don't even believe in the possibility of reasoned disagreement, and as such ascribe cynical motives to those who think about things a different way. . . . That the explainers and data journalists so frequently get things hilariously wrong never invites the soul searching you'd think it would. Instead, it all just somehow leads us to more smugness, more meanness, more certainty from the

reporters and pundits. Faced with defeat, we retreat further into
our bubble, assumptions left unchecked.[22]

In this passage, Rahn engages in just the kind of self-assessment
that humility requires. He admits that he and his fellow journalists
are blinkered. He laments the arrogance of dismissing those "on the
other side." Then, he suggests some first steps toward improvement:

> Our theme now should be humility. We must become more
> impartial, not less so. We have to abandon our easy culture of
> tantrums and recrimination. We have to stop writing these know-
> it-all, 140 character sermons on social media and admit that, as a
> class, journalists have a shamefully limited understanding of the
> country we cover. . . . We have to fix this, and the broken rea-
> soning behind it. There's a fleeting fun to gang-ups and group-
> think. But it's not worth what we are losing in the process.[23]

In short, Rahn thinks, he and his colleagues must own their intellectual limitations, including their biases, their ignorance, and their
mistakes. To do so would be a step toward intellectual humility.

How to Own It

Beyond simply admitting that we have them, there are at least three
ways to own our weaknesses. Sometimes we must determine to correct
our intellectual weaknesses—to shore up our ignorance, develop a new
skill, or learn to set aside our biases. Other times, we need to learn to
correct *for* our weaknesses, even when we can't correct the weaknesses
themselves. Still other times, we must accept our weaknesses and learn
to live with them. Let's consider these strategies in turn.

Correcting a weakness. Michael Inzlicht is a neuroscientist and
social psychologist who studies emotion, self-control, and prejudice. His field has been taking a lot of heat lately. Several high-
profile critiques allege that the scientific standards of his field

are *sub*standard. According to these critiques, researchers commonly base their results on small sample sizes, give undue credit to unreplicated studies, and use questionable statistical methods to get results that will be well published.[24] Inzlicht finds such critiques sobering. In light of them, he has launched a public inquiry into his own published studies. He has discovered several mistakes, and several ways to improve the reliability of his methods. He has resolved to "do better."

It's worth pausing to consider how remarkable this is. To get a sense of it, think of something about yourself that embarrasses you—a pimple, an unsightly mole, the mullet you wore for a decade. Now consider how you'd feel about voluntarily making that flaw known to the world. That's more or less how Inzlicht feels about revealing the flaws in his previous studies. But he thinks it's worth the pain. Over time, he reports, his research has become more scientifically robust:

> In contrast to my first 10 empirical papers, when I analyzed what were then my last 10 papers (published in 2014–2015), I discovered a more solid appearing set of studies. Though I suspect there were still puffs of smoke in there, I was trending in the right direction. By facing our problems head-on, by listening to our field's critics, I took small incremental steps to improve my research practices, and it appeared I was getting better.[25]

By seeking to overcome his past mistakes, Inzlicht displays one important way of owning intellectual weaknesses. He corrects his weaknesses by getting better at the very forms of reasoning with which, by his own lights, he previously struggled.

Correcting for a weakness.[26] Sometimes, our minds get stuck in ruts so deep we can't dig ourselves out. We can't improve our reliability by using the same methods and just being more careful. Instead, we need to address the same tasks and problems by using different strategies. Rather than correct a weakness, we must correct *for* it.

Here's an example. The Philosophy Department at Princeton University has a surprising practice for hiring new faculty: they base decisions solely on applicants' files. They don't conduct interviews of any kind. That might sound strange to us. If so, we're likely assuming that interviews provide information that is essential to discovering whether a candidate would flourish in the department. But this assumption doesn't withstand scrutiny. In dozens of studies, researchers have been able to find little evidence of a correlation between performance in interviews and later job performance. Interview performance doesn't reliably predict job performance. We can't tell from a good interview that a candidate will perform well. We can't tell from a bad interview that a candidate will perform poorly. And apparently, there's no clear way to improve in our ability. Interviews expose us to all kinds of "noise"—information about a candidate's looks, gender, and mannerisms that are not connected to job performance.[27] We tend to weigh such factors heavily nonetheless. In light of this, Princeton's philosophers stopped conducting interviews. They now make hires solely based on candidates' credentials. Realizing that they are not in a position to correct their limitations, they correct *for* them instead.

Accepting a weakness. Tommy has a dream of being a nuclear physicist. There's just one problem: he can't seem to keep up with the math the job requires. Now, he's not *bad* at math. His work ethic enabled him to maintain a B+ average through a college math major. At first, he mostly earned Cs on his exams. However, through hard work, he became proficient. When he took the Graduate Record Exam in preparing applications for his backup plan (an MA in math education), he scored in the 99th percentile. Tommy is far better at math than almost anyone you'd meet on the street. But that standard doesn't cut it for nuclear physics. To clear *that* bar, he'd need to be in more like the top 1% of the top 1%. Despite thousands of hours of additional study, Tommy just can't seem to get there. Disappointed but not downtrodden, he says to himself, "I guess I'm just not cut out to be a nuclear physicist.

That's too bad, but I won't hang my head. After all, not every good athlete makes the Olympics, either. I am limited in my mathematical ability. But I *am* better at math than most. And because I've had to work hard at it, I've learned to explain complex concepts simply. Perhaps teaching high school or college math would be a good fit for me."

Growing Humility through a Growth Mindset

Notice that Tommy only accepts his weaknesses *after* he has tested his abilities. That's important. If he had resigned himself to the fate of mediocre math performance after that first C, he would never have become a good mathematician. We can imagine some of his classmates giving up after similar early results. "I'm just not a math person" is their refrain. But facing the same adversity, Tommy keeps working. He refuses to think he's stuck in mediocrity. He believes he can do better. He works on his weaknesses; he *owns* them.

Tommy has what psychologist Carol Dweck calls a *growth mindset*. That is, he thinks of his intellectual lot—his knowledge and intellectual skills—as changeable through effort. He regards a poor exam performance as just that: one bad performance. In contrast, some of his classmates have a *fixed mindset*: they believe that their abilities can't be changed.[28] For them, every bad performance confirms not that they need to work harder, but that they're not gifted. It says something not just about how they did on one exam, but about who they *are*. Now, though Tommy *eventually* accepts his weaknesses, he is not too quick to do this. Instead, the lesson he draws from a poor performance is that he needs to work harder, so that he can do better on the next test. That mindset carries him through college, and his performance gradually improves until he's so good at math that his skills suggest an interesting and worthwhile vocation.

Tommy's growth mindset is central to his success. For one thing, it helps him persevere through academic challenges. For another, it enables him to assess and own his intellectual weaknesses. Here's why. If we have a fixed mindset, every performance is a judgment. It's an assessment not just of the abilities we happen to have right now, but of the abilities we're stuck with. When we see things this way, we naturally shy away from any situation that would reveal our weaknesses. Every assessment is a threat to our self-esteem. So we subtly steer clear from areas of ignorance; we avoid taking classes on subjects we find difficult; we're *crushed* when we have a poor performance in an area we thought was a strength. Consider the proverbial college freshman weeping over a B– on his first English paper. It would've been an A just four months earlier when he was a senior in high school. And he might have received effusive praise from his teachers: "You're so smart! This paper is brilliant! You're going places!" The lesson he draws from the B– is that he's not so smart after all. Had his previous teachers lied to him? And what will he do next? Some studies suggest that if he has a fixed mindset, he'll do one of two things. Either he'll put in *less* effort on the next paper (if he doesn't try, then a poor performance won't reveal his weakness); or he'll cheat. Either way, he won't likely gain an accurate perception of his weaknesses; and he probably won't own them.[29]

By contrast, a growth mindset allows us to see single performances for what they are: indications of our *current* knowledge and ability. That's all. A single poor performance doesn't tell us what our potential is, or who we are, or whether we're smart (or not). It only tells us that we don't have the knowledge or skill needed to perform well on a given task—*yet*. As Dweck notes, the "yet" makes all the difference. It leaves open the possibility that we can improve with further effort. A growth mindset lowers the stakes of the assessment. This leaves us free to admit our current weaknesses. It enables us to be honest about these limitations while signaling that probably, at least in some small way, we can do better. So, fostering a growth mindset enables us to acknowledge and own our intellectual limits. A growth mindset can foster humility.[30]

Humility's Mirror Image: Self-Confidence

To this point, we've been discussing the nature and importance of intellectual humility, the virtue needed to manage our cognitive weaknesses. But what about our intellectual *strengths*? Aren't they important? And can't we fall into vice if we don't manage them well? Yes, and yes. Managing our intellectual strengths is central to our avoiding many of the vices that oppose humility: pride, vanity, self-neglect, arrogance, and self-deprecation. Avoiding these vices, so far as our intellectual strengths are concerned, is the province of a virtue that mirrors humility: *self-confidence*.

Much of what we've said about humility also applies to self-confidence, once we change our focus from weaknesses to strengths. As with humility, it is helpful to think of self-confidence as having three components:

1. An appropriate degree of attention to our intellectual strengths;
2. An accurate—or at least reasonable—assessment of our intellectual strengths (registering our strengths *as* strengths); and
3. An effort to *own* our intellectual strengths.

A virtuously self-confident person displays each component consistently, as a matter of habit, and does so from good intellectual motives.

Take the first component. Paying too much attention to our strengths reflects pride. Caring too much about whether others notice our strengths displays vanity. And paying too little attention to our intellectual strengths bespeaks self-neglect.

Giving due attention to our strengths is one component of self-confidence. But due attention doesn't rule out inaccuracy. We can pay the right degree of attention to our intellectual strengths, yet over- or underestimate them. To underestimate our intellectual

Table 6.2   Self-Confidence as a Mean between Extremes

Sphere of activity	Vice (deficiency)	Virtue (mean)	Vice (excess)
Assessing our strengths	Self-deprecation	Self-confidence	Arrogance

strengths is self-deprecating; to overestimate them is arrogant. As table 6.2 depicts, self-confidence lies between the two.

The reason intellectual humility and self-confidence repel the same vices is that the two virtues concern such closely related activities—owning our weaknesses (humility) and owning our strengths (self-confidence). The two virtues partner together in the shared activity of managing our intellectual abilities.

To get a handle on the deficiency opposing self-confidence, recall Tommy's case. But now imagine that, after receiving his score on the Graduate Record Exam, Tommy is devastated. Suppose he's so fixated on his mild shortcomings that he fails to register his significant strength in mathematical reasoning. As he processes his disappointment, he says to a friend, "I stink at math. I'll never be able to do anything worthwhile in the field. I might as well just give up." As Tommy says this, he falls into self-deprecation. His assessment of his strengths is wildly out of step with reality. Though we might sympathize with him, we shouldn't think that Tommy's self-pitying assessment is virtuous. His self-deprecation is likely to cost him learning opportunities and keep him from passing his knowledge to others.

When it comes to self-confidence, arrogance is the excess vice. Recall the examples with which we began this chapter. Donald Trump's assessment of his foreign policy knowledge outstripped what he actually knew. Barring clairvoyance, there's no way he could've known more about ISIS, or national security, or diplomacy, than those with top-secret clearance and years of experience. In like manner, the Democrats and the press severely overestimated their knowledge of the political situation in the lead-up to November 2016.

These are galling examples, to be sure. It's easy to stew about them. But perhaps a wiser use of our time would be to ask ourselves whether we sometimes display a similar kind of arrogance. Consider these questions:

- Do I ignore the views of people I take to be my intellectual inferiors?
- Do I think I have nothing to learn from people whose moral or political views oppose mine?
- Am I unwilling to read new books about a subject because I regard traditional views as the last word?
- Am I unwilling to read old books about a subject just because those books are old?

If we find ourselves answering yes to such questions, it's worth considering whether we're overestimating our intellectual strengths. We should ask ourselves if—despite our strengths—we can still gain knowledge and understanding through others' input.

Like humility, self-confidence has a third component: *ownership*. Self-confident thinkers don't just attend to their intellectual strengths and assess them well; they *do* something about them. They exercise these strengths in order to learn new truths. They apply their abilities to preserve the knowledge they have. They share their knowledge and intellectual skills with others. They own these gifts and steward them wisely.

One More Trait of the Good Self-Manager

If you listen to people who are good at managing their weaknesses and strengths, you'll hear things like this:

"I made a mistake, and I must fix it."

"I'm not familiar with that idea. Can you share the basics with me?"

"I'm a little limited in that area, but I'm working on it."

"I'm pretty good at this. But I have a plan to get even better."

This is how humble and self-confident people sound. They know their liabilities and assets, and they manage them well. Now notice: such people would not be good at assessing their weaknesses and strengths without a commitment to respecting the truth about themselves. For without such a commitment, they might knowingly distort the truth about their knowledge and abilities. In other words, fully mature intellectual humility and self-confidence are impossible without *honesty*, the virtue we'll discuss next.

For Reflection and Discussion

1. Why, in the author's view, does humility require more than just being aware of our weaknesses?

2. Suppose you realize that you have an intellectual weakness. When should you correct such a weakness? When should you correct *for* it? And when should you simply accept it? See if you can provide a specific example for each category.

3. What is a growth mindset? Do you have one? If not, how might developing one help you develop humility?

4. How does humility differ from self-confidence?

5. Recall the archer-and-target image from previous chapters. The target has four quadrants: objects, occasions, means, and motives. To deepen your understanding of intellectual humility, apply these categories to your own case. What should you be humble about? When? How? And with what motivation? Consider similar questions about self-confidence.

Further Reading

Intellectual humility is currently the subject of vigorous academic study. Several different accounts of the trait are on offer. For a helpful introduction to these see Nancy Snow, "Intellectual Humility," in *The Routledge Handbook of Virtue Epistemology*, ed. Heather Battaly (New York: Routledge, 2019), 178–95. The view of humility developed in this chapter largely follows that of Dennis Whitcomb, Heather Battaly, Jason Baehr, and Daniel Howard Snyder, "Intellectual Humility: Owning Our Limitations," *Philosophy and Phenomenological Research* 94, no. 3 (2017), 509–39. For a prominent alternative see Robert C. Roberts and W. Jay Wood, *Intellectual Virtues: An Essay in Regulative Epistemology* (Oxford: Oxford University Press, 2007), chapter 9; also Ian Church and Peter Samuelson, *Intellectual Humility: An Introduction to the Philosophy and Science* (New York: Bloomsbury, 2016). For a psychologically rich and philosophically astute study of intellectual limitations, see Nathan Ballantyne, *Knowing Our Limits* (New York: Oxford University Press, 2019). For an illuminating discussion of virtues of intellectual limitation management, see Adam Morton, *Bounded Thinking: Intellectual Virtues for Limited Agents* (New York: Oxford University Press, 2012). For an accessible introduction to the psychology of cognitive limitations, see Thomas Gilovich, *How We Know What Isn't So* (New York: Free Press, 1991), and Richard Nisbett, *Mindware: Tools for Smart Thinking* (New York: Farrar, Straus and Giroux, 2015). For an accessible introduction to the growth mindset, see Carol Dweck, *Mindset: The New Psychology of Success* (New York: Random House, 2006). For empirical evidence of a link between growth mindset and humility, see Tenelle Porter and Karina Schumann, "Intellectual Humility and Openness to the Opposing View," *Self and Identity* 17, no. 2 (2018), 139–62. For a thought-provoking popular discussion of humility, see Leah Hager Cohen, *I Don't Know: In Praise of Admitting Ignorance (Except When You Shouldn't)* (New York: Riverhead, 2013).

Notes

1. The original video containing Trump's comments was retrieved from http://www.msnbc.com/morning-joe/watch/trump-my-primary-consultant-is-myself-645588035836; comments also quoted in Carol Giacomo, "Trump's Brain and U.S. Foreign Policy," *The New York Times*, March 16, 2016, retrieved from http://takingnote.blogs.nytimes.com/2016/03/16/trumps-brain-and-u-s-foreign-policy/?_r=0.

2. Quoted in Aaron Blake, "19 Things Donald Trump Knows Better Than Anyone Else, According to Donald Trump," *The Washington Post*, October 4, 2016, retrieved from: https://www.washingtonpost.com/news/the-fix/wp/2016/10/04/17-issues-that-donald-trump-knows-better-than-anyone-else-according-to-donald-trump/?utm_term=.c0b385e9e649.

3. Maxwell Tani, "Trump: I'm a 'Smart Person,' Don't Need Intelligence Briefings Every Single Day," *Business Insider*, December 11, 2016, retrieved from http://www.businessinsider.com/donald-trump-intelligence-briefings-skip-2016-12.

4. Frank Bruni in *The New York Times*, November 11, 2016.

5. David Catanese in *U.S. News and World Report*, November 11, 2016, retrieved from: https://www.usnews.com/news/the-run-2016/articles/2016-11-11/dnc-staff-arrogance-cost-hillary-clinton-the-election-vs-donald-trump.

6. John Cassidy in *New Yorker*, November 12, 2016, retrieved from https://www.newyorker.com/news/john-cassidy/media-culpa-the-press-and-the-election-result.

7. See Thomas Gilovich, *How We Know What Isn't So: The Fallibility of Human Reason in Everyday Life* (New York: Free Press), 77.

8. See Gilovich, *How We Know What Isn't So*, 77. See also Ola Svenson, "Are We All Less Risky and More Skillful Than Our Fellow Drivers?," *Acta Psychologica* 47 (1981), 143–48.

9. See Gilovich, *How We Know What Isn't So*, 77. See also Ruth C. Wylie, *The Self-Concept*, vol. 2: *Theory and Research on Selected Topics* (Lincoln: University of Nebraska Press, 1979), chapter 12.

10. See Gilovich, *How We Know What Isn't So*, 77. See also K. Patricia Cross, "Not *Can*, But *Will* College Teaching Be Improved," *New Directions for Higher Education* 17 (1977), 1–15. See especially p. 10.

11. One might object that if "average" is interpreted as a *mean*, it could turn out that many people are above average in their abilities and performance, and thus, that these studies are not evidence of overconfidence. For if some people are significantly below the mean, it could turn out that more than half of participants, or even most of them, are above it.

By way of reply, note three points. First, in the studies cited here, participants are not asked whether their abilities or performance place them above the mean. Rather, they are asked to rank themselves relative to others in a group or to locate their percentile rank. In such cases, when more than half of participants rate themselves above the 50th percentile, this is evidence of overconfidence. Second, it is a commonplace in the literature on overconfidence for theorists to claim that it is statistically *impossible* for more than half of participants in a given study to be above average. For instance, in an article surveying recent studies on self-assessment, David Dunning, Chip Heath, and Jerry M. Suls note, "On average, people say that they are 'above average' in skill," a judgment the authors say "defies statistical possibility." See "Flawed Self-Assessment: Implications for Health, Education, and the Workplace," *Psychological Science in the Public Interest* 5, no. 3 (2004), 69. This suggests that theorists are construing averages not as means, but as medians. Otherwise, we would have to suppose that a significant number of theorists who are trained in statistical methods are making very elementary errors, which seems unlikely. Third, as always, we should be careful in the conclusions we draw from studies like those discussed here. And while I don't claim that the studies provide decisive evidence of rampant overconfidence, I do think they provide enough evidence to raise the live possibility that many of us are more confident than we should be. Such a modest claim is enough for our purposes.

12. For discussion of the Lake Wobegon effect, see Gilovich, *How We Know What Isn't So*, 77–78.

13. The view of humility discussed in this chapter is heavily indebted to Dennis Whitcomb, Heather Battaly, Jason Baehr, and Daniel Howard-Snyder, "Intellectual Humility: Owning Our Limitations," *Philosophy and Phenomenological Research* 94, no. 3 (2017), 509–39. I am also indebted to Robert C. Roberts and Jay Wood, *Intellectual Virtues: An Essay in Regulative Epistemology* (Oxford: Oxford University Press, 2007), chapter 9. I depart from Roberts and Wood in taking recognition of limitations as central to intellectual humility, but I adopt their view that humility opposes pride, vanity, and arrogance.

14. Jane Austen, *Pride and Prejudice* (Hertfordshire: Wordsworth Classics, 1993), 17.

15. Anne Lamott, *Bird by Bird: Some Instructions on Writing and Life* (New York: Anchor Books, 1995), 208–9.

16. Attribution in *Reader's Digest*, September 1937.

17. I owe this phrase to Nathan Ballantyne. See his "Epistemic Trespassing," *Mind* 128, no. 510 (April 2019), 367–95.

18. "Hey Bill Nye! Does Science Have All the Answers or Should We Do Philosophy, Too?," *Big Think*, February 22, 2016, retrieved from http://bigthink.com/videos/bill-nye-on-philosophy.

19. Olivia Goldhill, "Bill Nye, the Science Guy, Says I've Convinced Him That Philosophy Is Not Just a Load of Self-Indulgent Crap," *Quartz*, April 15,

2017, retrieved from https://qz.com/960303/bill-nye-on-philosophy-the-science-guy-says-he-has-changed-his-mind/. All quotations in this paragraph are from Goldhill's article.

20. G. K. Chesterton, *Orthodoxy* (San Francisco: Ignatius Press, 1995), 37. Quoted in Philip Dow's *Virtuous Minds: Intellectual Character Development* (Downers Grove, IL: InterVarsity Press, 2013), 70.

21. See Whitcomb et al., "Intellectual Humility," for discussion of the many ways we can own, or fail to own, our limitations.

22. Will Rahn, "The Unbearable Smugness of the Press," *CBS News Online*, November 10, 2016, retrieved from http://www.cbsnews.com/news/commentary-the-unbearable-smugness-of-the-press-presidential-election-2016.

23. Rahn, "Unbearable Smugness."

24. For one such critique, see Daniel Engber, "Everything Is Crumbling," *Slate*, March 2016, retrieved from http://www.slate.com/articles/health_and_science/cover_story/2016/03/ego_depletion_an_influential_theory_in_psychology_may_have_just_been_debunked.html.

25. Inzlicht's account of his improvement project retrieved from http://michaelinzlicht.com/getting-better/2016/10/11/check-yourself-again, .

26. Thanks to Daniel Russell for helpful discussion of the difference between correcting a limitation and correcting *for* a limitation.

27. For discussion, see Richard Nisbett, *Mindware: Tools for Smart Thinking* (New York: Farrar, Straus and Giroux, 2015), 116–18.

28. Carol Dweck, *Mindset: The New Psychology of Success* (New York: Random House, 2006), 6–7.

29. Dweck, *Mindset*, 35–44.

30. For more on the relationship between humility and growth mindset, see Tenelle Porter and Karina Schumann, "Intellectual Humility and Openness to the Opposing View," *Self and Identity* 17, no. 2 (2018), 139–62. See also Jason Baehr, *Cultivating Good Minds*, chapter 6. Available at https://intellectualvirtues.org/cultivating-good-minds/ .

7

Honesty

Don't Distort the Truth

It was a Saturday night in Denver—June 24, 1899. Reporters from four Denver newspapers happened upon each other at the train depot. Al Stevens, Jack Tournay, John Lewis, and Hal Wilshire each represented one of the four Denver papers: the *Republican*, the *Denver Times*, the *Denver Post*, and the *Rocky Mountain News*. The tone was somber. There was nothing to report, and stories for the Sunday edition were due soon. Stevens piped up, "You guys can do what you want, but I'm going to fake. . . . It won't hurt anybody, so don't get sore." The other reporters decided to go along. Soon the foursome was drinking in the bar at the Oxford Hotel, trying to serve up a story. After several failed attempts, they settled on a story about China. This would prevent their being found out— China was a long way from Denver, and no one could be expected to refute their account. As long as the story was safe from inspection, they thought, why not make it a big one? And what's bigger in China than the Great Wall? The premise of the story was set: the Chinese government planned to tear down the wall in order to show its openness to trade with the West.

The reporters needed to supply supporting details and cover their tracks. They invented a group of American engineers who were stopping in Denver on the way to China, where they would plan a low-cost demolition of the wall. After proceeding to the Windsor Hotel, the reporters gained an accomplice in the night clerk, who let each of them sign a fake name to the guest list—one for each imaginary engineer. The reporters then coached the clerk: if anyone asks

The Excellent Mind. Nathan L. King, Oxford University Press (2021). © Oxford University Press.
DOI: 10.1093/oso/9780190096250.003.0007

about the traveling demolition men, say that they only talked to the press. The reporters now held a monopoly on fact-checking for the story. The Sunday papers were ready to roll. The headline: "Great Chinese Wall Is Doomed; Peking to Seek World's Trade!"

Within weeks, the story had reached across the United States, appearing in the nation's most widely circulated outlets. Lewis was surprised to learn that the hoax had been confirmed and embellished in a large East Coast paper, as a Chinese official visiting New York allegedly backed the story. From there, the spark jumped to China, where a group of traditionalists—the Boxers— were already angry with foreign interlopers. The Great Wall story set their rage ablaze. Hundreds of foreign missionaries and Chinese Christians were massacred, while the embassies in Peking were besieged. The lie of four Denver reporters had incited the Boxer Rebellion.

This story is commonly recounted in sermons about the destructive power of the tongue. Any homily recounting the hoax has great rhetorical power. And many ministers have pitched the story as having the added advantage of being true. Denver author Harry Lee Wilber brought the hoax into the popular consciousness in 1939 with an article in *North American Review*. Attesting to the story's truth, Wilber affirms, "This is how it happened."[1]

Only it isn't. It's true that the Denver reporters invented the story about the Great Wall's destruction. And it's true that the story reached several prominent American papers. But the link to the Boxer Rebellion is entirely made up, either by Wilber or by one of his informants. Wilber himself represents the whole story—including the bit about the Boxer Rebellion—as true. (His version of the story is entitled "A Fake That Rocked the World: An Authentic Story of Four Reporters Who Had to *Make* News.") But in reality, the Great Wall hoax had no link to the Boxer Rebellion. No scholarly account of the rebellion makes the connection. The rebellion in fact resulted from a mixture of famine, religious enmity, and patriotic zeal. The first hint of a connection between the hoax and the rebellion is in Wilber's article, which was written 40 years after the Denver reporters' tall tale was printed. It seems that either Wilber or someone in his chain of informants had manufactured another fake—a hoax about a hoax, dishonesty in the name of warning against dishonesty.[2]

Shocking as it is, the Great Wall story has nothing on today's episodes of dishonesty. Public trust in news media is in decline.[3] Sometimes, the seeds of doubt are sown by politicians who accuse the media of proffering "fake news" in order to cover their deceptions, or who supply their own "alternative facts" to do the same. In other cases, reporters deserve all the mistrust that comes · their way. *New York Times* writer Jayson Blair forfeited a promising career when it was discovered that he had plagiarized or made up some 600 of his stories.[4] NBC News anchor Brian Williams's reputation was damaged when he fabricated a story about falling under enemy fire on a helicopter ride during the second US war in Iraq.[5] As a result of such incidents, the media invests heavily in fact-checking departments in order to save its tarnished image.

Then there's the academy. Among college students, three recent studies report cheating rates of 70%, 86%, and 60%.[6] In another study of 472 students, only three reported that they had not cheated in any of nine ways listed on a questionnaire. 78% of these students reported having cheated often in at least one of those ways, including getting exam questions from someone who had taken the test (94%), copying from another student's test (90%), and taking a test for someone else (68%).[7] That's just exams. When it comes to student papers, plagiarism rates are also much higher than desirable. In one study of 71,300 college undergraduates, 62% admitted to cheating on written assignments.[8] To counter this trend, professors equip themselves with the latest honesty technology. They use websites and courseware such as turnitin.com and SafeAssign to ensure that students don't filch their written work. Some brazen students strike back by using secret paper mills and anti-anti-plagiarism services like cheatturnitin.com. There ensues an escalating arms race between cheating students and the teachers determined to keep them honest.

Alas, the professors themselves don't always avoid such fudgery. In 2002, independent reporters discovered several instances of plagiarism in the work of bestselling historian Stephen Ambrose. In writing such books as *The Wild Blue, Citizen Soldiers, Nixon: Ruin and Recovery, 1973–1990,* and *Crazy Horse and Custer,* Ambrose had lifted entire passages, word for word, from other authors' works, without proper attribution. His defenders excused the first alleged thefts as the honest mistakes of a busy writer pressed against publishing deadlines. But further digging unearthed a sustained pattern of plagiarism going back to Ambrose's early career. (Ambrose did mention the original works in his footnotes. But he passed off the writing itself as his own—a breach of honesty for which any student would expect to be punished.) Though some view Ambrose's offenses as minor, a haunting question lingers: if he was willing to deceive about the originality of his work, might he have been willing to stretch the truth about his historical narratives as well?[9]

If we're inclined to wag a finger at such incidents, that's a sign that we value intellectual honesty. For to value honesty is to reject its opposites: lying, bluffing, bullshitting, and their ilk. And, as we'll see, a better understanding of these misdeeds can yield a better understanding of honesty. As we sort through the varieties of dishonesty, we'll find clues about the nature of honesty itself. Sifting the intellectual rubbish will reveal where the treasure may be found.

Two points before we begin. First, though our main focus will be *intellectual* honesty, in practice, it is hard to separate this sort of honesty from its moral cousin. Both kinds of honesty involve a disposition to avoid distorting the truth. And the actions of the intellectually honest person and the morally honest person are likely to coincide, thereby making it unclear whether one virtue or the other—or both—are at work in a given case. If we demand a distinction between the two, however, it seems to come down to motivation. The intellectually honest person is motivated by a desire to convey and not distort the truth *because* she cares about truth as such. The morally honest person need not care about the truth in precisely the same way. She might instead be motivated to speak the truth and avoid distorting it because she wants to respect others, to avoid harming them, to be kind to them, or the like.[10] Of course, a person could have both motivations at the same time.

Second, in contrast to the intellectual virtues we've explored thus far, it is not clear that honesty is to be found in a mean between extremes. How could someone be *too* committed to speaking the truth and avoiding distortion? (One might point to people who say too much, or overshare, in the name of honesty—people who spout detailed and accurate accounts of their friends' faults, for instance. But that seems more a social vice than an intellectual one.) In any case, our account of honesty won't rely on the idea that the virtue is flanked by vices of deficiency and excess. Better to stick to reality than to try to squeeze every virtue into a preset mold.

How to Be Dishonest

We can get a handle on what honesty is by surveying some varieties of its opposite, dishonesty.

Any such survey naturally starts with *lying*.[11] We're all familiar with liars who utter falsehoods. But just saying something false doesn't suffice for lying. Consider an unwitting pastor who buys into Wilber's story and tells her congregation that the Great Wall hoax caused the Boxer Rebellion. She says something false. The hoax didn't cause the rebellion. But our pastor isn't lying. She doesn't *know* that what she's saying is false; she doesn't even *believe* she's saying something false. Perhaps she should've checked her facts more carefully, but she hasn't been dishonest. In order to lie, she must believe that she's uttering falsehood. As *Seinfeld's* George Costanza puts it, "It's not a lie . . . if *you* believe it."[12]

As it turns out, even *knowingly* saying something false isn't quite enough for a lie. An actor on stage can say lines that he knows are false; he needn't therefore be lying. Recall the iconic scene in *Star Wars: The Empire Strikes Back,* when Darth Vader reaches out to Luke Skywalker (Mark Hamill) and says, "Luke, I am your father." James Earl Jones, the voice of Vader, is saying something he knows to be false—he's not Hamill's father. But this isn't a lie. The audience knows that Jones is just acting. He's not "in the game" of trying to communicate the sober truth about his family ties. And the audience knows this. There's no lie here, because there's no intention to deceive. On the traditional view, to *lie* is to say something we know (or at least believe) to be false in order to deceive someone else—to get them to believe the falsehood asserted.[13]

Lying is a familiar kind of deception, but it's not the only kind. Sometimes, we can *bluff:* we can intend to deceive either by saying something true but misleading, or by not saying anything at all. Both varieties of bluffing are common in academic settings, especially competitive ones. Consider:

Scene 1: Dave is a college freshman. He's taking an ancient philosophy course, and class is about to start. Today's reading assignment was the first book of Plato's *Republic.* Dave didn't do the reading; he only read the *CliffsNotes.* The professor asks Dave what he thought about Socrates's objection to the idea that justice is giving people what they are owed. Dave answers in light of the *CliffsNotes:* "I think Socrates is right. If I borrowed a knife from a friend who then became insane, it wouldn't be just for me to return the knife. Someone might get hurt." Dave does not admit that he didn't do the reading. By his words, he intends to get others to think he did, though he stops short of saying that he did. He thereby misleads the class into thinking he did the reading.

Scene 2: The case is just as before, except that Dave did not even read the *CliffsNotes.* Instead, he spent the weekend watching football. The professor offers an interpretation of Socrates's objection to the idea that justice is giving people what they're owed. Intending to appear prepared, Dave simply nods along, saying nothing. He thereby misleads the class into thinking he did the reading.

In both cases, Dave bluffs the class into a false belief about his having done the reading. Yet he never asserts the falsehood he's trying to get others to believe. Instead, he exploits the expectation that students will do the assigned reading. That expectation, combined with what Dave says (in case 1) or doesn't say (in case 2) misleads the others. In the first case, Dave says something true (that he believes Socrates's objection is good), in order to get others to believe that he did the reading. Dave's bluffing speech, in the context, amounts to *falsely implying* that he did the assignment. In the second case, Dave misleads without saying a word. He doesn't admit that he didn't do the reading, but he does nod along—and this leads others into falsehood. In both cases, Dave misrepresents what he knows (he doesn't know as much about *Republic* as he's letting on) or his actions (he didn't read *Republic*), or both.

So much for lying and bluffing. Let's talk *bullshit*. In his bestseller, *On Bullshit*, Harry Frankfurt identifies this as a separate species of dishonesty:

> What bullshit essentially misrepresents is neither the state of affairs to which it refers nor the beliefs of the speaker concerning that state of affairs. . . . The bullshitter may not deceive us, or even intend to do so, either about the facts or about what he takes them to be. What he does necessarily attempt to deceive us about is his enterprise. . . . [T]he fact about himself that the liar hides is that he is attempting to lead us away from a correct apprehension of reality. . . . The fact about himself that the bullshitter hides, on the other hand, is that the truth-values of his statements are of no central interest to him.[14]

On Frankfurt's view, the bullshitter has no interest in the truth about what he's discussing. He is only interested in getting what he wants, or in portraying a certain image, or in furthering some other such goal. In order to achieve this goal, he misrepresents the truth about his internal state. He acts like he cares about the truth, but is motivated by some other end—say, wealth or power. Speaking in a context where listeners expect him to tell the truth (he's not engaged in a "bull session"), the bullshitter deceives about his intentions. In this way, he acts dishonestly. Concerning truth, Frankfurt says, the bullshitter "pays no attention to it at all. By virtue of this, bullshit is a greater enemy of the truth than lies are."[15] To put it in a word—Oxford Dictionaries' word of 2016—the bullshitter is *post-truth*.

In this connection, consider the spectacle of convenient "forgetting." Imagine a professor who, for years, has given the same tired arguments for his views while traveling the world and speaking to different audiences. At every stop, and in print, the professor encounters objections to these arguments—evidence that the arguments need to be revised or even abandoned. But instead of addressing these problems, the professor simply plows forward as if he's never heard them. Perhaps some audiences are still persuaded that he's interested in the truth—that his arguments are the fruit of honest inquiry. But those who know about the unacknowledged objections usually detect an unpleasant scent.

Some people bullshit as they defend their views. Others bullshit by the way they ask questions. This happens at academic conferences all the time. It usually goes like this. The speaker gives a paper on some topic. Then the Q & A period begins. Someone in the back asks a question that on its face is sincere, but on second glance is asked only to make the speaker look stupid—or the questioner look smart. The same sort of thing happens in college classrooms. Students have a knack for asking pithy questions that are hard to answer in a way that is both brief and satisfying. Usually, they ask because they hope the teacher can shed some light on the topic at issue. But sometimes, they ask just in order to "stump the professor."

The difference between earnest questions and bullshit questions is often revealed after someone offers an answer. Of course, the earnest questioner needn't *accept* the speaker's answer. Some answers are bad, after all. But what if, after hearing a considered reply, the questioner ignores it? Or goes on as if the answer had never been given? In those cases, it's a good bet that the questioner is bullshitting. In speaking of such cases, 18th-century writer George Horne remarks,

> Many and painful are the researches sometimes necessary to be made, for settling points of that kind. Pertness and ignorance may ask a question in three lines, which it will cost learning and ingenuity thirty pages to answer. When this is done, the same question shall be triumphantly asked again the next year, as if nothing had ever been written on the subject. And as people in general, for one reason or another, like short objections better than long answers, in this mode of disputation (if it can be styled such) the odds must be ever against us; and we must be content with those of our friends who have honesty and erudition, candor and patience, to study both sides of the question.—Be it so.[16]

So far, we've discussed forms of dishonesty that have an outward focus. They concern the ways we might misrepresent the truth to others. Here is another possibility: perhaps we can deceive ourselves. Examples might include the following:

- Deliberately ignoring or suppressing evidence against our views, so that we remain convinced that these views are true;
- Intentionally setting a higher evidential "bar" for contrary views than for our own, so as to make it harder to believe contrary views than it should be; and
- "Justifying" our views or attitudes in ways we would reject if others were to do the same, while telling ourselves our justifications are perfectly respectable.

If we're humble, we'll beware of our vulnerability to these kinds of self-deceit. For we might be more motivated to commit them than we realize. As psychologists Robert Abelson and Thomas Gilovich note, we tend to speak of our beliefs in the same ways we speak of our possessions—namely, in terms of *ownership:*

> We describe the formation of beliefs with numerous references to possession, as when we say, "I *adopted* that belief," "he *inherited* the view," "she *acquired* her conviction," or, if a potential belief is rejected, "I don't *buy* that." When someone believes in something, we refer to the fact that "she *holds* a belief," or "he *clings* to his belief," When a belief is "given up," we say that "he *lost* his belief," "she *abandoned* her convictions," or "I *disown* my earlier stand."[17]

We treat our beliefs like we treat our things. Thus, we are strongly motivated to protect them—to keep them intact. If we're not vigilant, this might lead us to deceive ourselves to that end.

Honesty, Dishonesty, and Truth

Plagiarism, lying, bluffing, bullshitting, and self-deception are all failures to respect the truth:

- Plagiarists distort the truth by representing someone else's work as their own.
- Liars distort the truth by saying something they believe to be false in order to deceive others.
- Bluffers (of the sort we discussed) distort the truth by misrepresenting their own knowledge or what they have done.
- Bullshitters distort the truth by misrepresenting their own commitment to knowing and speaking the truth.
- Self-deceivers (of the sort we discussed) distort the truth by misrepresenting the truth to themselves.

In all these ways, and in others we won't discuss, dishonest people fail to revere the truth. Instead, they distort it. As philosopher Christian Miller suggests, it's this distortion that unites the varieties of dishonesty and places them under a single heading.[18] That acts of dishonesty are united in this way helps us to see what honesty is. A commitment to representing the truth (as we see it) accurately is the core of honesty itself. More on that point in a moment.

First, an important aside: the notion of truth needed to make sense of honesty and dishonesty is fairly traditional and common-sensical. Let C stand for any claim. On this view of truth, the claim C is true if and only if C describes things the way they are. The claim *The cat is on the mat* is true if and only if the cat is on the mat. The claim *There's beer in the fridge* is true if and only if there's beer in the fridge. The claim *I was writing my book yesterday* is true if and only if I *was* writing my book yesterday. Dave's implied claim, *I did the reading assigned for class*, is true if and only if he did the reading. And so on. On this way of thinking, truth is determined by the way things are, and not by our beliefs, desires, conceptual schemes, or social mores.

To see why our account of honesty suggests something like this notion of truth, we need only explore examples. If I tell my wife I was writing my book yesterday but I was really watching TV, I lie to her. With deceptive intent, I tell her something I believe to be false, and what I tell her *is* false because I wasn't writing yesterday. I said I was doing one thing, but I was doing another. Likewise, when Dave bluffs a peer into thinking that he did the reading, his deception is deceiving because he *didn't* do the reading. He says he did the reading, but he didn't. The bullshitter similarly misrepresents his own motivations. He tries to get us to believe—to think it's true that—he's interested in the truth. But he's not.

These examples of dishonesty don't make much sense if, as some people today are fond of saying, all truth is subjective, or relative, or "socially constructed"—determined by what we believe. For as we saw earlier, my claim to have been writing my book was false not because of what anyone thought, but because I *wasn't* writing. And if I was writing, my claim would've been true, independent of what anyone believed about it. Similarly, Dave's implicit claim to have done the reading was false because he didn't do the reading— not because of what anyone believed about this claim. If he'd done the reading, his claim would've been true—regardless of what anyone believed. The bullshitter's implicit claim to care about truth wasn't made false by anyone's beliefs or conceptual framework. It was false because he didn't care about the truth. If he'd cared, his claim would've been true, even if no one else believed it.

These examples make trouble for the oft-repeated claim that we have recently discovered truth to be subjective, or relative, or socially constructed—wholly dependent on what we think. Our common-sense grasp of dishonesty suggests that truth depends on the way things are. Paradoxically, the nature of deception provides a clue about the nature of truth.[19]

What Honesty Is

Honesty stands in contrast to all kinds of deception, and it is time we consider it directly. It will help to start with some examples of the virtue in action.

In her book *I Don't Know*, Leah Hager Cohen examines our natural desire to avoid embarrassment about our ignorance. "How easily," she says, "we fall into the pattern of using deception as a shield against feeling uncomfortable."[20] In contrast to this pattern, Cohen describes her friend, Mary:

> You know when you're with people you want to impress, people you find a little intimidating? Maybe you're feeling kind of dumb, like you don't really belong with them. You're worried you'll be found out. And somebody mentions a writer or the title of a book in this tone like, *Naahh-turally you know what I'm talking about.*

And even though you have no clue, you do that little thing where you narrow your eyes and purse your lips and give this thoughtful nod. . . . You know what Mary does in that situation? . . . She says, "I don't know that book." She says, "I've never heard of that person."[21]

Mary admits her ignorance. She refuses to distort the truth, though this might cost her respect or social standing. She's *honest*. (We can detect intellectual humility and courage in this example, too. Mary owns her limitations despite her fear of being found out. But what underlies Mary's humility and courage is her honesty. Her commitment to the truth helps her curb her fear and own her ignorance.)

Here's another example. The logician Gottlob Frege published the second volume of his book *The Basic Laws of Arithmetic* in 1903. It was the culmination of a lifetime's work on the bedrock of mathematics. Just before the book's release, Frege received a letter from a young Bertrand Russell. The letter, written in response to Frege's first volume, argued that the work suffered from a crippling weakness—it entailed a contradiction. The problem is now known as Russell's Paradox. A lesser scholar might have been enraged. But rather than scold Russell for impertinence, Frege instead published an appendix acknowledging the error Russell had observed.

Frege's work is highly influential today. His many insights can be incorporated into logical systems that omit his fatal flaw. But for our purposes, what stands out is Frege's honesty. He refused to ignore the problem with his system, or to paper over it with confusing language. Nor did he omit mention of Russell's objection in the hope that no one would notice. Quite the opposite: he published the embarrassing truth for all to see. If there was egg on his face, Frege himself had cracked it. In an oft-quoted letter to a friend, Russell reflects,

As I think about acts of integrity and grace, I realize that there is nothing in my knowledge to compare with Frege's dedication to the truth. His entire life's work was on the verge of completion, much of his work had been ignored to the benefit of men infinitely less capable, his second volume was about to be published, and upon finding that his fundamental assumption was in error, he responded with intellectual pleasure clearly submerging any feelings of personal disappointment. It was almost superhuman and a telling indication of that which men are capable if their dedication is to creative work and knowledge instead of cruder efforts to dominate and be known.[22]

Above, our study of dishonesty revealed that every instance of this vice involves a lack of respect for truth—a willingness to distort it. The examples of Mary and Frege display the opposite inclination. For in these examples we see a healthy respect, even a reverence, for truth. Both thinkers value the truth, and indeed value it more than they value their own reputations. In light of these examples, we might even characterize honesty as a reverence for the truth— a commitment to express the truth as one sees it and to avoid distorting it.

This is a good start. Honesty requires reverence for truth, a commitment to representing things as one sees them and not distorting them. But on closer inspection, such reverence isn't quite enough for the virtue of honesty. To see why, recall that virtues like intellectual honesty are *character traits*. As such, they don't just involve our motivations (like reverence for truth). They also involve what we *think* and how we *act*. Thus, at least when she's reflecting on the matter, the honest person will think that truth is valuable. She will think that she should tell the truth when called upon (perhaps except under extreme circumstances). She'll think that dishonest people are flouting their obligations to others. As for her behavior, she won't leave her reverence on the couch. Rather, she will be disposed to behave in ways that reveal her truth-oriented motives and thoughts, and her aversion to duplicity. She'll tell the truth when called upon; she'll avoid lying, bluffing, bullshitting, and the like.

In light of all this, we may characterize virtuous intellectual honesty as follows:

> *Intellectual honesty* is a disposition to express the truth (as we see it) through our thought, speech, and behavior, to avoid intentionally distorting the truth (as we see it), and to do so because we revere the truth and think it is valuable. [23]

Again, it's the motive-oriented feature—a reverence for truth itself—that distinguishes intellectual honesty from moral honesty. (Moral honesty is motivated by a concern for moral ends— say, to avoid harming people or to be kind to them. It doesn't require a motivation for truth as such.) It's also a motivation for truth that makes the difference between merely honest behavior and the virtue of intellectually honesty. To be intellectually honest, our penchant for avoiding distortion must be motivated by reverence for truth itself. If we avoid all duplicity just so that others think we're honest, we might behave honestly, but we won't have the virtue.

Our account gives us a working understanding of intellectual honesty. Important questions remain. Will the honest person *always* tell the truth? Are there circumstances in which she may justifiably lie or mislead? Could she distort the truth *sometimes* without thereby failing to be an honest person? These questions deserve prolonged attention. But given our aims, we can only make a start on them. Nevertheless, a few brief points may prove helpful.

First, do honest people always tell the truth? Clearly not. As we saw earlier, the honest person avoids *intentionally* distorting the truth. This is an important qualifier. For while it seems clear that we sometimes have access to the truth, sometimes we don't. Merely misrepresenting the truth does not suffice for dishonesty. There are such things as honest mistakes, after all. Dishonesty requires an *intention* to deceive. By contrast, the honest person reliably intends to be truthful.

Are there exceptions? Does the honest person *always* avoid misrepresenting the truth as she sees it? The question divides itself. First: are there cases in which an honest person will *justifiably* distort the truth as she sees it? Second: does a single act of *unjustified* dishonesty mean that a person lacks the virtue of honesty?

There is a centuries-long debate about whether deception is ever justifiable. We cannot enter that debate here. Fortunately, for our purposes, we don't need to.[24] Even those who think that deception is *sometimes* permissible think that it is so only in rare or extreme situations—say, in order to save a life. Such thinkers agree that most lies are wrong—both intellectually and morally. They agree that we should avoid deceptions of the Denver reporter variety. So it seems that all parties concur with the following: lying and other forms of deception are rarely, if ever justified. Barring extreme circumstances, the honest person will rarely deceive. Deception will rarely, if ever, express her character. All can agree with that point, and with our general account of honesty, even if disagreement remains about whether deception is justifiable in some cases.

What about uncharacteristic, unjustified deceptions? Everyone will agree that unjustified deception occurs. (Recall those Denver reporters.) Does the fact that someone commits a single act of dishonesty thereby disqualify that person from being honest—from having the virtue of honesty?

No. An honest person will not *characteristically* distort the truth as she sees it. Most of the time, and in many situations in which telling the truth is hard for her, she'll tell the truth. But a single deception need not mean she's not an honest person. Consider an analogy from the world of golf. PGA Tour player Phil Mickelson is an excellent putter. He makes 99% of his putts from three feet or less.[25] This is an excellent mark. It's a virtue of a golfer to putt as well as Mickelson does. But occasionally, perhaps especially in high-pressure situations, he misses. This doesn't mean he's not a good putter. Likewise, a single lie doesn't necessarily mean a person lacks the virtue of honesty; still less does it mean that she has the vice of dishonesty. Even so, an honest person will reliably tell the truth as she sees it. And other things being equal, the more reliably she does this, the more honest she is.

A Team of Virtues

Recall Frege's intellectual honesty—his fervent desire to get and speak the truth, and to avoid distortion, even in the face of professional loss and embarrassment. Throughout his career, that virtue worked alongside others. For instance, Frege would never have developed his logical system without the curiosity that motivated his inquiry. Nor would he have produced such exacting work without intellectual carefulness. He would not have been able to admit a major mistake in his life's work without intellectual humility. Finally, he would not have finished his life's work without a disposition to overcome obstacles to knowledge. Frege faced an exceptionally difficult project, coupled with neglect and discouragement from others. He pressed on anyway. That is to say, Frege owed much of his success to intellectual perseverance, the virtue we'll discuss next.

For Reflection and Discussion

1. How does the author distinguish lying, bluffing, and bullshitting from each other? Would you draw these distinctions in the same ways?
2. What examples of intellectual dishonesty do you see exhibited today? As you answer, try to identify several different varieties.
3. Do your social or intellectual circles reward honesty? Or do they reward dishonesty? As you answer, try to specify the ways in which your circles reward either trait.
4. Is self-deception really possible? If so, how?

5. Assuming that self-deception is possible, reflect on the idea that we treat our beliefs like we treat our possessions. In light of this idea, in what areas might you be vulnerable to self-deception?

Further Reading

There is alarmingly little philosophical work available on intellectual honesty. For an exception, see Louis Guenin, "Intellectual Honesty," *Synthese* 145, no. 2 (2005), 177–232. The account of *intellectual* honesty developed in this chapter is adapted from the account of honesty defended in Christian B. Miller, "Honesty," in *Moral Psychology*, vol. 5: *Virtue and Character*, ed. Walter Sinnott-Armstrong and Christian B. Miller (Cambridge, MA: MIT Press, 2017), 237–73. See also Alan Wilson, "Honesty as a Virtue," *Metaphilosophy* 49, no. 3 (2018), 262–80. For a thorough discussion of the nature of lying and deception see James Edwin Mahon, "The Definition of Lying and Deception," *Stanford Encyclopedia of Philosophy*, ed. Edward N. Zalta, Winter 2016 ed., available online for free. For a brief but illuminating account of bullshit, see Harry Frankfurt, *On Bullshit* (Princeton: Princeton University Press, 2005). For lively and learned discussions of truth, relativism, and social constructionism, see Michael P. Lynch, *True to Life: Why Truth Matters* (Cambridge, MA: MIT Press, 2004) and Paul Boghossian, *Fear of Knowledge: Against Relativism and Constructivism* (New York: Oxford University Press, 2006). For an articulation of a sophisticated version of relativism, see John MacFarlane, "Making Sense of Relative Truth," *Proceedings of the Aristotelian Society* 105 (2005), 321–39. For an empirically informed discussion of academic dishonesty, see Christian B. Miller, "Honesty, Cheating, and Character in College," *Journal of College and Character* 14, no. 3 (2013), 213–22. Self-deception is a fascinating and puzzling topic in its own right. I have not done it justice here. For a helpful introduction see Ian DeWeese-Boyd, "Self-Deception," *Stanford Encyclopedia of Philosophy*, ed. Edward N. Zalta, Fall 2017 ed., available online for free.

Notes

1. The story to this point follows that of Wilber, "A Fake That Rocked the World: An Authentic Story of Four Reporters Who Had to *Make* News," *North American Review* 247, no. 1 (Spring 1939), 21–26.

2. Those interested in learning the *real* story of the Boxer Rebellion should consult Anthony E. Clark, *Heaven in Conflict: Franciscans and the Boxer Uprising in Shanxi* (Seattle: University of Washington Press, 2015); also Joseph W. Esherick, *The Origins of the Boxer Uprising* (Berkeley: University of California Press, 1988).

3. For details, see the recent Gallup survey, "Indicators of News Media Trust" (Gallup, 2018), retrieved from https://www.knightfoundation.org/reports/indicators-of-news-media-trust

4. I first learned of this story from Philip Dow, *Virtuous Minds* (Downers Grove, IL: InterVarsity Press, 2013), 62. See also a series of letters to the editor, "Betrayal of Trust: The Jayson Blair Scandal," *New York Times*, May 13, 2003; Rem Rieder, "The Jayson Blair Affair," *American Journalism Review*, June 2003, retrieved from http://ajrarchive.org/Article.asp?id=3019; and "Corrections to Articles by Jayson Blair," *New York Times* June 11, 2003. I glean these sources from Dow's volume.

5. Paul Farhi, "NBC Removes Williams for 6 Months over 'Misrepresented' Events in Iraq," *Washington Post*, February 10, 2015.

6. See Helen Klein, Nancy Levenburg, Marie McKendall, and William Mothersell, "Cheating during the College Years: How Do Business Students Compare?," *Journal of Business Ethics* 72 (2007), 197–206; also Donald McCabe, Kenneth Butterfield, and Linda Treviño, "Academic Dishonesty in Graduate Business Programs: Prevalence, Causes, and Proposed Action," *Academy of Management Learning and Education* 5 (2006), 294–305; and Carter Rokovski and Elliot Levy, "Academic Dishonesty: Perceptions of Business Students," *College Student Journal* 41 (2007), 466–81. For directing me to these sources, I am indebted to Christian B. Miller's paper "Honesty, Cheating, and Character in College," *Journal of College and Character* 14, no. 3 (August 2013), 213–22. I closely paraphrase Miller in this paragraph.

7. Suncana Taradi, Milan Taradi, Tin Knezevic, and Zoran Dogas, "Students Come to Medical Schools Prepared to Cheat: A Multicampus Investigation," *Journal of Medical Ethics* 36 (2007), 666–70. Cited in Miller, "Honesty, Cheating," 214.

8. Statistic provided by the International Center for Academic Integrity, retrieved from https://academicintegrity.org/statistics/, .

9. On the Ambrose story see David D. Kirkpatrick, "As Historian's Fame Grows, So Do Questions on Methods," *New York Times*, January 11, 2002; David Plotz, "The Plagiarist: Why Stephen Ambrose Is a Vampire," *Slate*, January 11, 2002, retrieved from http://www.slate.com/articles/news_and_politics/assessment/2002/01/the_plagiarist.html; and Mark

Lewis, "More Controversy for Stephen Ambrose, *Forbes,* January 9, 2002, retrieved from http://www.forbes.com/2002/01/09/0109ambrose.html.

10. For this way of drawing the distinction, I am indebted to Alan Wilson, "Avoiding the Conflation of Moral and Intellectual Virtues," *Ethical Theory and Moral Practice* 20 (2017), 1037–50.

11. For a fuller survey of these varieties, see Louis M. Guenin, "Intellectual Honesty," *Synthese* 145 (2005), 177–232.

12. *Seinfeld,* season 6, episode 15: "The Beard," NBC Studios, 1995.

13. For further discussion of this point see Michael P. Lynch, *True to Life: Why Truth Matters* (Cambridge, MA: MIT Press, 2005), 147–48. My Vader/ Skywalker example is adapted from an example of Lynch's. Please note: the account of lying discussed in this chapter will work for our purposes, but is subject to technical problems. The most straightforward of these is the problem of bald-faced lies—lies that are so clearly untrue that they don't involve an intention to deceive. For a thorough discussion of lying and deception, see James Edwin Mahon, "The Definition of Lying and Deception," *Stanford Encyclopedia of Philosophy,* ed. Edward N. Zalta, Winter 2016 ed., retrieved from https://plato.stanford.edu/entries/lying-definition/.

14. Harry Frankfurt, *On Bullshit* (Princeton: Princeton University Press, 2005), 53–55.

15. Frankfurt, *On Bullshit,* 61.

16. George Horne, *Letters on Infidelity,* in *Standard Works Adapted to the Use of the Protestant Episcopal Church in the United States,* vol. 5, ed. William R. Whittingham (New York: New-York Protestant Episcopal Press, 1831), letter 8, 272. I first learned of Horne's remarks from Tim McGrew.

17. Thomas Gilovich, *How We Know What Isn't So: The Fallibility of Human Reason in Everyday Life* (New York: Free Press, 1991), 86.

18. I owe the suggestion that all acts of dishonesty involve distorting the facts or the truth to Christian B. Miller. See his "Honesty," in *Moral Psychology,* vol. 5: *Virtue and Character,* ed. Walter Sinnott-Armstrong and Christian B. Miller (Cambridge, MA: MIT Press, 2017), 237–73. Miller argues that all varieties of honesty involve a disposition to avoid intentionally distorting the facts. The account of honesty developed in this chapter is heavily indebted to Miller's work. Miller includes cheating, stealing, and promise-breaking within the scope of dishonesty. He's right to do so, but with the exception of plagiarism as a form of cheating, I've elected not to discuss these examples here.

19. In the last few paragraphs, I've suggested that in order to make sense of honesty and dishonesty, we need to think of truth as determined by the way things are. Philosophers will rightly recognize an affinity for the

correspondence theory of truth here. And some philosophers are apt to wonder whether more "minimalist" views of truth (which are officially silent on what makes propositions true) can handle the examples discussed in these paragraphs. I am somewhat skeptical about the prospects for such minimalist views. But they are not my main target here. I would not be alarmed to discover that minimalist theories can handle the cases I discuss in this chapter. My aim is simply to show that radical versions of relativism and social constructionism about truth have difficulty accommodating our common sense judgments about dishonesty. If the argument of these paragraphs does nothing more than apply pressure to these views, it will have done its job. Thanks to Daniel Howard-Snyder and an anonymous referee for helpful discussion here. Alas, I fear I haven't fully addressed either of their concerns.

20. Leah Hager Cohen, *I Don't Know: In Praise of Admitting Ignorance (Except When You Shouldn't)* (New York: Riverhead, 2013), 4.

21. Cohen, *I Don't Know*, 10–11. I first came across this passage in Dennis Whitcomb, Heather Battaly, Jason Baehr, and Daniel Howard-Snyder, "Intellectual Humility: Owning Our Limitations," *Philosophy and Phenomenological Research* 94, no. 3 (2017), 510.

22. Quoted in Scott Soames, *The Analytic Tradition in Philosophy*, vol. 1: *The Founding Giants* (Princeton: Princeton University Press, 2014), 129.

23. The discussion of the nature of honesty in this section of the chapter relies on Miller, "Honesty." Part I of Miller's paper makes clear several possible conditions for honesty that are subject to controversy. For instance, Miller considers whether virtuous honesty requires good motivations for honest behavior, and whether the virtue requires access to facts or the truth. Where my account takes a stand on such issues, I do not claim that Miller would take a similar stand.

24. For one important perspective see Immanuel Kant's treatment of lying in his "On a Supposed Right to Lie because of Philanthropic Concerns," in *Grounding for the Metaphysics of Morals with On a Supposed Right to Lie Because of Philanthropic Concerns*, trans. James W. Ellington (Indianapolis: Hackett, 1993). See also *Grounding*, sections 402–3 and 429–30.

25. Data retrieved from the PGA Tour's statistics tracking website. Mickelson's numbers are available at https://www.pgatour.com/content/pgatour/stats/stat.341.y2019.html.

8

Perseverance

Overcome Obstacles

The path toward knowledge is often littered with obstacles. No one knew this better than Helen Taussig (1898–1986). A founder of infant heart medicine, she pioneered a technique, the Blalock-Taussig surgery, which saved the lives of countless "blue babies," whose complexion revealed a deadly heart defect. Her research laid bare the dangers of thalidomide, a prenatal sedative that caused infants to be born without limbs. After studying the drug's devastating effects on German babies, Taussig successfully campaigned to prevent its release in the United States. For her lifelong advocacy of infant care, in 1964 she received the Presidential Medal of Freedom—the highest possible honor for an American civilian—from President Lyndon Johnson. Taussig went on to become the first female president of the American Heart Association.[1]

If you had known Helen as a child, you would not have predicted such grand outcomes. As an infant, she contracted tuberculosis. As a result, she only attended school half-time for over two years of her early education. Her mother died when she was just eleven. As if this weren't enough, Taussig battled learning disabilities that hampered her ability to read, spell, and recognize numbers. Her father, a Harvard academic, worried that she would not finish grammar school. Despite this, he tutored her extensively, providing instruction and encouragement. By the time she was an undergraduate at Radcliffe College and then at Berkeley, her academic work was excellent and still improving. However, Taussig was beset

The Excellent Mind. Nathan L. King, Oxford University Press (2021). © Oxford University Press.
DOI: 10.1093/oso/9780190096250.003.0008

with self-doubt. Her trouble reading, self-diagnosed as dyslexia, continued to slow the learning process—an obstacle she overcame through increased effort.[2]

Upon graduating from college, Taussig opted to pursue a career in medicine. In addition to the standard rigors of med school admissions, she faced resistance that had nothing to do with her qualifications. At Harvard, women weren't allowed to attend the medical school. Seeking a workaround, Taussig considered applying to the School of Public Health, which admitted women. Her hopes were dashed when she learned that women who completed coursework could not thereby earn a degree. She pressed the dean about the policy: "Who is going to be such a fool as to spend four years studying and not get a degree?" "No one, I hope," he replied. She shot back boldly, "I'll not be the first to disappoint you."[3] She would seek her education elsewhere.

After supplementary studies at Boston University, whose medical school also did not admit women as MD candidates, Helen was accepted to the medical school at Johns Hopkins University. She completed her MD in 1927, having already published articles in medical journals.[4] At the urging of her mentors, she opted for a specialty in pediatric cardiology, an unexplored field at the time. As she put it, she "galloped" into a field that some saw as a dead end, but that she knew was live with opportunity.[5]

Without the work of others to draw upon, Taussig was forced to start collecting data without knowing how she would use it. Within ten years, she had amassed an unprecedented supply of information about children's heart defects. This took an impressive display of perseverance—all the more so because by the age of thirty-one, Taussig had begun to lose her hearing. She was a heart doctor who could not listen to a heartbeat! At first she addressed the problem by adding an amplifier to her stethoscope. When that stopped working, she honed her skills at feeling for the pulse. She supplemented readings taken by feel with blood pressure readings and images from an electrocardiogram machine. She combined all this information to gain a fuller picture of each infant's heart health, a task Helen called her "crossword puzzle."[6]

In developing the revolutionary Blalock-Taussig surgery, Helen encountered resistance from male colleagues. As of the early 1940s, specialists had become adept at closing the ductus arteriosus, an opening that joins two important blood vessels in the heart. This passage remains open while the fetus is in the womb, but is supposed to close when the infant's lungs mature enough to breathe air. However, in some patients, the ductus remains open. As a result, not enough blood enters the lungs. This in turn can cause an oxygen deficit in the blood, making the patient appear blue. It was clear that in some infants, closing the ductus provided a health benefit. However, Taussig noticed that other patients—those with more than one heart defect—often benefited from an *open* ductus. She mentioned this to Dr. Robert Gross, the Harvard surgeon who had invented the ductus-closing surgery. She suggested that surgery to open the ductus might benefit patients who fit a certain profile. He chafed against the idea: "Madame, I close ductuses, I do not create them."[7] Helen persisted in the face of this dissent, discussing her idea with Alfred Blalock, chief surgeon at Johns Hopkins. With the help of painstaking research by technical specialist Vivien Thomas, Taussig and Blalock outlined the steps required for the surgery. Blalock performed the first surgery in 1944. It quickly became apparent that, for some patients, the procedure caused an immediate and dramatic benefit. Taussig recounts with joy the third surgery, performed on a six-year-old boy whose cheeks turned from blue to pink immediately:

> I suppose nothing would ever give me as much delight as seeing the first patient change from blue to pink in the operating room. . . . There the little patient was with bright pink cheeks and bright lips. Oh, what a lovely color. . . . The child woke up, looked at Dr. Blalock, blinked his eyes a little, and said, 'Is the operation

over, may I go now?' . . . And from that day on he was raring to go and we realized we had won.[8]

When Taussig and her colleagues published the results of the first three surgeries, they set off a cascade of developments, including the founding of several pediatric heart clinics.

Alongside Gross and Blalock, Taussig led increasing numbers of specialists into her field. She wrote a central textbook on infant heart health, *Congenital Malformations of the Heart,* and engineered a program at Johns Hopkins devoted to the specialty. Taussig saw over 100 students through an education more systematic and targeted than the one she had been left to cobble together.[9] She continued her research even after her retirement in 1963, publishing 40 papers in her last 23 years.[10] From start to finish, hers was a life spent overcoming obstacles to knowledge.

Intransigence and Irresolution

Not everyone shows such perseverance. Picture a promising student who gives up on his math homework after five minutes. He doesn't "get it" right away, so he heads outside to shoot hoops. Or imagine an aspiring writer who is perpetually off-task, setting composition aside to binge-watch her favorite TV show. For any number of reasons, some of us quit on our intellectual projects before we should. Or we keep going, but do so half-assedly. This sort of behavior is a sign of *intellectual irresolution*, a vice that opposes the perseverance we see in Helen Taussig.

Irresolution is not the same as indifference. Intellectually indifferent people don't care about truth or knowledge. By contrast, irresolute thinkers may believe that knowledge is valuable, and they may want to gain it. What sets them apart is that they reliably fail to overcome—or even try to overcome—the obstacles that keep them from knowledge. As a matter of habit, they yield to discouragement, distraction, and other hurdles. While not all such yielding bespeaks vice (we all need a break sometimes), the irresolute are in the habit of giving up sooner than they should.

At the other end of the spectrum are the *intellectually intransigent*, who give up too late or not at all. Among their ranks is anyone still searching for El Dorado, the fountain of youth, the edge of the Earth, or a recipe for turning base metals into gold. Now, it's not like these quests and projects were inherently bad; some of them were worthy, at least at the start. But the questers veered away from virtue when they continued their projects long after getting strong reason to think that the projects were hopeless.

Intellectually Virtuous Perseverance

Irresolution is a vice of deficiency, intransigence a vice of excess. As table 8.1 suggests, intellectually virtuous perseverance is the mean that lies between them.

The mean for perseverance is a matter of displaying excellence in behavior, thought, and motivation (and, we might add, emotion). Virtuously persevering thinkers

- continue in their intellectual projects with serious effort, despite obstacles that make it difficult for them to get, keep, or share knowledge;
- think wisely about which projects to pursue, and for how long, and by what means;

Table 8.1 Perseverance as a Mean between Extremes

Sphere of activity	Vice (deficiency)	Virtue (mean)	Vice (excess)
Overcoming obstacles	Irresolution	Perseverance	Intransigence

- desire to overcome obstacles for the sake of knowledge; and
- react to obstacles in emotionally appropriate ways, not in extreme or irrational ways. They may be disappointed by their failures, but they are not crushed.[11]

Let's think a bit more about each of these elements.

Carrying On: Perseverant Behavior

Perseverant thinkers continue in their intellectual tasks. They keep seeking knowledge, or holding onto it, or sharing it. They *act* for the sake of knowledge (and truth and understanding).

Often, acts of virtuous perseverance show up in the midst of a specific inquiry—a concerted attempt to discover new truths or knowledge. Recall Helen Taussig gathering her data, taking vital signs by palpation to make up for her hearing loss. Or Tycho Brahe staying up late night after night to observe the stars and planets. Or Isaac Newton struggling diligently for years to invent the calculus needed for his physics.

These are pictures of virtuous perseverance in *inquiry*. But similar acts show up in other venues. Sometimes we need perseverance in order to gather background knowledge or skills *before* a specific inquiry can begin. As we saw earlier, Helen Taussig had to overcome dyslexia on the way to gaining the education needed for her medical research. Consider now another Helen—Helen Keller. An illness during her early years left Keller blind and deaf. As we all know, she would overcome these obstacles, earning a BA and becoming an advocate for women and people with disabilities. But before she could even conceive of these projects, the young Keller had to learn how to give and receive communication. Anne Sullivan, herself nearly blind, taught Keller by spelling words into the student's hands, using the sense of touch as a proxy for sight and hearing. Once Keller understood the method, she demanded that

Sullivan teach her signs for more objects. Within hours, Keller had learned some thirty words. She never slowed down. Of the early relationship between Keller and Sullivan, Van Wyck Brooks writes,

> Anne was already observing certain traits of Helen that were to become more marked as time went on—for one, the pertinacity and the love of perfection that accompanied her singleness of purpose. She was unwilling to leave a lesson if she did not understand it all, and even at the age of seven she would never drop a task until she had mastered it completely.[12]

Keller's condition required her to learn perseverance while still young. She would apply the trait for the rest of her life.

Sometimes we need perseverance not to *get* knowledge, but to *keep* it. Consider Ray Bradbury's *Fahrenheit 451*, which transports us to a dystopian world where books are illegal. Society is beset by war, addicted to trifling entertainment, and averse to thinking. Fire departments, in our world charged with putting out fires, are ordered to start them. Their main targets? Books and those who own them. The protagonist, Guy Montag, is a fireman on the run. Authorities have caught him with intellectual contraband—books he has stolen while on the job. As he flees his pursuers, Montag happens upon a group of nomadic intellectuals devoted to the difficult task of preserving classic works. One of them describes the group like this: "Thousands on the roads, the abandoned railtracks, tonight, bums on the outside, libraries inside. . . . Each man had a book he wanted to remember, and did."[13] The group members don't own books—that would make them vulnerable to search and arrest. Instead, each person commits a book, word by word, to memory. Someone memorizes the works of Thoreau. Someone else picks Thomas Paine. Machiavelli. The Bible. *Gulliver's Travels*. Having memorized the book, each human library then burns it to destroy evidence of the crime. "All we want to do," Montag's acquaintance says,

is keep the knowledge we think we will need intact and safe. . . .
We'll pass the books on to our children, by word of mouth, and let
our children wait, in turn, on the other people. . . . And when the
war's over, someday, some year, the books can be written again,
the people will be called in, one by one, to recite what they know
and we'll set it up in type until another Dark Age, when we might
have to do the whole damn thing over again. But that's the won-
derful thing about man; he never gets so discouraged or disgusted
that he gives up doing it all over again, because he knows very
well it is important and *worth* doing.[14]

Preserving knowledge is a great good—especially compared to
losing it. But we often want to do more. We want to *share* the knowledge we've preserved. And rightly so. After all, knowledge is the
kind of gift that does not diminish for being shared. In this way, it is
unlike other gifts. If you give me some of your money or your candy
bar, there will be less of it left for you. Knowledge isn't like this. If
you share your knowledge with me, you still have it all the same.[15]
    Such sharing often requires perseverance. Recall our discus-
sion of the suffragists from chapter 5. Thinkers like Elizabeth Cady
Stanton and Susan B. Anthony had formulated sound arguments
for women's rights as early as the 1840s. The arguments themselves appealed to the same rational principle of equality extolled in
America's founding documents: all humans are equal, and so should
have equal rights. At the advent of the movement, some feminists
believed their case for suffrage was so compelling that few would
balk. Simply lay out the arguments for suffrage, they thought, and
women would get the vote. Ignorance was the primary impediment
to suffrage, and the transmission of knowledge could remove it. In
recalling her early efforts, an eighty-year-old Stanton wrote, "I was
always courageous in saying what I saw to be true, for the simple
reason that I never dreamed of opposition. What seemed to me true
I thought must be equally plain to all other rational beings. Hence
I had no dread of denunciation."[16] But as they began to share their

arguments, suffragists encountered fierce resistance. Opponents of suffrage insisted that women could exercise more power as mothers than as political agents, and that women's "gentler nature" rendered them unfit for public life. It would take more than half a century for the suffragists' appeals to gain traction against such views—an obstacle that required Stanton, Anthony, and their colleagues to take what can only be described as "the long view."[17]

Effort, Obstacles, and Difficulty

The exemplars of perseverance we have thus far considered had this in common: they kept going. That's important. But as our exemplars make clear, and as we'll explore further below, merely continuing in our tasks isn't enough to make us models of perseverance. We can continue in a task with minimal, lollygagging effort. (At any rate *I* can. Every semester, I squander large quantities of time while grading my students' papers. I begin well enough. But my energy fades quickly. I soon find myself checking sports scores or eating several chips after every paper—and then after every page. My "work" becomes less and less virtuous as the time passes.) Virtuously perseverant thinkers don't do such things. They continue

with serious *effort*
despite *obstacles* to their success
that make success *difficult*.

Effort. Obstacles. Difficulty. Resistance to these factors is part of what makes perseverance excellent.

Obstacles to knowledge are as diverse as weeds in a garden—and just as annoying. Some obstacles are internal to us. These include our fears, self-doubt, depression, discouragement, procrastination, boredom, lack of skill or knowledge, mental limitations, and the like. Other obstacles encroach on us from the outside: injustice, poverty, physical and emotional threats, social distractions, technological distractions, and so on. To show intellectually virtuous perseverance, we must try to overcome such obstacles in the effortful pursuit of truth, knowledge, and understanding.

For our continued pursuits to be virtuous—excellent as opposed to unremarkable—the obstacles in question must make it hard for us to achieve our goals. There's nothing excellent about continuing in an easy task. Virtuous perseverance requires that we take on intellectual tasks that are difficult for us. *For us*: a one-size-fits-all approach won't work here. What is hard for one thinker may not be hard for another. Recall Helen Taussig's struggle with dyslexia. Her condition made reading difficult for her in a way that it was not difficult for, say, her father. Likewise, completing a basic chemistry experiment might be hard for a freshman student, but not for a seasoned professor. The difficulty of an obstacle, in short, depends both on a thinker's current abilities and on features of the task itself. Whenever such difficulty stretches a thinker's abilities, opportunities for perseverance aren't far to seek.

One last point about obstacles. Though they make it difficult for us to reach our goals, paradoxically, they sometimes end up helping us succeed. Today we know J. K. Rowling as a stunningly successful author whose stories both entertain us and instruct us about human life, friendships, and character. Famously, she was not always so. Rowling wrote the manuscript for *Harry Potter and the Philosopher's Stone* while on state assistance. She recounts being "as poor as it is possible to be in modern Britain, without being homeless."[18] Rowling was so strapped for cash that she could scarcely afford a folder in which to submit the manuscript. The book was rejected by a literary agent, and then by twelve different publishers, before Bloomsbury Press finally accepted it.[19] With these struggles in the background, consider Rowling's musings about failure, delivered in her 2008 Harvard commencement speech:

> You might never fail on the scale I did, but some failure in life is inevitable. It is impossible to live without failing at something, unless you live so cautiously that you might as well not have lived at all—in which case, you fail by default. Failure gave me an inner security that I had never attained by passing examinations. Failure taught me things about myself that I could have learned no other way. I discovered that I had a strong will, and more discipline than I had suspected.[20]

Rowling does not simply say that failure ultimately led to success—though that would be instructive enough. Rather, she attests that failure wrought changes in her intellectual character that helped make her ultimate success possible. Applied to our knowledge-seeking, keeping, and sharing projects, Rowling's remarks reveal the importance of setting ourselves difficult intellectual tasks.

Wise Thinking

A task's being difficult does not, by itself, make it worth doing. If it did, it would be virtuous to persist in tasks we know to be impossible—and that can't be right. Indeed, even short of impossibility, wisely chosen difficulty has its limits. It's not always a good idea to persist in the face of difficulty. As W. C. Fields purportedly quipped, "If at first you don't succeed, try, try again. Then quit. There's no point in being a damn fool about it."[21] To persevere virtuously, we must make sure that our projects are not just difficult, but well chosen. (Here we do well to recall the target image from previous chapters. The factors we're about to explore help determine the appropriate objects and occasions for perseverant behavior. They help us to see which intellectual projects we should select, and for how long we should continue them.)

Prospects

At a minimum, for us to choose a project well, we must have some reason to think it can succeed—that it can move us closer to getting, keeping, or sharing knowledge. This is where the El Dorado searchers and alchemists go wrong (at least if they're still trying). They have very strong reasons for thinking that their projects will fail. If there were a lost city of gold or a recipe for turning lead into gold, we'd know by now. Those who pursue such projects can do so only by ignoring strong evidence that their efforts are doomed. Wise thinkers don't do this. They weigh the reasons for thinking their projects will succeed against the evidence pointing to failure. And they don't pick projects without some chance of success.

This doesn't mean that in order to be well chosen, a project's success must be more likely than not. Even in science, a researcher often has little more than a hunch about a hypothesis, which needs to be tested and retested in order to be confirmed. It's not just that there's no *guarantee* of success in science. It's that there's often no way of telling, up front, whether experimentation is likely to yield a new discovery. Unless we want to banish most of science to the gulag of intransigence, we shouldn't think that wisely chosen projects must be likely to get results. *Somewhat* likely, sure—but perhaps not especially so.

Value

Wisdom in choosing our projects involves something beyond their probability of success: namely, their potential intellectual *value*. Think about Newton laboring to develop the calculus. Or Brahe braving the cold to observe the stars. Or Taussig overcoming sexism while doing her research on the Blalock-Taussig surgery. Or Montag stumbling through the difficulty of memorizing the entire book of Ecclesiastes. These thinkers' projects aren't wisely chosen solely on account of their prospects for success. They are chosen because of their potential to deliver or preserve something valuable. It is a great good for scientists to be able to measure objects over the course of time and change (Newton's calculus). It is valuable to understand the layout of the physical universe (Brahe's aim). It is important that doctors discover new ways of saving patients' lives (Taussig's surgery). And it is good to learn ancient wisdom well enough to pass it along to others (Montag's memorization). Wisely chosen intellectual projects must pass this test: *if* they succeed, they'll deliver, preserve, or transmit something of intellectual value.

Here's a further point along similar lines. Over the course of our lives, we might have hundreds of opportunities to take up projects with the promise of something valuable and a reasonable chance of success. But life is short, and our mental resources are limited. We can't undertake all of the potentially valuable intellectual projects that come our way. So we must choose from among competing goods. Choosing wisely, then, requires more than just thinking through our prospects for success and the value of the project before us. It requires us to think about what else we could be doing instead. To borrow a phrase from the economists, virtuous perseverance requires that we consider the *opportunity cost* of our projects.

Roles

The wise inquirer considers not only which intellectually valuable projects she can undertake; she also considers what *other* inquirers are doing, and what work she is uniquely suited to do. Recall Taussig's decision to become an infant heart doctor. At the time of her decision, many in the medical community were convinced that pediatric cardiology was a dead end. Taussig thought otherwise. She thought that someone ought to carry out the work. More than this, she was convinced that she was particularly suited for an important task that others had neglected. If there had been hundreds of qualified researchers already doing the same work, it may have been sensible for Taussig to choose a different specialty. But in light of her circumstances, she determined not that *someone* needed to study infants' hearts, but that *she* had to do it. Her case is an example of an important principle: the practically wise thinker considers her *role* in the intellectual community, then selects and persists in her projects accordingly.

All of this is bound to seem potentially helpful but vaguely un-satisfying. We've seen that wise thinking about our intellectual projects, and thereby virtuous perseverance, requires us to consider several factors: prospects for success, potential value, opportunity costs, and community role. But how exactly is this supposed to go? Just how likely must success be in order for a project to count as wisely chosen? How valuable must it be, relative to other projects? And how many other people must be taking it on? Is it better to hop on board a mature project with lots of bright people? Or to forge ahead into unexplored territory?

Again, there's no tidy formula for practical wisdom. But we needn't fret over this, for two reasons. First, even if we don't yet have all the right answers about practical wisdom, we've isolated the right kinds of questions. We've thereby taken a step toward wise thinking. Second, the main reason the questions just above don't yield easy answers is that, as stated, they're far too general. In real life, if we're thinking well, our questions about our projects won't look like this:

If I am to pursue a well-chosen project, how likely must success be? How valuable must the prospective knowledge be?

Instead, they'll look more like this:

Given that (i) my proposed research on the reproductive habits of sea turtles has a decent chance of success, and (ii) it could yield important knowledge, and (iii) it's more compelling to me than my other opportunities, and (iv) my training in marine biology has prepared me for it, should I forge ahead with a new set of experiments?

Fortunately, whereas questions in the first set are extremely hard to answer, questions in the second set are often easier. Knowing the details of our particular situation, and knowing which factors the wise person will consider, can help us to choose our projects well. (Similar remarks apply to our choices about how long to continue in these projects.) None of this means it is *easy* to make wise decisions. But it does suggest that the process isn't a complete mystery.

Motivations and Emotions

Like other intellectual virtues, intellectual perseverance involves our motivations and emotions.

Perseverant thinkers are motivated to overcome obstacles in order to get the truth, to accumulate knowledge, to gain understanding—and to keep and share these goods. They *want* knowledge, and they want others to have it, too. They're willing to overcome obstacles to make sure this happens. These desires animate the intellectual perseverance we see in Taussig, Keller, Stanton, Anthony, Montag, and Rowling. They make up the motivation component of perseverance.

Often, virtuous perseverance involves an emotional aversion to obstacles. Keller was frustrated with her inability to communicate. Stanton and Anthony were angry when otherwise decent men rejected their arguments for suffrage. Montag was daunted by the task of memorizing an entire book. Rowling was discouraged because publishers rejected her work.

In all these cases, the relevant emotional response was appropriate. The thinkers were right to be frustrated or angry or discouraged. But they did not let these emotions get the best of them. Keller used her frustration to fuel further learning. Montag did not allow his state to descend from daunted to despairing. Stanton and Anthony did not become so irate that they ceased giving rational arguments. Rowling didn't let herself become so despondent that she gave up. These thinkers illustrate an important facet of intellectually virtuous perseverance: it requires an appropriate emotional response to the obstacles before us. Virtuous perseverance rules out emotional responses that are so irrational, long-standing, or extreme that they hamper the pursuit of intellectual goods.

The cases just mentioned show that sometimes an appropriate emotional response to an obstacle is a negative one. However, virtuous perseverance does not require that our emotional state be, on the whole, negative.[22] Sometimes we can be so inspired to seek knowledge that our excitement overwhelms negative responses to obstacles. Taussig, for example, did struggle with discouragement and self-doubt. But these negative emotions were minor chords in an overall positive tune. As physiologist Laura Malloy notes,

> [Taussig's] insight and perseverance were nurtured by her early experiences of hardship, the passion and pleasure she found in her intellectual life, and the understanding that being an outsider can present opportunities as well as limitations. . . . Though Taussig achieved both recognition and social change during her career, her primary motivation was the personal need to find an arena where she could work and learn. This pragmatic strategy allowed her to overcome insecurities, to reshape disappointments into opportunities, and to persist when options seemed discouragingly limited.[23]

Taussig was consumed with getting knowledge, so she used her passion and wit to find ways around the obstacles in her way. When she was rejected at Harvard, she tried Boston University. When that didn't work out, she tried Johns Hopkins. When her research in physiology was discouraged there, she found another place within the university to continue her work. When other fields seemed closed to her, she "galloped" into pediatric cardiology—all in order to learn. Throughout the process, her passion for knowledge outweighed the emotional burden of discouragement.

Why Perseverance Matters

Until now, we've been considering what perseverance *is*. Let's pause and consider why it is important.

For starters, perseverance played a major role in the success stories we've already discussed. And the heroes and heroines of our chapter are not alone. A veritable chorus of history's best and brightest joins together in a hymn to perseverance. Thus, Plutarch: "Perseverance is more prevailing than violence; and many things which cannot be overcome when they are together, yield themselves up when taken little by little."[24] Goethe croons, "In the ideal realm all depends on bursts of enthusiasm; in the real world what matters is perseverance."[25] Victor Hugo praises perseverance as the "secret of all triumphs."[26]

Recent research in psychology suggests that such claims are more than just fodder for warm fuzzies and cheesy inspirational posters. They enjoy empirical support. In her bestselling book, *Grit*, and in several psychological studies, Angela Duckworth extolls the benefits of grit, which she describes as passion and perseverance for long-term goals. Duckworth argues that grit is a powerful predictor of success across a wide range of activities. To summarize just two of the interesting results:

- *Performance at elite colleges*: In a study of 138 undergraduates conducted at the University of Pennsylvania, gritty students outperformed their less gritty peers, as measured by GPA— even though they had lower SAT scores.[27]

- *Performance in the Scripps National Spelling Bee*: Grit positively predicted advancement to later rounds of the competition. Moreover, gritty finalists outperformed their less gritty peers in part because of their grit—they spent much more time practicing spelling words than their opponents did.[28]

These results dovetail with previous empirical findings. Thus, while one might quibble about a study here or there, the cumulative case for the value of perseverance is harder to undermine; it involves a larger number of respected studies. For instance, Warren Willingham and colleagues tested the efficacy of "follow-through" among 3,500 students from nine different colleges. They found that follow-through—purposeful, continuous commitment in an activity—was a better predictor of a student's achieving a leadership position than either SAT score or high school rank. Follow-through was also the best predictor of significant accomplishment in science, art, communication, and other fields.[29] These results fall in line with still earlier work. In 1892, Francis Galton gathered biographical information on prominent people from various fields, including judges, politicians, poets, musicians, and painters. He found that success in these fields resulted not just from talent, but from "ability combined with zeal and with capacity for hard labor."[30] Similarly, in 1926, Catharine Cox analyzed the biographies of 301 eminent "geniuses." Importantly, the estimated IQ of these figures only moderately impacted their level of eminence (their rank on the list). Other traits, including perseverance, seem to have made a larger difference.[31]

It would be foolish to conclude that talent is unimportant. Innate ability, IQ, and the like are undeniably important factors in success in many areas, not least the intellectual realm. But a wealth of research—along with common sense—suggests that they're not the *only* important factors. Traits like grit and perseverance often enable less talented people to surpass their gifted peers, and to fare better than those with equal talent. More to the point, they help us do valuable things—not the least of which is to learn.

What does this mean for our study of intellectually virtuous perseverance? The most immediate conclusion is that perseverance can be valuable. It's a strong predictor of success, including intellectual success. This in turn suggests that if we want to gain truth and knowledge, we should try to foster intellectual perseverance in ourselves. Such a conclusion is right—at least when properly parsed. Not all perseverance is virtuous. Persevering can be intransigent. We can continue in unworthy tasks (El Dorado hunting), or with impure motives (prestige, money, or good grades); or we can ignore practical wisdom and choose a worthy task when we should've chosen one that's even better. Not all grit is good—a point Duckworth herself is eager to make.[32] But provided we choose and continue our projects wisely, perseverance is often a key to achievements whose value will last.

Becoming Overcomers

We now have a sense of what perseverance is, and why it is good. How do we get it?

This question has many good answers. We can develop perseverance through practice, and by thinking about inspiring stories like those told in this chapter. We can commit to doing hard things over the long haul. We can choose to enter cultures that value grit and perseverance. We can find like-minded friends who will encourage us to stick with our projects. More on strategies like these in chapter 12.

For now, let's focus on one more insight from the psychologists. In chapter 6, we met Carol Dweck.[33] You'll recall that she and her colleagues developed the idea of a *mindset*. By way of review:

- Thinkers with a *fixed mindset* believe that intelligence is a static quality. You either have it or you don't, and specific performances reveal which it is. Successes are evidence that you're smart. Failures are evidence that you're not.
- Thinkers with a *growth mindset* believe that intelligence is malleable, and that it can increase with effort. They view successes as evidence of hard work, and as an invitation to try a more challenging task. They see failures as opportunities to learn, and as evidence that they need to try harder or try different strategies.

Visit any school, and you'll hear both mindsets expressed. You'll hear students say things like "I'm just not cut out for geometry," or "I'm not very smart," or "I'm not wired to understand poetry." Maybe you'll hear a teacher say, "This batch of students isn't as gifted as last year's." Or you'll hear an administrator say, "Next year's incoming class has the highest average SAT in the history of our college. It's a *smart* class." Remarks like these betray a fixed mindset. If you visit a good school, they aren't the only kind you'll hear. You'll also hear things like this: "I'm disappointed in my grade on the last exam; I need to work on my weaknesses." Or, "Plato's *Republic* is a difficult text. I hope that reading it a second time will help me understand it better." Or, "Could you direct me to the University Writing Center? I need to get better at structuring my essays." Or, "I like this group of students. I'm excited to see where their efforts take them." These comments reflect a growth mindset.

Dweck and her colleagues report that students with a growth mindset persist longer in their intellectual tasks than their fixed-mindset peers do. In one study involving 20 New York City schools, students were nearly unanimous in reporting that learning a growth mindset increased their tenacity. In another study of NYC middle-schoolers, a growth mindset improved the perseverance and performance of students transitioning into seventh grade. Because this transition is often difficult, many students were already showing declining grades—especially in math. Participants were divided into two groups: a control group in which students were taught only study skills, and an experimental group in which students were taught both study skills and a growth mindset. After each group attended six instructional workshops, those in the control group continued to show declining grades. By contrast, those in the growth mindset group became motivated to apply their study skills, and their math scores increased. Moreover, their teachers— who did not know which students were in the growth mindset group—were asked to observe any changes they saw in student performance. Teachers were three times as likely to note positive changes in the "growth mindset" group as in the control group.[34]

We should exercise care in what we infer from results like these. But Dweck's research at least suggests a strategy that's worth trying: we can seek to develop perseverance by fostering a growth mindset. In Dweck's view, mindsets can be altered. We can help others develop a growth mindset by praising them not for their intelligence, but for their effort. And we can encourage them through difficulty by prompting them toward increased effort and better strategies. Perhaps we can do the same for ourselves. We can tell ourselves that increased effort will increase our intellectual abilities. We can dare to imagine ourselves conquering intellectual challenges, and cultivate the belief that effort can help us succeed. Perhaps if we can develop a growth mindset, we'll be more likely to persevere in our intellectual tasks, and thereby raise our odds of learning.

Perseverance and Other Virtues

Intellectual perseverance doesn't just help us succeed in our efforts to get, keep, and share knowledge. It helps us develop other intellectual virtues. As we've seen, perseverance is the virtue needed to overcome obstacles to knowledge. With this in mind, consider these challenging activities:

- Avoiding distractions to cultivate a healthy appetite for knowledge
- Reasoning carefully
- Thinking for ourselves
- Avoiding lying, bluffing, and bullshitting
- Considering new views, especially when they contradict our own beliefs
- Discussing controversial topics wisely and winsomely
- Defending our views in the face of fears and threats to our well-being

In one way or another, all of these activities are hard. In each of them, there are bound to be obstacles to knowledge: titillating cell phone apps, ingrained tendencies toward biased or self-serving thought, pressures from our community, temptations to stretch the truth, the desire to ignore dissent, rude discussion partners, and so on. But if this is right, then intellectually virtuous perseverance overlaps heavily with virtues like curiosity, carefulness, autonomy, honesty, open-mindedness, firmness, fair-mindedness, and charity. To exercise any of these virtues, we must overcome obstacles, and thus, we must act with perseverance. This point is nowhere better illustrated than with intellectual courage, the virtue needed to persist in the quest for knowledge despite threats. It is to that virtue that we'll turn next.

For Reflection and Discussion

1. Make a list of the obstacles Helen Taussig faced in her career. Compare and contrast these obstacles, and see if you can group them into helpful categories. What does this exercise reveal?

2. How does intellectual perseverance differ from its vice counterparts, intransigence and irresolution?

3. The author lists several examples of intellectual intransigence and irresolution. See if you can come up with two or three examples of your own. Do the same with examples of intellectually virtuous perseverance.

4. What factors determine whether an act of intellectual perseverance is a virtuous one?

5. The author suggests that fostering a growth mindset can increase our tendencies to persevere in intellectual tasks. How might this point apply to you? Be as specific as you can.

Further Reading

For a thorough, insightful discussion of intellectual perseverance, see Heather Battaly's paper "Intellectual Perseverance," *Journal of Moral Philosophy* 14, no. 6 (2017), 669–97. See also Nathan King, "Erratum to: Perseverance as an Intellectual Virtue," *Synthese* 191, no. 15 (2014), 3779–801. (This is the definitive version of "Perseverance as an Intellectual Virtue," which was marred by typesetting errors.) Finally, see King, "Intellectual Perseverance," in *The Routledge Handbook of Virtue Epistemology*, ed. Heather Battaly (New York: Routledge, 2019), 256–69. On the related topic of grit, see Angela Duckworth, *Grit: The Power of Passion and Perseverance* (New York: Scribner, 2016). On growth mindset see Carol Dweck, *Mindset: The New Psychology of Success* (New York: Ballantine Books, 2006). For more on failures of perseverance, see Heather Battaly, "Quitting, Procrastinating, and Slacking Off," in *Vice Epistemology*, ed. Ian James Kidd, Heather Battaly, and Quassim Cassam (New York: Routledge, 2020). For numerous edifying stories of intellectual perseverance, see Rachel Swaby, *Headstrong: 52 Women Who Changed Science—and the World* (New York: Broadway Books, 2015). See also Margot Lee Shetterly, *Hidden Figures: The American Dream and the Untold Story of the Black Women Mathematicians Who Helped Win the Space Race* (New York: HarperCollins, 2016).

Notes

1. I first learned of Taussig's story from Rachel Swaby, *Headstrong: 52 Women Who Changed Science—and the World* (New York: Broadway Books, 2015), 19–22. The vignette sketched in this chapter relies on Swaby's work, and

on Laura Malloy's essay "Helen Brooke Taussig (1898–1986): A Biography of Success," in *Women Succeeding in the Sciences: Theories and Practices across Disciplines*, ed. Jody Bart (West Lafayette, IN: Purdue University Press, 2000), 1–24.

2. Malloy, "Helen Brook Taussig," 12ff.
3. Malloy, "Helen Brooke Taussig," 14.
4. Malloy, "Helen Brooke Taussig," 16.
5. Malloy, "Helen Brooke Taussig," 17.
6. Malloy, "Helen Brooke Taussig," 4–5.
7. Malloy, "Helen Brooke Taussig," 7.
8. Malloy, "Helen Brooke Taussig," 8.
9. Swaby, "Helen Taussig," 22; Malloy, "Helen Brooke Taussig," 9.
10. Malloy, "Helen Brooke Taussig," 10.
11. I owe this point to Heather Battaly. For further discussion, see Battaly, "Intellectual Perseverance," *Journal of Moral Philosophy* 14, no. 6 (2017), 669–97.
12. Van Wyck Brooks, *Helen Keller: Sketch for a Portrait* (New York: E.P. Dutton, 1956), 17.
13. Ray Bradbury, *Fahrenheit 451* (New York: Del Rey Books, 1953), 153.
14. Bradbury, *Fahrenheit 451*, 152–53.
15. I owe this point to Carol Simon.
16. Quoted in Vivian Gornick, "Elizabeth Cady Stanton, the Long View," in *Elizabeth Cady Stanton: Feminist as Thinker*, ed. Ellen Carol DuBois and Richard Cándida Smith (New York: New York University Press, 2007), 26.
17. I glean this phrase from the title of Gornick's essay.
18. J. K. Rowling, "The Fringe Benefits of Failure, and the Importance of Imagination," *Harvard Gazette*, June 5, 2008, retrieved from http://news.harvard.edu/gazette/story/2008/06/text-of-j-k-rowling-speech/.
19. Allison Flood, "J.K. Rowling Says She Received 'Loads' of Rejections before Harry Potter Success," *The Guardian*, March 24, 2015.
20. Rowling, "The Fringe Benefits."
21. This remark is widely attributed to Fields. I have not been able to verify it.
22. See Battaly, "Intellectual Perseverance," for what may be a different perspective here.
23. Malloy, "Helen Brooke Taussig," 1, 17. Several pages lie between the ellipsis and the rest of the quotation, but I place the two passages together to paint a fuller picture of Taussig's attitudes.
24. Plutarch, *Sertorius*, section 16, trans. John Dryden. Retrieved from The Internet Classics Archive: http://classics.mit.edu/Plutarch/sertoriu.html,

accessed August 28, 2019. Plutarch reports this quotation as spoken by the Roman general Sertorius.

25. Quoted in Johann Wolfgang von Goethe, *Maxims and Reflections* (New York: Penguin Classics, 1998), 121.

26. Victor Hugo, *The Man Who Laughs* (Scotts Valley, CA: CreateSpace, 2016), 148.

27. Angela Duckworth, Christopher Peterson, Michael D. Matthews, and Dennis R. Kelly, "Grit: Perseverance and Passion for Long-Term Goals," *Journal of Personality and Social Psychology* 92, no. 6 (2007), 1087–1101. See especially 1098.

28. Duckworth et al., "Grit," 1098.

29. Duckworth et al., "Grit," 1099.

30. Duckworth et al., "Grit," 1088. Galton's insights on perseverance are separable from his maligned work on eugenics. We should embrace the former and repudiate the latter.

31. Duckworth et al. "Grit," 1088.

32. See Angela Duckworth, *Grit: The Power of Passion and Perseverance* (New York: Scribner, 2016), 148–49.

33. Readers interested in further details about the material in this section should consult Carol Dweck, *Mindset: The New Psychology of Success* (New York: Ballantine Books), chapters 1–3.

34. For further details, see Carol Dweck, Gregory M. Walton, and Geoffrey L. Cohen, *Academic Tenacity: Mindsets and Skills That Promote Long-Term Learning* (Bill and Melinda Gates Foundation, 2014), 15–17, retrieved from https://ed.stanford.edu/sites/default/files/manual/dweck-walton-cohen-2014.pdf.

9

Courage

Persist Despite Threats

At the advent of the Cold War, the US military spent millions of dollars to develop supersonic aircraft. The planes themselves were impressive feats of engineering. Their ejection systems? Not so much. Despite earnest efforts, the units were reliable in just three out of four ejections. That may not sound so bad, except that the unlucky fourth pilot was killed while ejecting.[1] The military was losing pilots, and it was happening fast. Something had to be done.

Colonel John Paul Stapp (1910–1999) would be the one to do it. John Paul was the son of Baptist missionaries, who named the boy after their two favorite apostles.[2] As a youth, he was small, and bookishly eccentric. Both traits made Stapp a target for bullies. But he was scrappy enough to earn the nickname "Demon Stapp" for standing up to schoolyard toughs, showing the pluck that would later make him famous.[3]

After finishing a BA in zoology at Baylor University, Stapp enrolled in Baylor's master's program in experimental zoology. It was 1931. The world was mired in the Great Depression. Desperately poor, Stapp lived in the basement of a condemned dormitory, and then in the biology lab. For food, he trapped pigeons, picked pecans, and barbecued lab rats and guinea pigs.[4]

As if this bleak existence weren't challenging enough, Stapp also had firsthand experience with tragedy. Upon returning from Christmas break during his sophomore year at Baylor, he learned that his girlfriend had been killed when a drunk driver ran a red light and plowed into her parents' car.[5] Later, as a graduate student

The Excellent Mind. Nathan L. King, Oxford University Press (2021). © Oxford University Press.
DOI: 10.1093/oso/9780190096250.003.0009

at the University of Texas, Stapp was driving to a science convention in St. Louis when he witnessed a fatal car crash. Attending a man who would die of his injuries, Stapp noticed that "he hit his head against the left support of the windshield and cut a groove clear to the brain."[6] Just two months after witnessing the accident, Stapp received word that his own brother, Wilford, had been badly injured in a crash.[7] Such accidents were part of a troubling national trend in 1930s America. In 1934 alone, some 35,000 Americans died in automobile accidents.[8]

Later in life, when faced with the problem of the deadly ejection seats, Stapp drew resolve from all this suffering and hardship. He fixed his eyes on one goal: to discover how to make things safer.

To get the knowledge he needed, Stapp would need intellectual courage. In an age before reliable crash-test dummies, experiments on ejection and harness systems required human subjects. To protect his fellow researchers, Stapp selflessly volunteered as subject in his own harrowing trials. In a test designed to reveal the threshold for surviving a wind blast after an ejection, he climbed into a fighter jet piloted by Chuck Yeager. Without oxygen, the two of them climbed to a height of over 20,000 feet. They then accelerated to a speed of 575 mph—with the canopy removed. At that speed, the wind blast was so sharp that it shredded Stapp's flight jacket, though he was unharmed.[9] In another experiment, Stapp rode a rocket-propelled sled down a railway track, reaching a land speed record of 639 mph, literally faster than a speeding bullet. By design, at the end of the track, his sled plowed into a shallow pool of water. The rapid deceleration subjected his body to over 46 g's—more than double what some scientists thought would break every bone in the human body.[10] In his many jet flights and sled runs, Stapp risked his life in the course of scientific inquiry. He endured a broken wrist, wind blast blisters, a cracked tailbone, torn rib cartilage, a damaged retina, and at least two suspected concussions.[11] His work was central to the development of life-saving harnesses that have long been used not only in supersonic aircraft, but also in ordinary automobiles. Sometimes regarded as the father of automobile safety restraint systems, his work has saved countless lives. Though his childhood faith waned in his later years, when summing up his life's work, Stapp said, "I have the missionary spirit. When asked to do something I do it. I took my risks for information that will always be of benefit. Risks like that are worthwhile."[12]

Not long after Stapp's courage brought safety to the skies, Ruby Bridges (1954–) put her bravery on display in an altogether different context—one blaring not with thundering rockets or screeching sleds, but with angry voices. As a six-year-old first-grader in 1960, Bridges was the first African American student to attend the previously all-white William Frantz Public School. Following the passage of *Brown vs. Board of Education* in 1954, New Orleans schools received a mandate for integration. But some officials sought to stall the effort by writing especially difficult entrance exams. If all black students failed the exams, they thought, integration could be halted.[13] Despite these appalling efforts, a handful of black students passed. Bridges was among them, and she was assigned to attend William Frantz. Upon hearing the news, many whites objected vehemently, pulling their children from the school rather than allowing them to attend with a black student.[14] The segregationists' protests were so menacing that Bridges required four federal marshals as armed escorts to ensure her safe arrival. Day after day, she ascended the school's steps to the sound of racial slurs.[15] One woman threatened to poison Ruby, screaming every morning, "I'm going to poison you. I'll find a way."[16] Another protester put a black doll in a tiny wooden coffin in order to intimidate the tender child.[17]

She was aware of the threats surrounding her. But Bridges deftly managed her fear in the pursuit of knowledge. Her teacher, Barbara Henry, said of Ruby, "She didn't seem anxious or irritable or scared. She seemed as normal and relaxed as any child I've ever taught."[18] Charles Burks—one of the marshals charged with protecting Ruby—noted, "She never cried. She didn't whimper. She just marched along like a little soldier."[19] By year's end, Ruby had learned so much that her performance outpaced that of most other children her age. In seeking a better education despite physical threats, Bridges shows us what intellectual courage looks like in action.

Courage Plays on Different Stages

Stapp sought very specific knowledge in the midst of well-designed inquiries. Bridges sought foundational knowledge that would support her future efforts to learn. Both showed intellectual courage as they pursued new knowledge. However, as we saw in our discussion of intellectual perseverance, sometimes a virtue is needed not just to get knowledge, but also to *keep* it. The point holds for intellectual courage as well.

Consider Winston Smith, the main character of George Orwell's *1984*. Smith has a mid-level job at the Ministry of Truth, an organ of the ruling Party. The Ministry's task is to rewrite history and eliminate memories of the world before Big Brother came into power. Smith "changes" any fact, large or small, that could threaten an "orthodox" interpretation of reality. Citizens must fall in line, not just in their behavior, but also in their thinking. Everyone is surveilled for evidence of *thoughtcrimes*: writing in a diary, thinking a rebellious thought, or asking a certain kind of question. Such offenses are punishable by death. Smith comes to hate this mental prison. Through a surprising turn of events, he learns a truth that conflicts with the Ministry's official narrative. He acquires a secret document, "the book," which he reads furtively in order to learn the truth about history, and to learn how the Party might be overthrown. Smith's mental life is fraught with turmoil. He no longer trusts the Ministry, but finds himself ill-equipped to prove that its views are mistaken. All the while, he comforts himself with a single certainty: He *knows* that 2 + 2 = 4, and he can't be forced to say otherwise. Or so he thinks.

When imprisoned for thoughtcrimes, Smith finds himself subject to torture. His tormentor, O'Brien, intends to make it clear to Smith that *whatever* the Party says is true, and is true *because* the Party says so. Smith is kicked, beaten, elbowed, and restrained. He's hooked up to a machine that triggers searing pain throughout his body at the turn of a dial. Using all the horrid techniques at his disposal, O'Brien chisels away at Smith's worldview, including his beliefs about the existence of a world outside his mind, and even belief in his own existence. O'Brien chides Smith:

"Do you remember," [O'Brien] went on, "writing in your diary, 'Freedom is the freedom to say that two plus two make four'?"

"Yes," said Winston.

O'Brien held up his left hand, its back toward Winston, with the thumb hidden and the four fingers extended.

"How many fingers am I holding up, Winston?"

"Four."

"And if the Party says that it is not four but five—then how many?"

"Four."

The word ended in a gasp of pain. The needle of the dial had shot up to fifty-five. The sweat had sprung out all over Winston's body. The air tore into his lungs and issued again in deep groans which even by clenching his teeth he could not stop. . . .

"How many fingers, Winston?"

"Four."

The needle went up to sixty.

"How many fingers, Winston?"

"Four! Four! What else can I say? Four!"[20]

Readers of *1984* know there's more to the story. But resisting as far as he does is enough to earn Smith a place among the intellectual courage all-stars.

Smith's case lies at the boundary between two venues in which intellectual courage can show itself. It is unclear whether Smith is fighting to keep *believing* that $2 + 2 = 4$, or to resist O'Brien's efforts to make him *say* otherwise. The difference is worth flagging, because it is unclear to what extent our beliefs are under our direct control. (To test this, try to get yourself to believe—really believe, not just say—that there is a pink elephant balancing on a stool ten feet in front of you. Unless you're currently at the circus, such a feat is probably hard for you to accomplish.) If, as many philosophers and psychologists think, our beliefs aren't directly "up to us," then perhaps we shouldn't think of Smith's courage as an attempt to keep *believing* in the face of threats. We might instead think of it as an effort to keep O'Brien from making him *say* that $2 + 2 = 5$.

However we think of Smith's case, there are others in which intellectual courage is exercised when people *share* their knowledge or defend their beliefs in public settings. For example:

- Susan B. Anthony (discussed in chapter 5) once stared down a rabble of men armed with guns and knives in order to deliver her message about suffrage.
- Suffragists such as Alice Paul endured imprisonment, solitary confinement, hunger strikes, and forced-feedings in order to raise awareness about women's rights.[21]
- Civil rights advocates like Martin Luther King Jr. gave their lives professing the truth that all humans are of equal value.[22]
- German resistance leaders Hans and Sophie Scholl were executed by guillotine for producing and distributing anti-Nazi leaflets during World War II.[23]

Such cases are among the most familiar and inspiring examples of courageous knowledge-sharing in action. If we want to know what intellectual courage is, we do well to spend time learning about and reflecting on them.

Fears or Threats?

Intellectually courageous people are motivated to persist despite threats, and to do so for the sake of knowledge. This is the positive motivational part of intellectual courage.

There is often a negative part. In many cases, intellectually courageous people act in the face of *fear*—fear that pushes back against the desire for knowledge.[24] As he sought to maintain his belief that $2 + 2 = 4$, Winston Smith was terrified at the threats of torture and death. He feared that O'Brien's cronies would continue to beat him, or that the torture machine would snap his spine. In defending her views on suffrage, Alice Paul feared public speaking. Indeed, she feared it more than she feared being arrested.[25] Sophie Scholl feared the consequences of speaking out against the Nazis.[26] Further examples abound.

Clearly, fear is present in many cases of intellectual courage. Further, to learn that our exemplars of courage are afraid is seemingly to learn something fundamental about their situations, and about their courage. It seems that fear is not an incidental feature of these cases. Perhaps this kind of point explains why Aristotle includes fear as a defining feature of courage:

In the field of Fear and Confidence, the mean is Courage; . . . the one who exceeds in confidence is called Rash, and the one who shows an excess of fear and a deficiency of confidence is called Cowardly.[27]

It follows from this view that courage requires fear.

However, with some trepidation, I suggest that we reject this view. For starters, a common or important feature of the members within a class need not be an *essential* feature. Most dogs have four legs. But if we come across a three-legged terrier, we don't conclude from its lack of a fourth that it is not a dog. Similarly, it doesn't follow from fear's being a prominent feature in many cases of courage that it is essential. Perhaps we should be open to the possibility of courageous people who are unafraid, even in the midst of their courageous actions. Maybe courage doesn't require fear, after all.

Let's pause to unpack this idea. To begin, even some thinkers who *do* think courage is closely related to fear will admit that not every *act* of courage involves acting despite fear. Philosophers Robert Roberts and Jay Wood imagine someone inoculated against fear by repeated acts of courage, so that he is no longer afraid when navigating threats to his well-being:

> A person who has repeatedly faced down fear and thus become courageous may have become fearless in some of the circumstances in which he acts courageously. Despite the absence of actual fear, we still call him courageous, for at least two reasons. First, he has *achieved* fearlessness in this kind of circumstance *by* facing perceived threats on earlier occasions. . . . An essential condition of the virtue—courage's relation to fear—can be met without the condition being met in every action in which the virtue is exemplified, because the trait carries the relation to fear in its history. Second, the circumstance is the kind in which many people would feel fear. It is a circumstance in which the agent risks some significant harm or loss.[28]

The sort of case Roberts and Wood imagine isn't just possible. Sometimes, it actually occurs. For example, repeated bouts of danger and simulated danger hardened John Paul Stapp against fear. While training for upcoming tests, Stapp regularly climbed into a centrifuge machine designed to expose pilots to increased gravitational forces. With regular use of the machine, Stapp reports, "Gradually, I felt myself being conditioned against the subjective threat of extinction, the fear of dying."[29] During later field tests, Stapp was often irritable, and was always scrupulous about safety. But he never showed fear. Now, it is always possible that he was putting up a false front. But even if we assume that he was not—if we assume he really *wasn't* afraid—we can still count him as acting courageously.

Not all *acts* of courage involve fear. That much seems clear. But we might still wonder, doesn't *having* intellectual courage as a character trait require that a person experience fear *at some point*? Isn't the experience of fear necessary for the development of courageous character?

It seems likely that in most cases, fear *does* play a crucial role in courage's development. However, it would be a mistake to think that, therefore, a courageous character absolutely requires exposure to fear. To see why this would be mistaken, imagine Stapp risking his life in order to learn how to make a safe ejection seat. Or picture Alice Paul preparing to give a speech or endure a horrific forced-feeding. Or Martin Luther King Jr. preparing to march in Selma, Alabama. Now suppose we were to discover previously unknown documents about these people. Suppose the documents confirmed much of what we know to be true: Stapp, Paul, and King were well aware of the dangers they faced. They managed their reactions to these threats with wisdom and good judgment. They valued truth so much that they acted for its sake despite threats to their well-being. They persisted despite threats, and did so at the right times, in the right ways, and for the right reasons. They did all of this consistently. Now imagine our documents revealed something unexpected: these heroes and heroines had never experienced fear of any kind. Everything else needed for courage was present in their lives and characters, but fear was absent. Should learning this lead us to deny that these people were intellectually courageous? Perhaps not. But if not, then fear is not essential to courage.

This exercise suggests that intellectual courage is fundamentally a disposition to persist in intellectual activity, for the sake of truth, knowledge, or understanding, while enduring perceived *threats* to one's well-being.[30] Our judgments about apparent threats are more central to courage than our emotional reactions to such threats. Indeed, the whole point of honing our emotions in order to fear the right things is that fear can be a helpful guide to good judgments about danger. Well-trained fear helps us avoid and manage threats. But if such fear is valuable for that reason, then it's our judgment about the threats, and not the fear itself, that really matters.

Here's another way to see the point. We can at least imagine cases of courage in which exposure to fear plays no role. But it seems impossible to imagine genuine cases of courage without an actor who knows—or at least reasonably believes—that acting for the good will require encountering some risk or threat. At least for my part, if I imagine Stapp's entire dangerous career but subtract all fear from it, his case seems an atypical case of courage. But if I imagine his whole career and then subtract his awareness of physical threats, his safety consciousness, and his painstaking double-checking, he no longer seems courageous at all. He just seems oblivious. The core of courage—including intellectual courage—is persistence despite threats in the service of something good.

One last point about threats. To say that intellectual courage requires acting in the face of threats is not to say that the threats themselves must be intellectual. The "intellectual" in "intellectual courage" refers to the *goals* of intellectually courageous actions. Intellectually courageous thinkers face threats for the sake of truth and knowledge. Sometimes the threats themselves are intellectual. For instance, the prospect of forming false beliefs about important issues is a kind of threat, and a distinctively intellectual one. Another example: black students who lived before school integration faced an intellectual threat in being denied equal access to education—a problem that continues to threaten many students today. Examples like these show that some threats are, properly speaking, *intellectual* threats. But in other cases—say, those of Stapp and Alice Paul and Sophie Scholl and Martin Luther King

Jr.—the relevant threats concern bodily or psychological harm. In such cases, our exemplars show intellectual courage not because they face intellectual threats, but rather, because they conquer non-intellectual threats in order to gain or share knowledge.

Intellectual Courage: Virtuous and Otherwise

Not all acts of intellectual courage are *virtuously* courageous. To see this, recall that intellectual virtues involve not just patterns of behavior, but also patterns of thought and motivation. To be virtuous, those patterns must be excellent. They must accord with proper objects, occasions, means, and motives (recall the target image from previous chapters).

First, we can act courageously out of a desire for unimportant truths and trivial knowledge. Our acts of courage can take the wrong objects. When they do, they aren't virtuous. Consider the popular TV show and film series *Jackass*. The show's actors routinely conduct dangerous experiments, as we say, "just to see what happens." In one stunt, cast member Steve-O is pierced through the cheek with a fishhook. He then hurls himself into shark-infested waters to see how he'll fare as human bait. He survives, though scathed and shaken.[31] In another scene, actors are shot at close range with riot bullets, apparently so they can discover how this feels.[32] In yet another, cast member Ryan Dunn shoves a toy car up his rectum in order to see how the doctor examining his X-rays will react.[33] In a twisted, backward sense, these are displays of intellectual courage. But they aren't virtuous ones. These attempts to gain knowledge reflect poor judgment.

Second, we can act "courageously" when the occasion doesn't call for it. Suppose we loudly and firmly announce our view that 2 + 2 = 4 when no one is challenging it, and when other matters are pressing. That's not an act of virtuous courage. It's just foolishness. If we are virtuously courageous, we won't go around repeating indiscriminate displays of "courageous" behavior in irrelevant contexts. Instead, we'll act courageously as the occasion demands, and only as it demands.

Third, we can act courageously through unwise means. Imagine that Stapp's experiments had not required human subjects. (Imagine that he had excellent test dummies at his disposal.) In that case, his courage could not have been virtuous because putting his life at risk would not have been necessary for getting the knowledge he sought. It's one thing to persist in a dangerous scientific experiment. It's another to persist in an experiment that is unnecessarily dangerous. The former act may be virtuous. The latter is not.

Finally, we can act courageously, but do so from a bad or selfish motive. A medical researcher can study a dangerous disease solely to learn how to produce a biological weapon, or just in order to win prestige. A political activist can speak the truth in the face of oppression just in order to consolidate power within the movement. A student can overcome the threat of being overlooked by making a controversial claim in class, but do so only to appear bold. These aren't virtuous acts of intellectual courage.

All of this shows that there's more to intellectually virtuous courage than just persisting in intellectual activity while under threat. Virtuous acts of intellectual courage require the right objects, occasions, means, and motives. Only acts that meet these requirements are virtuously courageous. If acts of courage were archers' arrows, only these would hit the mark. And only when thinkers are disposed to hit the mark consistently do they have intellectually virtuous courage as a matter of character.

Vice Counterparts

Finding excellence in facing threats involves considering the objects of our knowledge and the occasions on which we act, along

Table 9.1 Courage as a Mean between Extremes

Sphere of activity	Vice (deficiency)	Virtue (mean)	Vice (excess)
Persisting despite threats	Cowardice	Courage	Rashness

with our means and motives. Getting clear on these factors helps us to see how and why intellectual courage is excellent. But the details are complex enough that it will help to have a convenient shorthand—namely, the idea that intellectually virtuous courage stands between two vices. The deficiency is *cowardice*, which gives too much weight to threats, and thereby leads a person to quit a project too soon. The excess is *rashness*, which weighs threats too lightly, thereby leading a person to persist beyond what is wise. Table 9.1 depicts these traits.

Intellectual cowards weigh threats too heavily, or the value of intellectual goods too lightly. They don't ask their questions for fear of mild ridicule. They keep excellent manuscripts in their drawers rather than risking rejection from a publisher. They silence themselves during class given the slightest possibility that their idea won't meet with their peers' approval. And so on.

Intellectually rash inquirers make the opposite mistake. Recall the *Jackass* stunts just discussed. Here we have inquirers seeking knowledge in the face of threats. They have courage, after a fashion, but their "courage" is not virtuous. Steve-O needlessly hooks his cheek and then hurls himself into dangerous waters, in order to gain some trivial knowledge and a bit of fame.[34] That's not intellectually *virtuous* courage. Given the relative triviality of the knowledge they seek compared to the great risk of swimming with sharks (while bleeding from the cheek), the Jackasses weigh the relevant threats too lightly. Their project is a dangerous, unworthy pursuit—an exercise in intellectual rashness.

To be virtuously courageous, we must thread the needle between cowardice and rashness. But note: finding this mean is not a matter of seeking a precise midpoint between the two traits. As Aristotle argues in his discussion of moral courage, courage is closer to rashness than to cowardice.[35] Consider a soldier who runs into a flurry of machine gun fire without a clear reason (he's not trying to save a wounded platoon member, for instance). He doesn't act with virtuous courage. He acts rashly. But he is closer to virtuous courage than the soldier who cowers in his foxhole during a lull in the battle, while his wounded mates need help. Likewise, despite their rashness, the Jackasses come closer to intellectually virtuous courage than intellectual cowards do. For, despite lacking the right objects, means, and motives for inquiry, they at least try to gain knowledge despite threats. They *act*. And while there is much more to intellectual courage than behavior, there is not less.

Courage, Conformity, and Us

To this point, we've focused on the nature of intellectual courage—on what it *is*. Supposing that we're right about the nature of the trait, how many of us have it? It's hard to tell for sure. But a famous experiment by Solomon Asch (1907–1996) sheds some disturbing light on the matter.

Asch wanted to learn about the effects of social pressure on personal opinion and verbal affirmation. Can group pressure change what people believe? Or at least what they say they believe? To find out, Asch ran several experiments with a similar setup. Eight or so people enter a room for what is presented as an experiment on visual judgment. Participants are shown cards like those in figure 9.1, and asked to match the line on the left-hand card with one of the lines on the right-hand card.

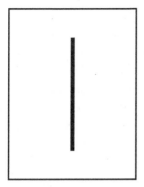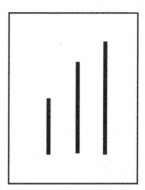

Figure 9.1 Line Cards

On their own, subjects are extremely accurate in their judgments, making errors just 1% of the time. The matter of which lines match in length is not ambiguous; it is totally clear to the subjects. As the experiment opens, all participants are asked to report to the rest of the group which lines match. Everyone agrees. This is repeated for a few rounds, and still everyone agrees. Then, suddenly, all but one of the participants gives the obviously *wrong* answer. Unbeknownst to the only real subject of the experiment, the rest of the group is "in" on a psychological ruse: they have been instructed to give unanimous and obviously incorrect answers at predetermined times.

Imagine yourself as the subject at this moment. It is obvious to you which lines match. Yet everyone in the room has given an answer implying that you're wrong. In just a moment, it will be your turn to report your answer. Will you stand up to the unanimous majority and say what you (rightly) think is true? Or will you give in to the obvious social pressure and say something that's clearly false? Will you let the threat of embarrassment get to you? Do you have the courage to stand up to the majority?

Over the course of many trials, about 75% of subjects deferred to the unanimous but wrong answer at least once. That is, only one in four subjects consistently gave the correct answer, irrespective of the majority opinion. The rest caved at least some of the time. On average, subjects conformed to the unanimous majority in about one-third of the trials. If these results are representative of the total population, they suggest that many of us can be counted on to speak the truth in the face of unanimous dissent only two-thirds of the time. The great majority of us will sometimes affirm what we know to be false in the face of social pressure.[36] (You might wonder if the subjects who gave in suffered more from doubt in their senses than from a fear of embarrassment. But Asch tested this hypothesis. He asked subjects to write down their answers privately instead of speaking them. They continued to give correct answers in this condition, despite unanimous dissent. Thus, the group dynamic didn't change their beliefs; it changed what they were willing to say.)[37]

It would be hasty to conclude that few among us are intellectually courageous.[38] For one thing, a quarter of subjects consistently resist the majority. If that 25% is representative of the general population, there may be millions of intellectually courageous people among us, Asch's experiments notwithstanding. But Asch does seem to show that a lot of us are sometimes disturbingly fragile in our ability to stand up for our beliefs. This is sobering in itself. Unless we have some special reason to think we are among the stout minority, we should look for opportunities to grow in intellectual courage—especially as this applies to our willingness to champion what we believe.

Intellectual Courage for Regular People

Few of us can reasonably aspire to the levels of courage displayed by Stapp, Bridges, Smith, Paul, the Scholls, or King. And Asch's experiments suggest that many of us are not as courageous as we ought to be. When it comes to the relation between intellectual courage and "regular people," is there anything other than depressing news?

There is. First, though our heroes and heroines display remarkable persistence despite threats, even they have their limits. For example, (spoiler ahead) Winston Smith ends up yielding in the face of O'Brien's abuse. After enduring beatings and mechanized torture, along with much verbal abuse, Smith finally says that $2 + 2 = 5$. This does not mean that he lacks courage, even virtuous courage. For, time after time, despite the threat of terrible pain, he persists for the sake of the truth. He is courageous even though he does not ultimately succeed in his efforts. This kind of case shows that genuine intellectual courage—even *paradigmatic courage*—need not be invincible. Virtue requires excellence, not perfection. For those of us who aren't perfect, this should come as good news.

Second, intellectual courage comes in degrees, and we can acquire it in greater measure. Even in fairly mundane settings, there is ample opportunity for us to grow in intellectual courage by "putting on" the trait—by acting courageously even if we don't yet have the virtue. Consider the following settings and activities:

- our classrooms
- our meeting rooms
- our relationships
- examining our cherished beliefs

All of these venues provide occasions for practicing intellectually courageous acts—for threats abound in all these areas. A classmate might sneer if we ask a question that shows our ignorance; we can practice courage by asking anyway. A boss might dismiss our idea for a change to company policy; we can practice courage by speaking up despite the threat. An acquaintance might mock our political position on an important topic; we can lean into courage if we graciously stand our ground. We ourselves might experience loss and grief if honest questioning shows that our treasured beliefs are false; we can act courageously by sticking with the inquiry. As long as we do it wisely, acting for the sake of truth in the face of danger can lead us toward intellectually virtuous courage. Over time, by performing acts of courage in different settings, we may come to acquire such courage as a trait of character. We may practice courage with such consistency that it becomes a part of who we are.

Third, even if we never acquire intellectually virtuous courage as a character trait, isolated acts of courage can be worthwhile. Asking a single hard question can lead us from ignorance to knowledge. Our boss might accept our good idea rather than ignore it. A friend might end up understanding our perspective more thoroughly than if we'd remained silent. An honest examination of our own beliefs might keep us from a harmful falsehood, or confirm a treasured truth. I'm sure you can think of further examples. Here's one that is dear to me. When I was in graduate school, I had a friend who worried that he wasn't cut out to be a college professor. He had done well in his studies, and was nearing the end of his PhD thesis. But with the job market looming, he hadn't yet published anything in a professional journal. (This is a near requirement for getting a job in my field.) Worse, my friend knew that journal reviewers are often vicious in their treatment of an author's manuscript—a kind of rejection bound to breed further discouragement. At the urging of a professor, and as an exercise in intellectual courage, my friend submitted a paper to a top-tier journal. Though afraid, he was eager to share his knowledge and contribute to inquiry within the field. Within a few weeks, the paper was accepted. The point: even before we have undergone enough practice to *be* courageous people, we should seek opportunities to *act* as if we were courageous. Provided we choose our opportunities wisely, we can reap the benefits of brave acts even in the midst of our training. To do so is risky, of course. But the coward's way comes with its own risks. If we take it, we risk missing opportunities—including opportunities to get, keep, and share knowledge.

Courage and Outward-Looking Virtues

In this chapter, we have focused on the nature and benefits of intellectually virtuous courage, a trait central to our ability to conduct our inquiries, hang on to our knowledge, and stand up for our beliefs in the face of threats. We have emphasized the *personal* benefits of such courage, the ways in which it helps us achieve our intellectual goals. However, like many other virtues, intellectual courage can have an outward focus, too. Stapp's courage helped safety restraint manufacturers learn how to save lives. Bridges's courage helped other black children face down menacing racism in order to gain a better education. Alice Paul's intellectual courage helped change America's mind about suffrage. And so on. This *communal* aspect of intellectual virtue is vitally important. Thus, in the next two chapters, we will turn to four intellectual virtues that are central to excellent intellectual functioning in communities: open-mindedness, fair-mindedness, charity, and— perhaps surprisingly—firmness.

For Reflection and Discussion

1. The author discusses three different ways in which intellectual courage can be expressed. What are these? See if you can think of your own example of each.

2. Do some research and learn about dangerous experiments in the history of science. (It is easy to find examples online, and in popular science texts.) Try to accumulate three or four examples. Upon completing this task, use the archer-and-target image to consider whether or not the experimenters displayed intellectually virtuous courage. That is, consider the objects, occasions, means, and motives involved in the experiments.

3. How might one argue that the performers in the *Jackass* stunts aren't actually acting with intellectual rashness?

4. What specific threats do you face in your own quest to gain knowledge? In your efforts to keep and share knowledge? How might you improve in your ability to persist despite these? Try to answer in terms of specific acts you could perform.

Further Reading

For a detailed philosophical treatment of intellectual courage, see Jason Baehr, *The Inquiring Mind: On Intellectual Virtues & Virtue Epistemology* (Oxford: Oxford University Press, 2011), chapter 9. See also Robert C. Roberts and W. Jay Wood, *Intellectual Virtues: An Essay in Regulative Epistemology* (Oxford: Oxford University Press, 2007), chapter 8. The account of intellectual courage developed in this chapter owes much to these works. There is much to be gained from reading the biographies of intellectually courageous people. On John Paul Stapp, see Craig Ryan, *Sonic Wind: The Story of John Paul Stapp and How a Renegade Doctor Became the Fastest Man on Earth* (New York: W.W. Norton, 2015). On Ruby Bridges, see Ruby Bridges, *Through My Eyes* (New York: Scholastic, 1999). On Alice Paul, see Katherine H. Adams and Michael L. Keene, *Alice Paul and the American Suffrage Campaign* (Urbana: University of Illinois Press, 2008). See also the film *Iron-Jawed Angels* (HBO Films, 2004). On Martin Luther King Jr. see Martin Luther King, Jr., *The Autobiography of Martin Luther King, Jr.*, ed. Clayborne Carson (New York: Warner Books, 1998). On Hans and Sophie Scholl see Annette Dumbach and Jud Newborn, *Sophie Scholl and the White Rose* (Oxford: Oneworld, 2006). See also George Orwell, *1984* (New York: Signet Classics, 1949).

Notes

1. Craig Ryan, *Sonic Wind: The Story of John Paul Stapp and How a Renegade Doctor Became the Fastest Man on Earth* (New York: Liveright, 2015), 1.
2. Ryan, *Sonic Wind*, 9.
3. Ryan, *Sonic Wind*, 14.
4. Ryan, *Sonic Wind*, 19.
5. Ryan, *Sonic Wind*, 16–17.
6. Ryan, *Sonic Wind*, 25.
7. Ryan, *Sonic Wind*, 26.
8. Ryan, *Sonic Wind*, 26.
9. Ryan, *Sonic Wind*, 153. (I have converted the aircraft speed from the 500 knots Yeager reports to a more familiar rate of 575 miles per hour.)
10. Ryan, *Sonic Wind*, 110, 207, and 377.
11. Ryan, *Sonic Wind*, 147, 157, and 183.
12. Quoted in the entry on John Stapp at the New Mexico Museum of Space History, retrieved from http://www.nmspacemuseum.org/halloffame/detail.php?id=46, accessed August 28, 2019.

13. Ruby Bridges, *Through My Eyes* (New York: Scholastic, 1999), 10.
14. Bridges, *Through My Eyes*, 20.
15. Bridges, *Through My Eyes*, 13–22.
16. Bridges, *Through My Eyes*, 22.
17. Bridges, *Through My Eyes*, 20–21.
18. Quoted in Robert Coles, *The Story of Ruby Bridges* (New York: Scholastic, 1995). There are no page numbers in this book.
19. Quoted on *PBS News Hour*, February 18, 1997.
20. George Orwell, *1984* (New York: Signet Classics, 1949), 249–50.
21. See Katherine H. Adams and Michael L. Keene, *Alice Paul and the American Suffrage Campaign* (Urbana: University of Illinois Press, 2008), chapter 8.
22. See Martin Luther King Jr., *The Autobiography of Martin Luther King, Jr.*, ed. Clayborne Carson (New York: Warner Books, 1998).
23. See Annette Dumbach and Jud Newborn, *Sophie Scholl and the White Rose* (Oxford: Oneworld, 2006).
24. I borrow this point from Robert C. Roberts and W. Jay Wood, *Intellectual Virtues: An Essay in Regulative Epistemology* (Oxford: Oxford University Press, 2007), 217.
25. Adams and Keene, *Alice Paul*, 11.
26. Dumbach and Newborn, *Sophie Scholl*, 60.
27. Aristotle, *Nicomachean Ethics*, 1107a 33ff., trans. J. A. K. Thomson (New York: Penguin, 1976), 103.
28. Roberts and Wood, *Intellectual Virtues*, 217–18.
29. Ryan, *Sonic Wind*, 66.
30. For further discussion of the claim that the persistence despite perceived threats, not *fears*, is the locus for intellectual courage, see Jason Baehr, *The Inquiring Mind: On Intellectual Virtues & Virtue Epistemology* (Oxford: Oxford University Press, 2011), chapter 9. I glean the main point of this section, and my account of intellectual courage, from Baehr. See also Robert C. Roberts and W. Jay Wood, *Intellectual Virtues: An Essay in Regulative Epistemology* (Oxford: Oxford University Press, 2007), chapter 8.
31. *Jackass Number Two* (MTV Films and Paramount Pictures, 2006).
32. *Jackass Number Two.*
33. *Jackass: The Movie* (MTV Films and Paramount Pictures, 2002).
34. A referee helpfully suggested that Steve-O's chief motive may be to make the audience laugh. Perhaps that's right. Even so, it seems clear that trivial knowledge is also among Steve-O's motives. Perhaps his act is comedically virtuous yet intellectually vicious.

35. See *Nicomachean Ethics*, Book II, section 8.
36. For more on Asch's research see Asch, "Opinions and Social Pressure," *Scientific American* 193 (1955), 31–35; also Douglas Mook, "Solomon Asch on Conformity," in Mook, *Classic Experiments in Psychology* (Westport, CT: Greenwood Press, 2004), 325–29. I derive the statistics in this section from Mook's summary, which reports on a wider range of trials than does Asch's original.
37. See Mook, "Solomon Asch on Conformity," 327.
38. For an empirically informed challenge to the claim that people have intellectual virtues, see Mark Alfano, *Character as Moral Fiction* (Cambridge: Cambridge University Press, 2013), part II. For a reply to the challenge see Jason Baehr, "The Situationist Challenge to Educating for Intellectual Virtues," in *Epistemic Situationism*, ed. Abrol Fairweather and Mark Alfano (Oxford: Oxford University Press, 2017), 192–215; also Nathan King, "Responsibilist Virtue Epistemology: A Reply to the Situationist Challenge," *Philosophical Quarterly* 64, no. 255 (2014), 243–53.

10

Open-Mindedness and Firmness

Transcend and Maintain Your Perspective

In chapter 8 we met Helen Taussig. She overcame childhood illness, grief, dyslexia, deafness, and sexism on her way to becoming a prominent cardiologist and the president of the American Heart Association. Hers was a tale of intellectual perseverance. But as we'll see, there were other virtues at work in the story.

As Taussig set out to heal "blue babies," so-called for their unhealthy hue, she encountered starkly different responses to her ideas. Taussig, recall, suggested that infants with multiple heart defects might benefit from an opening of the ductus arteriosus, a vessel that supplies blood to the lungs. In some patients, she thought, surgery to create such an opening would increase blood flow to the lungs, resulting in better oxygenation. When Taussig broached the idea, doctors dismissed her. Harvard pediatric surgeon Robert Gross told her bluntly, "Madame, I close ductuses. I do not create them."[1] From the time she first made her suggestion, Taussig would have to wait two years for anyone to take it seriously. It seemed that many doctors were intent on closing not just ductuses, but also their own minds. It was then that Taussig floated her idea to Dr. Alfred Blalock, head of surgery at Johns Hopkins. Physiologist Laura Malloy recounts the upshot of the meeting: "Blalock, known for his openness and flexibility, was intrigued by [Taussig's] ideas."[2] He set out to test her hypothesis. Alongside technical specialist Vivien Thomas, Blalock developed the idea into a surgical procedure. Two years of animal testing revealed the merits of the technique—the Blalock-Taussig surgery—that would save the lives of many infants.

The Excellent Mind. Nathan L. King, Oxford University Press (2021). © Oxford University Press.
DOI: 10.1093/oso/9780190096250.003.0010

Blalock had been right to take Taussig's idea seriously. He'd been right to keep an open mind.

A Puzzle

Much as we might admire Blalock's open-mindedness, some among us are of two minds about the trait. At least in my circles, open-mindedness presents a bit of a puzzle. On the one hand, many of my friends seem to think that open-mindedness is a cure-all for diseases like intolerance, bigotry, and spoiled discourse. On the other hand, I rarely have a conversation about it without hearing slogans like, "If you don't stand for something, you'll fall for anything" or "Don't be so open-minded that your brains fall out." When it comes to open-mindedness, many of us are open-minded, but uneasy.[3]

If we venture just a step beyond the slogans, we find familiar characters waiting. We find closed-minded ostriches, unwilling to consider anything different from what they already think. Their heads are buried firmly in the sand. We also find indiscriminate thinkers, who seem willing to take most *any* idea seriously—even if it has no merits. We find wishy-washy, flip-flopping, spineless thinkers, who abandon their well-confirmed beliefs at the drop of a hat. And we find rigid dogmatists who dismiss any evidence that challenges their views.

One reason for ambivalence about the value of open-mindedness is that it can seem unclear what distinguishes these characters from each other. We don't want to be closed-minded, but we're unsure whether we can be open-minded without becoming indiscriminate. We don't want to be spineless, but we don't want our convictions to turn us into inflexible know-it-alls. What gives?

In this chapter, we'll try to sort through the confusion by considering the nature of two important virtues: open-mindedness and firmness. The former virtue helps us to transcend our perspective.

The latter helps us maintain it. If all goes well, our inquiry will transform ambivalence into clarity.

What Open-Mindedness Is Not

Let's start by getting clear about what open-mindedness is not. By exploring some plausible but mistaken ideas about the virtue, we can work toward a more accurate understanding of it.

One such idea is that open-mindedness requires neutrality. Peter Gardner states the view like this: "To be open-minded about an issue is to have entertained thoughts about that issue but not to be committed to or to hold a particular view about it."[4] By way of illustration, he says,

> I am open-minded . . . about whether soft drugs should be legalized, about whether Britain should become a republic, and about whether the salmon season in England should be extended. I have thought about these things, I have even listened to some of the arguments about them, but I have no views, certainly no firm views, for or against.[5]

Now, it's true that neutrality can express open-mindedness. We might consider some evidence for and against an idea, suspend judgment, and remain open-minded as we await further evidence. However, this doesn't mean that being open-minded *just is* being neutral, or even that it requires neutrality. We can show open-mindedness toward ideas even when we think they're wrong. A city planner may be confident that a proposed building will disrupt traffic flow, but remain open to the possibility that it won't. A scientist may be strongly inclined to hold fast to a well-confirmed theory, but nevertheless take seriously the possibility that it is wrong. Religious leaders might hold their religious beliefs with high confidence, yet remain open to evidence that these beliefs are false. Such people, we may suppose, are open-minded about their beliefs. But they are not neutral. So, open-mindedness can't be the same thing as not having a view. It doesn't even *require* neutrality.[6]

That's a good thing, too. For if open-mindedness required neutrality in all we believe, perhaps the only people who could be open-minded would be extreme skeptics: people who don't believe (or disbelieve) any claim, but instead suspend judgment about everything. For most of us, such a stance is a nonstarter. To be sure, all of us suspend judgment sometimes. We shrug our shoulders and say, "I don't know what to think." And that's sensible—for sometimes our evidence is divided or negligible. At times like those, suspending judgment is the reasonable thing to do. Despite this, we know that we not only have, but *should* have beliefs about many topics. (Feel free to fill in your own examples here.) All-out skepticism is an intellectually costly position—it entails that we don't know, and shouldn't believe, *anything*. Thus, the neutrality model of open-mindedness is itself too expensive. If we order open-mindedness as it appears on the neutralist's menu, we'll be stuck with the bill for skepticism.[7]

There's more bad news for the neutrality model. In addition to being unnecessary for open-mindedness, neutrality isn't sufficient, either. Suppose Johnny is hell-bent on staying neutral about whether gun control is a good idea. No matter what evidence comes in on either side, he'll remain neutral—he won't believe that gun control is a good idea, nor will he deny this. He will suspend judgment. In taking this stance, Johnny has effectively committed to ignoring incoming evidence, no matter what it suggests. Surely this isn't open-minded of him. If anything, doesn't this seem like a clear case of *closed*-mindedness? If so, then open-mindedness can't be a matter of fence-sitting.

If open-mindedness isn't neutrality, what is it? Here's another idea. Perhaps open-mindedness is really a matter of assessing the evidence for and against our views in a reasonable way. Educational theorist William Hare explains the view:

A person who is open-minded is disposed to revise or reject a
position he holds if sound objections are brought against it, or,
in the situation in which the person presently has no opinion on
some issue, he is disposed to make up his mind in light of available evidence and argument as objectively and as impartially as
possible.[8]

At first blush, this view has a lot going for it. After all, an open-
minded person *will* change views in light of new evidence. This
is part of what makes open-mindedness different from closed-
mindedness. Hare's view also helps us to see how open-mindedness
differs from indiscriminate thinking. The indiscriminate flip-
flopper might change views without any evidence at all—say, due to
social pressure or out of a desire for popularity. Not so the virtuous,
open-minded thinker. In short, thinking of open-mindedness as
the reasonable assessment of evidence at least helps us distinguish
open-mindedness from its opposites.

But on reflection, this view of open-mindedness can't be
right. It succeeds in highlighting a key feature of the intellectually virtuous thinker: she respects her evidence. However, this is
not unique to open-mindedness. It's also a feature of virtues like
carefulness and humility. It's just what rational thinkers do. This
is very good, of course. But it doesn't help us understand what
makes open-mindedness different from other virtues. For the exercise of these virtues also involves believing what our evidence
supports. As an account of open-mindedness, this model is far
too general.[9]

What Open-Mindedness Is

We need an account of open-mindedness that helps us to see not
just how this trait differs from vices like closed-mindedness, but
also how it differs from virtues like carefulness and humility. In his

book *The Inquiring Mind*, Jason Baehr develops such an account. He states it like this:

> An open-minded person is characteristically (a) willing and (within limits) able (b) to transcend a default cognitive standpoint (c) in order to take up or take seriously the merits of (d) a distinct cognitive standpoint.[10]

A *virtuously* open-minded person will satisfy these conditions in a way that reveals her motivation for truth, knowledge, and understanding.

Let's unpack several features of open-mindedness that fall out of this account. These features will help fill in the profile of a thinker who has this virtue.

First, to think open-mindedly, we must be willing and able to transcend our default perspective on an issue. Both willingness and ability are important here.[11] Consider:

> *Willing Will*: Will strongly desires to consider new and contrary viewpoints. He genuinely wants to learn about alternative perspectives, and to take their merits seriously. But he is constitutionally unable to do so. Whenever he encounters a view that differs from his, biases and blind spots keep him from seeing its merits. Though he wants to be open-minded, he never adopts a different view in light of new evidence. Instead, he always distorts or dismisses evidence that runs against his views. He even ignores evidence for new views that don't conflict with his own. He doesn't do any of this consciously or maliciously. It's just the way his mind works.

> *Able Abe*: Abe is perfectly capable of transcending his own perspective. If he tried, he could successfully get past his biases and blind spots in order to take new and contrary ideas seriously. The trouble is, he just doesn't want to do it. Abe is unwilling to consider the merits of any ideas other than the ones he already

affirms. He thinks he has got the truth-market cornered, and sees no need to consider any evidence that suggests otherwise.

If we're to be open-minded, we must not be like Will or Abe. We must be *both* willing to transcend our perspective (unlike Abe) and able to do so (unlike Will). Open-mindedness requires a willing ability to consider perspectives distinct from our own. And across a wide range of relevant situations, an open-minded person can be expected to display open-minded behavior—her willingness and ability will spring into action as she seeks to transcend her own perspective.

Second, *transcendence*, as we'll think of it here, is a willing ability to take seriously the merits of alternative views. This kind of transcendence is perfectly compatible with our continuing to hold our beliefs. To transcend our perspective, we need not give up that perspective. We need not become wishy-washy or dial back our beliefs so that we're not confident in them. For example, we can confidently hold to our political views even while we consider evidence that we might be wrong. (Of course, that evidence *might* demand that we change our views once we consider it. But this isn't given at the outset. We don't have to give up our beliefs *in order* to take other ideas seriously.) Indeed, the project of transcending our perspective is mainly focused not on *our own* beliefs, but rather, on our understanding of *others'* beliefs. We can consider views other than our own in order to understand them better or to clear away our misconceptions. None of this need involve, say, a radical political, religious, or moral conversion on our part.

A third point: "distinct from" doesn't imply "contrary to." Sometimes open-minded people haven't yet formed beliefs about the issues they are considering. As Baehr notes, an impartial judge will not have formed a belief about the defendant's guilt or innocence prior to hearing testimony. Because she does not yet have a belief about the matter, the testimony of the court cannot run contrary to her beliefs. Yet she can and should hear the testimony open-mindedly.[12] Open-minded thinkers are willing and able to consider views that conflict with their own. But open-mindedness is not just for conflict resolution.

Fourth, being *virtuously* open-minded requires that we take alternative views seriously for the sake of a specific intellectual goal. We must act for the sake of truth, knowledge, or understanding. For instance, a political liberal may try to "think" like a conservative for the purposes of "getting inside" that perspective in order to understand it. A conservative may do the same in order to understand the liberal mind. An atheist may try to think like a theist for much the same reason; and vice versa. A parent may transcend grown-up understandings of the world in order to understand a child's mind. The point is that if we're open-minded, our efforts to transcend our own perspective will aim at things like gaining new true beliefs and finding knowledge.

Open-Mindedness and Its Rivals

A deficiency of openness is easy to disdain, at least when we see it in other people. When we bristle against closed-minded jerks, we pay a back-handed compliment to open-mindedness. Consider this case:

> *The Echo Chambers*: Pat is a college student with firmly progressive views on abortion, euthanasia, healthcare, free speech restrictions, the proper structure for a government, and so on. She reads regularly on these topics. Pat prides herself on using sources that are reliable; and in her view, "reliable" means "progressive-leaning." She shares her opinions on social media, where most of her "friends" and "followers" have beliefs that align with hers. Pat rarely encounters anyone whose views conflict with her own. When she does, she dismisses her dissenter as a "right-wing nutjob." Meanwhile, across campus, Chris is blogging in

defense of his strongly conservative views. Like Pat, he has firm views on abortion, euthanasia, healthcare, free speech, political power, and the like. His views are, in almost every way, the opposite of Pat's. But his habits are similar. He gets his news exclusively from conservative media sources. Most of his real friends and social media followers are conservatives. He rarely encounters a real-live progressive. And when he does, he dismisses the person as a "muddleheaded hippie." When he hears reports about events that cast his favored political party in a bad light, he dismisses them as "fake news."

Pat and Chris are closed-minded. They fail to take the merits of alternative views seriously. All of their evidence points in one direction—the direction of their views. Whether consciously or unconsciously, they have selected it for just this purpose. Their problem is not so much that they are mean as that they are sheltered. Thus, from a certain perspective, their dismissal of the opposition is understandable. Given the evidence they have, it really *does* appear that their views are the only reasonable option. Their habits put them in a position from which they can see, at most, half of the relevant evidence. Because of this, it really does seem to them that all of the evidence supports what they believe. This in turn leads them to dismiss dissenters as crazy or irrational. How, they think, could anyone be so dense as to miss the obvious truth? It's easy to see how their habits of mind make for bad contributions to public discourse.

Pat and Chris live in *echo chambers*—socially isolated places in which only one side of an issue may be heard (thus, the "chamber") and in which everyone says basically the same things (thus, the "echo").[13] To see why this is unfortunate, consider a famous allegory from Plato's *Republic*.[14] Plato describes an underground cave in which prisoners sit chained, facing a wall, their heads restrained. Behind them is a fire that sheds light on the wall, along with people moving puppets in order to cast shadows. The prisoners can see only the shadows; they can't see the solid objects that cast them. As a result, they come to believe that the shadows on the wall are real—indeed, that they are *ultimately* real. There is evidence all around them that reality is solid, but their restraints keep them from seeing this. At last, one fortunate prisoner gains freedom. He escapes the cave, and comes, gradually and painfully, to see things as they are. When he returns and tries to save the others from their illusions, they sneer at him and try to do him in.

Plato's Allegory of the Cave leaves the reader pitying the prisoners it describes, and rooting for the escapee. It also prompts a haunting question: What are *my* "caves"? For their part, Pat and Chris are like Plato's prisoners in this crucial respect: there is evidence all around them that reality is more than they think it is—but they are blind to this evidence. The main difference is that Plato's prisoners have been restrained from birth. Pat and Chris, by contrast, have restrained themselves. Their evidence is biased in the direction of their own political views, and this by their own selection. So it's no wonder that contrary views—and the people who hold them—seem strange and irrational. It's no wonder they don't take such views seriously. To a significant extent, they have built their own caves.

The Echo Chambers case is sadly realistic. Perhaps many of us can identify friends or relatives who resemble Pat or Chris. Or perhaps many of us resemble them ourselves. In any case, some emerging evidence suggests that characters like them are all too common. In a recent study, both conservatives and liberals displayed a motivation to avoid learning about political views that opposed their own. When offered a choice of reading material, a majority of people opted to read material that aligned with their views (for a chance to win $7) rather than read opposing material (for a chance to win $10). Given the choice, conservatives and liberals were no more motivated to learn about the political opposition than to take out the trash.[15] Such motivations lead to actions—"clicks," podcast subscriptions, and so on—that help create echo chambers once they are filtered through the algorithms that dictate what we see on our screens.[16]

We rightly shudder at the conditions and choices that give rise to closed-mindedness. But of course, it's not *always* virtuous to take alternative views seriously. There are some ideas to which we should remain closed. For educated people, openness to the possibility of a flat Earth or to Holocaust denial is not a sign of intellectual virtue. Nor is it virtuously open-minded to think we might be wrong about whether we exist or about whether there's a world outside our minds. Such openness would be excessive.

Virtuous open-mindedness is a mean between deficiency and excess. On the one hand, not to take any new or contrary views seriously would be a deficiency in our intellectual character. Like Pat and Chris, we'd be closed to the world around us, embodying the slogan, "I already know what I believe, don't confuse me with the facts." On the other hand, we could be excessively open, taking views seriously even when they have no merits. As table 10.1 suggests, virtuous open-mindedness lies between these vices.

Several questions arise here. Granted we should sometimes take alternative views seriously and sometimes not, how can we tell the difference? When does ignoring an idea bespeak closed-mindedness? When does taking an idea seriously bespeak indiscriminateness? *Where do we draw the line?*

We'll address these questions in a moment. But first, let's clarify what's at stake. If we lacked a fully precise way to distinguish virtuous open-mindedness from its competing vices, we would be left unsure what judgments to make about certain borderline cases.

Table 10.1 Open-Mindedness as a Mean between Extremes

Sphere of activity	Vice (deficiency)	Virtue (mean)	Vice (excess)
Transcending our perspective	Closed-mindedness	Open-mindedness	Indiscriminateness

And that would be unfortunate. (Indeed, because I doubt we have a precise way to draw the lines between open-mindedness and its opposing vices, I'd say that we *are* in a somewhat unfortunate situation.) But how unfortunate exactly? After all, many things are vague to some degree. We seem to get by despite this. For example, how many grains of sand are needed for a *pile*? It's hard to tell. There's no number—17, 220, 1,022, or 2,200—that marks the exact divide between piles and non-piles. Likewise, there's no height—say, 5'9" or 5'10"—that makes every human male above it tall and every male below it not tall. Piles and tallness are vague. But this doesn't shake our confidence that there are clear cases of piles and non-piles, or tall and non-tall people. Rather, we can identify obvious examples of piles of sand (say, the Michigan sand dunes) and clear cases of tall people (say, LeBron James). And we can do all this without perfect precision in our ideas of *pile* and *tall*.[17] Similarly, as long as we can identify clear cases of closed-mindedness, open-mindedness, and indiscriminateness, we needn't be greatly worried about vagueness at the boundaries of these traits.

Nevertheless, it will help to consider some ways to clarify when being open-minded is virtuous and when it is not.[18] Here's one:

- *Support for new or contrary ideas.* A virtuously open-minded thinker realizes that it is impossible to take seriously every perspective. So, when new and contrary views appear on her radar, she'll take them seriously only if they have (or appear to have) something going for them. Unless she has reason to think they might be true, she won't tend to take seriously—much less adopt—views that are radically at odds with her own. To do so would be indiscriminate.

This guideline enables us to dismiss the worry that being open-minded will automatically force us to adopt views that threaten our cherished beliefs. Virtuous open-mindedness requires considering new and contrary views only if and insofar as these views have (or appear to have) intellectual merits. If they don't, we needn't take them seriously. Thus, given a proper understanding of open-mindedness, the worry disappears. (If, on the other hand, new or contrary views clearly *do* have something going for them, we'd be foolishly closed-minded to ignore this.)

Here's another suggestion:

- *Prospects for gaining understanding.* A virtuously open-minded thinker tends to focus on transcending her perspective in ways that promise to yield valuable knowledge and understanding. This might in principle require her to take seriously views that are somewhat implausible and at odds with her own. But she will do so only if the exercise has the prospect of being illuminating. She won't waste her open-mindedness on ideas that are clearly trivial. This, too, would be indiscriminate.

These guidelines, of course, don't deliver a step-by-step decision process for determining when open-mindedness is virtuous. They're not meant to. Instead, they specify the *kinds* of considerations that can make the difference between virtuous and non-virtuous open-mindedness. And that, coupled with our ability to make good judgments about clear cases of closed-mindedness and indiscriminateness, is enough for our purposes. We've drawn the needed distinctions without drawing precise lines around the things distinguished.

With this account of the virtue before us, we can now see how open-mindedness differs both from other virtues and from vices like closed-mindedness and indiscriminateness. Open-mindedness differs from other intellectual virtues because it concerns its own distinctive sphere of activity—namely, transcending one's perspective.[19] And this virtue differs from its opposing vices because it involves excellent activity within this sphere.

Intellectual Firmness: Maintain
Your Perspective

Whereas open-mindedness concerns *transcending* our own perspective, intellectual firmness concerns *maintaining* it. Open-mindedness enables us to take seriously the merits of other ideas. Firmness enables us to hold fast to those of our beliefs that are true and well supported. Both are important. Without a willing ability to consider new ideas, we're largely stuck with the beliefs we currently have, even if they're false. Without a disposition to hang on to our credible beliefs, we'll too easily give up beliefs that are true.

It's easy to see how open-mindedness might serve us well not only as individuals, but also in communities. After all, we like being around people who are willing to consider the merits of *our* ideas! But it is at least initially puzzling to hear that intellectual firmness can serve us well in communities. Won't this trait lead us to plug our ears when we should be listening? Or to dig in our heels when we should be moving forward? How could firmness be anything but a detriment to our intellectual communities?

To see how it could, consider a classic case. Isaac Newton published his famous *Principia Mathematica* in 1686. Just a century later, his theory of gravitation was widely accepted and strongly confirmed. It was the master theory that seamlessly explained both the orbits of the planets around the Sun and the behavior of falling bodies on Earth. Newton lit the candle that illuminated the entire universe, resulting in endless praise from his fellow inquirers. Despite this fanfare, however, Newton's theory was imperfect. Newton himself knew that the theory incorrectly predicted the path of the Moon's orbit. But he didn't abandon the theory on account of this. (The problem was resolved in the 18th century, when Alexis Clairault found an error in one of Newton's calculations.) Shortly thereafter, latter-day Newtonians faced another problem: Uranus had just been discovered, and its orbit conflicted with the theory's predictions. The planet's orbit wobbled in a way Newton's theory said it shouldn't. Now, it's practically a commonplace that good scientists are open to evidence against their theories. So it was not an option for the Newtonians to ignore this anomaly. What were they to do? The core of Newton's theory—including his inverse-square law—was strongly confirmed. Despite this, something was clearly wrong somewhere in the theory. They could reasonably ignore neither the evidence for the theory nor the evidence against it. Thus, in a display of open-minded firmness, the Newtonians came up with a novel solution: they surmised that there must be another planet, as yet unobserved, that was disturbing the orbit of Uranus. This allowed them to admit that there was a problem with a peripheral part of their theory (the predictions involving Uranus's orbit) while retaining the core of the theory itself. As it turned out, the Newtonians were not only *rational* in proceeding this way, they were *right*: the discovery of Neptune vindicated their reluctance to drop the theory at the first sign of trouble.[20]

This episode illustrates the general truth that scientific progress requires both openness to new evidence and a certain amount of stability. If members of a scientific community never examine new or contrary evidence, their views become stagnant. If their theories are false, they remain stuck in falsehood. But if they abandon their theories on account of a single anomaly, they will constantly pick up the pieces of their views, without any prospect of arranging those pieces into a coherent picture. They will give up even their *true* beliefs, and won't maintain the kind of collaboration a research program requires. To maintain a community of researchers, they must hold fast to some common commitments. Collaborative intellectual projects require intellectual firmness.

To underscore and extend this last point, consider social justice movements—for instance, the suffrage and civil rights movements discussed in earlier chapters. Without firmness, the participants in those movements might have abandoned the truths central to their causes—namely, that women and people of color have the same moral rights, and deserve the same legal rights, as white

Table 10.2 Firmness as a Mean between Extremes

Sphere of activity	Vice (deficiency)	Virtue (mean)	Vice (excess)
Maintaining our perspective	Spinelessness	Firmness	Rigidity

males. Such abandonment would have deprived these participants of true beliefs. It would also have crippled the moral communities and causes that were founded on these truths. In short, intellectual firmness is a virtue particularly suited to fighting oppression; indeed, it is not clear how oppression can be fought without it.

As table 10.2 depicts, firmness stands between two vices.

At one end of the spectrum lies a deficiency, a vice Robert Roberts and Jay Wood call "flaccidity." Here we have the mental equivalent of a muscle that will not tense when it is supposed to, so that its owner is easily toppled, or is unable to brace for impact.[21] This vice sometimes goes by other, more familiar names—"looseness," "flabbiness," and my preferred term, "spinelessness."

At the other end of the spectrum is the vice of *rigidity*—a feature of a mind that has become calcified to the point of immobility. A rigid thinker is like a muscle that, due to cramping, cannot function properly. It remains tightly contracted, unavailable for action. Likewise, rigid thinkers are set in their ways. They can't properly consider the possibility that they are wrong.[22]

Dogmatism is a special—or not so special—variety of rigidity. To see the possibility of other varieties, notice that a person could be rigid in her view not because she especially *cares* to hold fast to her beliefs (as a dogmatist does), but because she is simply too *lazy* to consider alternatives. Intellectual rigidity comes in at least two varieties, dogmatism and laziness, that vary according to their motivations.

By contrast with the spineless or rigid mind, the firm mind is both supple enough to navigate changing intellectual environments with agility *and* solid enough in its core convictions to stay balanced throughout the movements. Or, to borrow another metaphor from Roberts and Wood, intellectual firmness allows us to maintain the right kind of grasp of reality.[23] A firm grip is neither so loose that important objects can be jerked away easily, nor so tight that it cannot release what needs to be let go. It can be varied depending on what it's hanging onto, and as the occasion demands. It can grasp a small bird without crushing it, or cling to a rescue line with ferocious strength. Our minds should be a little like that.

How Dogmatism and Spinelessness Are the Same

Earlier in this chapter, we explored the mean between closed-mindedness and indiscriminateness. More recently, we have considered the mean between spinelessness and rigidity. It is natural to think that, as excesses and deficiencies, these vices are very far from each other. What could be further from refusing to take new ideas seriously than taking seriously every new idea we hear? What could be further from dogged steadfastness than a willingness to give up our beliefs at the first sign of trouble? In sum, it's easy to see these vices of excess and deficiency as polar opposites. And in one respect this is right. Rigidly dogmatic people are usually far from wishy-washy or spineless.

But surprisingly, vices like closed-mindedness, dogmatism, and spinelessness share something in common: they lead people to ignore evidence. To see how this might go, consider two characters:

Dogmatic Don is a religious zealot who is completely convinced in all his beliefs about God, the universe, and morality. He knows that there are intelligent people who disagree with him on these issues, and knows that they have at least some evidence for their views—evidence he has not himself encountered. But he ignores all of this, telling himself that his own evidence makes it certain that he's right.

Spineless Steve has all kinds of evidence that would justify firm beliefs about God's existence, the universe, and various moral issues. His evidence—let's stipulate—would make it reasonable for him to hold confident views even in the face of significant counterevidence. But whenever Steve encounters someone who takes a different view on one of these topics, he immediately changes his opinion, adopting the belief of his most recent discussion partner. As a result, in the past year, Steve has been a Christian, a Muslim, a Buddhist, an agnostic, an atheist, an evolutionist, a young-Earth creationist, a pro-choicer, a pro-lifer, a Democrat, a Republican, a gun rights advocate, and a pacifist.[24]

To help us see how Don and Steve are making a common mistake, it will help to mark the difference between two kinds of evidence— what we might call *direct evidence* and *indirect evidence*.[25] Here are some examples of direct evidence:

- A good argument for God's existence is direct evidence that God exists.
- A good argument against God's existence is direct evidence that there is no God.
- A good argument for the pro-choice position is direct evidence that this position is morally correct.
- A good argument for the pro-life position is direct evidence that this position is morally correct.
- The way objects fall when dropped is direct evidence of Newton's theory of gravity.
- The bloody glove is direct evidence that the defendant is guilty.

In these cases, the evidence points directly toward some claim's being true (thus the term "direct evidence").

Indirect evidence is different. It does not bear directly on our beliefs about, say, God's existence, moral issues, or scientific theories. Instead, it's evidence about things like the character or quality of the direct evidence concerning those issues, or about how we are responding to it.[26] Is our direct evidence a large or small sample of the evidence that's available? Is it representative of the total evidence, or is it biased in some way? Are we well placed to assess it reliably? Indirect evidence answers questions like these. Such evidence is often indirectly relevant to the claim that is itself at issue. For example:

- If a large consensus of experts believes that a body of evidence suggests that the Earth is warming, this consensus is indirect evidence for global warming.
- If an informed, intelligent person believes that there are several good arguments for the pro-choice position, this is indirect evidence for that position.
- If an informed, intelligent person believes that there are several good arguments for the pro-life position, this is indirect evidence for that position.
- If I reasonably think that most people regularly ignore evidence against their political views, this is evidence that *I* ignore evidence against my views. It is thus indirect evidence against those views themselves. (It makes them less reasonable than they would be otherwise.)
- If I reasonably think that most people fail to account for their own biases in weighing evidence, this is evidence that *I* fail to account for my own biases. It is thus indirect evidence against those of my beliefs that are subject to bias. (It makes them less reasonable than they would be otherwise.)

Indirect evidence is important because it provides us with a clue about where the direct evidence points, or about whether we're assessing it correctly. And direct evidence is a clue about where the truth lies. So, in a roundabout way, indirect evidence is a clue to where the truth lies. As philosopher Richard Feldman puts it, "Evidence of evidence is evidence."[27]

If you're not yet convinced that indirect evidence is important, try this exercise. Pick some belief of yours that is controversial—something you believe, but which many intelligent, well-informed people deny. Maybe your belief concerns morality, or the law, or politics, or religion. You pick. Just be sure to choose a topic about which you're likely to have a lot of dissenters. Got it? Now, picture those dissenters. If it helps, envision them all arranged together, filling up a large football stadium or the US National Mall. Imagine them looking at you while chanting the refrain, "We're right. You're wrong!" for several minutes. Then, something surprising happens. The chanting stops. Everyone in the group approaches you, one by one, and announces that they've actually agreed with you all along. "Just kidding!" they say, "*Of course* your view is right. We were just trying to get a rise out of you." Would their confession make you more confident in your view than you were the moment before? If so, then you have the intuition that indirect evidence makes a difference for what you should believe.[28] Before the confession, you were taking your dissenters' views as indirect evidence against your belief. At the end of our imagined scenario, that evidence was removed, and this took away a powerful reason against your view. This in turn made your total evidence more strongly supportive of your original belief. Indirect evidence matters.

It bears emphasis that evidence—whether direct or indirect—is usually fallible. There are rarely "knockdown arguments" that provide such strong direct evidence for a view that you'd have to be a fool to deny it. And often, a body of direct evidence is mixed, so that we have to weigh the evidence, both pro and con, in order to come up with a reasonable summary judgment. Likewise, indirect evidence is usually fallible. An intelligent friend can misjudge the strength of the evidence. So can a lot of experts. And the fact that *many* or *most* people are beset with cognitive biases is not decisive proof that *you* are. The point of mentioning these varieties of direct and indirect evidence is not to say that they are decisive. It's just to say that they can't reasonably be ignored.

Let's return to Dogmatic Don and Spineless Steve. We're now in position to see that they're making the same sort of mistake. In his dogmatism, Don forms his beliefs solely on the basis of his direct evidence, but ignores his indirect evidence. In his spinelessness, Steve does the opposite: he constantly adjusts his opinions in response to his indirect evidence, but forgets about his direct evidence in the process. Don and Steve share this in common: *their vices are leading them to base their beliefs on less than their total evidence.* Different vices. Same mistake. The reason it *is* a mistake is that to the extent that their evidence is what makes their beliefs reasonable, it's their *total* evidence that matters.[29] Ignoring part of this evidence makes their beliefs less likely to be reasonable, and thereby less likely to be true, than if they considered the whole of their evidence.

Of Propositions and People

As we think about open-mindedness and firmness, it's sensible to focus on these virtues in connection with our beliefs about science, morality, politics, law, and religion. This is because open-mindedness and firmness are central to our ability to think well about such topics—especially when social pressures might tempt us to harden our views, or to alter them to fit ever-changing fashions.

But traits like open-mindedness aren't just relevant to our beliefs about difficult or controversial *topics*. They are relevant to our beliefs about other *people*. It is tempting, and all too easy, to think that only those "on our side" are intelligent, informed, sincere, and the like. Those on the other side, by contrast, are easily cast as dumb, ignorant, blinkered, or even evil. But we don't have to think of them in these ways. We can dare to transcend our views of those on the other side. We can imagine that they are smarter, more informed, more sincere, and more morally upright than our first judgments would suggest. We can emulate Abraham Lincoln who, remarking on someone of whom he had a bad first impression, is said to have declared, "I don't like that man. I must get to know him better."[30] As Lincoln suggests, if we *really* want to transcend our view of others, we might consider talking to them.

Evan Low and Barry Corey did just this. Low is a California State Assembly member and head of the LGBTQ Caucus, while Corey is the president of a conservative Christian college, Biola University. In the spring of 2016, the two found themselves at odds over assembly and senate bills designed to protect the rights of LGBTQ students. The bills promised to extend LGBTQ rights, but prompted religious conservatives to worry about their colleges' abilities to foster a traditional sexual ethic on their campuses. It looked like a zero-sum game: either the legislation would pass, to the boon of LGBTQ groups and the bane of religious conservatives; or it would fail, with the opposite result. It was human rights versus religious freedom—and something had to go.

At the outset of this tense situation, Low and Corey seemed destined to meet in battle as enemies. But then something unusual happened. As they report in a coauthored *Washington Post* article:

> Two leaders on opposite sides of a divisive ideological issue decided to talk to each other. We listened to each other's perspectives. We listened while wanting to learn rather than listening while waiting to respond.[31]

As a result, Low and Corey report,

> The collision began morphing into a cooperation. And now here we are. This time last year the two of us were foes in a religious liberty skirmish, but now we are friends.[32]

The formation of this friendship did not depend on either leader changing his view on the disputed issue (neither did). Rather, each changed his mind about the other, and about people "on the other side":

> Generous listening helped deconstruct some of the wrong impressions we had about the communities the other represented. . . . We both had notions that informed our initially defensive stances toward the other. It's amazing how quickly biases can be overcome when real relationships are prioritized, when you realize the person you once thought an adversary is in many ways like you, with a story and passions and fears, and a hope that we can make the world a better place.[33]

Because Low and Corey remained open-minded in their beliefs about each other, they were able to collaborate, discussing legislation that seeks to protect LGBTQ students while preserving religious freedom. Each also found an ally in efforts to combat sexual assault on college campuses, to make college more affordable, and to make higher education more accessible to first-generation students and other marginalized groups. Thus, they conclude, "Two people do not need to see eye-to-eye in order to work shoulder-to-shoulder."[34]

It is unrealistic to expect every conflict to resolve so happily. But neither should we strike a pessimistic note. After all, Low and Corey found themselves debating one of the most contentious issues in recent American history. And they found themselves tethered to convictions and social roles that might easily have made them into fierce and permanent enemies. If *they* can remain open-minded about each other, perhaps the rest of us have reason to hope—and to emulate their practices.

Toward Fair-Mindedness and Charity

What if someone was open-minded enough to take alternative views seriously, but then applied biased standards in evaluating those views? Or what if someone gave a devastating, even-handed criticism of a view, but failed to acknowledge a simple way to fix that view? These possibilities are all too realistic. And they signal that our study of community-related intellectual virtues hasn't quite reached its end. In light of this, let's finish our gallery by sketching portraits of two final virtues that are central to improving our public discourse: fair-mindedness and charity.

For Reflection and Discussion

1. The author considers and rejects two models of open-mindedness. What are these models, and what reasons does the author offer for rejecting them? Do you find these reasons convincing?
2. What are the key components of open-mindedness? Illustrate each component with an example.
3. Schedule a meeting over coffee with someone whose views on an important topic differ from yours. (It will help if the other view has at least some merit.) During the discussion, try to learn as much as you can about the merits of the view. As you do this, seek to remain open-minded in your beliefs about the other person.
4. Set aside an hour and read Plato's Allegory of the Cave. (See *Republic*, Book VII.) With the allegory as a backdrop, consider what intellectual caves you might inhabit. How might open-mindedness help you escape these caves?
5. Try to develop an example of someone who is virtuously firm in a belief, but who ends up being wrong (the belief ends up being false).

Further Reading

For a detailed philosophical discussion of open-mindedness see Jason Baehr, *The Inquiring Mind: On Intellectual Virtues & Virtue Epistemology* (Oxford: Oxford University Press, 2011), chapter 8. See also Wayne Riggs, "Open-Mindedness," in

Virtue and Vice: Moral and Epistemic, ed. Heather Battaly (Malden, MA: Wiley-Blackwell, 2010); and James Spiegel, "Open-Mindedness and Intellectual Humility," *Theory and Research in Education* 10, no. 1 (2012), 27–38. For a detailed treatment of various benefits and limits of open-mindedness, see Jeremy Fantl, *The Limitations of the Open Mind* (Oxford: Oxford University Press, 2018). For a rich discussion of intellectual firmness see Robert C. Roberts and W. Jay Wood, *Intellectual Virtues: An Essay in Regulative Epistemology* (Oxford: Oxford University Press, 2007), chapter 7. On the topic of vagueness, see R. M. Sainsbury, *Paradoxes,* 3rd ed. (New York: Cambridge University Press, 2009), chapter 3. For the Allegory of the Cave, see Plato, *Republic,* Book VII. There is a large and growing literature on the intellectual significance of disagreement, a topic that deserves much more attention than I can give it here. For a helpful introduction see Bryan Frances and Jon Matheson, "Disagreement," in *The Stanford Encyclopedia of Philosophy,* ed. Edward N. Zalta, Winter 2019, ed., (available online for free). For an excellent and wide-ranging treatment of what I call "indirect evidence," see Nathan Ballantyne, *Knowing Our Limits* (New York: Oxford University Press, 2019).

Notes

1. Quoted in Laura Malloy, "Helen Brooke Taussig (1898–1986): A Biography of Success," in *Women Succeeding in the Sciences: Theories and Practices across Disciplines,* ed. Jody Bart (West Lafayette, IN: Purdue University Press, 2000), 7.
2. Malloy, "Helen Brooke Taussig," 7.
3. For help in noticing the tension addressed in this paragraph, I am indebted to Jason Baehr and Wayne Riggs. See Baehr, *The Inquiring Mind: On Intellectual Virtues & Virtue Epistemology* (Oxford: Oxford University Press, 2011), chapter 8; Riggs, "Open-Mindedness," in *Virtue and Vice: Moral and Epistemic,* ed. Heather Battaly (Malden, MA: Wiley-Blackwell, 2010), 173–88. I owe the "brains falling out" quotation to Baehr.
4. Peter Gardner, "Should We Teach Children to Be Open-Minded? or Is the Pope Open-Minded about the Existence of God?," *Journal of Philosophy of Education* 27, no. 1 (1993), 39. For the quotations from Gardner in this section, and for my critique of Gardner's view, I am indebted to James Spiegel. See his "Open-Mindedness and Intellectual Humility," *Theory and Research in Education* 10, no. 1 (2012), 27–38.
5. Gardner, "Should We Teach Children," 39.
6. See Spiegel, "Open-Mindedness and Intellectual Humility" for further discussion of this point. I rely on Spiegel for the main point of this paragraph.

7. On this point, I'm indebted to Spiegel, "Open-Mindedness and Intellectual Humility," 30.

8. William Hare, *Open-Mindedness and Education* (Montreal: McGill-Queens University Press, 1979), 9.

9. For this point, I am indebted to Wayne Riggs. See Riggs, "Open-Mindedness," 179ff.

10. Baehr, *The Inquiring Mind*, 152. The account of open-mindedness developed in this chapter follows Baehr's account closely, though I do not claim that Baehr would endorse all of the ways I unpack his account.

11. See Baehr, *The Inquiring Mind*, 152–53, for further discussion of this point.

12. Baehr, *The Inquiring Mind*, 143ff.

13. For more on echo chambers, see Kartik Hosanagar, "Blame the Echo Chamber on Facebook. But Blame Yourself, Too," *Wired*, November 25, 2016, retrieved from https://www.wired.com/2016/11/facebook-echo-chamber/.

14. See *Republic*, Book VII.

15. Jeremy A. Frimer, Linda J. Skitka, and Matt Motyl, "Liberals and Conservatives Are Similarly Motivated to Avoid Exposure to One Another's Opinions," *Journal of Experimental Social Psychology* 72 (2017), 1–12.

16. See Hosanagar, "Blame the Echo Chamber," on this theme. Hosanagar nicely balances the human and technological elements that lead to echo chambers.

17. There is a well-known paradox about vagueness lurking here: the sorites paradox. For a helpful introduction see R. M. Sainsbury, *Paradoxes*, 3rd ed. (Cambridge: Cambridge University Press, 2015), chapter 3.

18. See Baehr, *The Inquiring Mind*, chapter 8, section 4, for a more detailed discussion of these issues.

19. Such transcendence is, as Baehr puts it, the "conceptual core" of open-mindedness. See *The Inquiring Mind*, 148–49.

20. For further of discussion of this example, *Philosophy of Science: The Central Issues*, ed. Martin Curd and J. A. Cover (New York: Norton, 1998), 71.

21. Robert C. Roberts and W. Jay Wood, *Intellectual Virtues: An Essay in Regulative Epistemology* (Oxford: Oxford University Press, 2007), 184ff.

22. For an illuminating discussion of rigidity as an intellectual vice, see Roberts and Wood, *Intellectual Virtues*, 193ff.

23. Roberts and Wood, *Intellectual Virtues*, 184.

24. My sketch of Spineless Steve is inspired by Roberts and Wood's "bright college freshman." See *Intellectual Virtues*, 188.

25. Philosophers often use the labels "first-order evidence" and "higher-order" evidence instead of "direct evidence" and "indirect evidence."

26. The examples of indirect evidence considered here are (a) evidence about our direct evidence, and (b) evidence about our responses to our direct evidence. These, I think, are the central cases of indirect evidence. There could be others. For instance, we could have evidence about the evidence concerning our direct evidence. Such evidence would, I suppose, be doubly indirect. For ease of explication, I leave this possibility to the side in the main text. Thanks to an anonymous referee for alerting me to the possibility.

27. Richard Feldman, "Evidence of Evidence Is Evidence," in *The Ethics of Belief*, ed. Jonathan Matheson and Rico Vitz (Oxford: Oxford University Press, 2014), 284–300.

28. Thanks to Fritz Warfield for helpful discussion of this kind of example.

29. The view developed in this section relies heavily on Thomas Kelly's recent work on the epistemology of disagreement. In particular, I make use of Kelly's claim that those who fail to give proper weight to what I call "indirect evidence" and those who fail to give proper weight to "direct evidence" are making the same kind of mistake. See, e.g., Kelly, "Peer Disagreement and Higher-Order Evidence," in *Disagreement*, ed. Richard Feldman and Ted A. Warfield (Oxford: Oxford University Press, 2010), 111–74. See especially p. 141.

30. This quotation is attributed to Lincoln in numerous places. I have not been able to verify it.

31. Evan Low and Barry H. Corey, "We First Battled over LGBT and Religious Rights. Here's How We Became Unlikely Friends," *Washington Post*, March 3, 2017.

32. Low and Corey, "We First Battled."

33. Low and Corey, "We First Battled."

34. Low and Corey, "We First Battled."

11

Fair-Mindedness and Charity

Don't Do unto Others . . . / Do unto Others . . .

The satire paper *The Onion* recently ran the headline, "Online Activists Unsure about Offensiveness of Article, Figure They'll Destroy Author's Life Just in Case."[1] The headline is funny only because it studiously mimics real life. Anyone with a computer and an internet connection is familiar with the spectacle of *trolling*: the practice of using social media and online forums to post offensive, inflammatory, threatening, or demeaning comments. The perpetrators of these offenses—the trolls—assault the weak, the unpopular, and those who are simply different from them. They do it to gain power, to ruin others' days, or just for laughs and "likes."[2]

In today's internet jungle, anyone can play the role of predator— or prey. Vicious attacks can come from the Right or the Left. They can come from above (from the rich, famous, or powerful) or from below (from the rest of us). Those who defend liberal causes are dubbed "snowflakes," "social justice warriors," "communists," "loons," or "hippies." Those defending conservative causes are cast as "wingnuts," "racists," "sexists," "bigots," and the like. People on both ends of the political spectrum are called "fascists." Those with ties to elite institutions are dubbed "shills," while regular people are labeled "deplorables." And let's not forget the flexible terms applied to just about anyone: "idiot," "moron," "nutjob," and the like.

Incendiary discourse isn't confined to Facebook threads, Twitter feeds, or online comments sections. On our college campuses, students protest controversial speakers, or shout them down, or

The Excellent Mind. Nathan L. King, Oxford University Press (2021). © Oxford University Press.
DOI: 10.1093/oso/9780190096250.003.0011

riot in the streets. University presidents invite and then disinvite speakers. They give prestigious awards, then revoke them for political reasons. They live in fear that the next nationally televised dustup will occur on *their* campus. Debates will continue about who is right and who is wrong in all of this. We won't enter into those debates here. Instead, we'll focus on one fact that seems indisputable: our public discourse is ailing.

Ask yourself:

- Am I reluctant to discuss ethics, politics, religion, gender, sexuality, or other controversial topics?
- If so, why?

If you answered yes, you're not alone. A recent poll of the authors at *Time* magazine found that 80% had avoided writing about a disputed subject for fear of online backlash.[3] We might wonder: if that poll is representative of professional journalists, whose job it is to discuss tense topics, what are the numbers for the rest of us? And whatever the numbers are, what explains them?

For my money, I'm willing to bet that a lot of people will explain their uneasiness in terms like these (fill in your own blanks):

- I'm concerned that others will berate me if I express my view that _____.
- I fear that others will attribute bad motives to me if I say I believe _____.
- I worry that people will criticize me before they even try to understand why I think that _____.
- I believe _____. But I don't want to get lumped in with all of the people who have defended that view obnoxiously. I'm not one of "those people."
- I don't want my views about _____ to get me branded a _____.
- I'm afraid that discussing controversial issues will strain my relationships.

Sound familiar? Such responses come down to this: we're afraid that if we express our views, others will treat us unfairly. And if we're honest, most of us will admit that we haven't always been *entirely* fair to others—especially those whose beliefs differ from ours. If so, it will be worth our time to examine the virtue of *fair-mindedness*— its nature, its opposites, and the habits that foster it.

Fairness in Morality and Mind

Moral Fairness and Justice

We can get a basic grasp of fair-mindedness by considering an analogy to *moral* fairness or justice. (In what follows, we'll use the terms "justice" and "fairness" synonymously.) Let's start in familiar territory. Nearly everyone agrees that morally just or fair people don't intentionally harm others without good reason. Nor do they gain undue advantage over others. They don't assault injured people on the side of the road. They don't take what isn't theirs, or cheat others out of their retirement benefits. In their behavior toward others, they act in line with a time-honored precept:

> *Silver Rule*: Don't do to others what you wouldn't want done to you.

This rule sums up our concept of justice. It gives us a simple way to figure out, in a large class of cases, how we should *not* treat others. We imagine what we wouldn't want others to do to us, and thereby learn what we should not do to them. If we act accordingly, we act in line with justice.

What people want or don't want isn't what *makes* actions just or unjust. But we needn't think for long to gain a clue about what does. Unjust actions *harm* people, and deny them what they are *due*.

These concepts—harm prevention and desert—are central to our idea of moral justice or fairness. We want others not to harm us, and not to deny us what we are due. This explains why the Silver Rule tracks our judgments about justice so closely.

Moral justice comes in both individual and corporate varieties. A just society prevents harms to its citizens and ensures that all citizens receive their due. Political systems differ on exactly what each citizen is due. But any system should acknowledge that every citizen deserves at least

- protection from bodily harms;
- freedom from persecution or discrimination based on factors like race, gender, or religion; and
- freedom from arbitrary exclusion from opportunities to pursue education and well-being.

On the individual level, people who have the virtue of justice are disposed not to harm others bodily, and not to engage in arbitrary discrimination against them—for such acts harm their victims.

All of this describes how just people behave. But as we've seen throughout this book, there's more to virtues than behavior. Virtues also require right motives and patterns of thought. As far as motives go, just people don't act in accordance with the Silver Rule in order to get praise or recognition. Rather, they act justly because they care about others, or because they care about doing the right thing. As for patterns of thought, just people think it is wrong to harm others. They believe that others should not be denied what they are due. They understand that what we owe people, we owe to them because they are persons, or perhaps because we stand in some special relation to them (e.g., a parent to a child), or because we have promised them something. They recognize that it is wrong to ignore their obligations to others. In short, just people think well about justice.

Intellectual Fairness (Fair-Mindedness) and Justice

Our brief sketch of moral justice or fairness positions us to grasp the concept of *intellectual* fairness or *fair-mindedness*. This is the virtue of fairness as it applies to our knowledge-seeking, keeping, and sharing activities. We can start by stating the following rule:

> *Intellectual Silver Rule*: In intellectual activities, don't do to others what you wouldn't want done to you.

What, as thinkers, don't we want done to us? To borrow a phrase from Miranda Fricker, we don't want to be harmed or wronged *in our capacities as knowers*.[4] Thus, intellectual justice or fairness is a matter of our doing what we can to ensure that others aren't harmed in that capacity. Such harms include, among other things:

- unequal access to information or education;
- misrepresentation of our views;
- an unequal opportunity to express our views or be taken seriously; and
- biased assessments of the evidence for our views; and
- blameworthy, inaccurate, or unreasonable assessments of our intelligence, our intellectual character, or our motives.

These are distinctively *intellectual* harms in that they concern our ability to get, keep, or share knowledge. Fair, just thinkers avoid harming others in these ways.[5]

A central feature of the fair-minded thinker is *even-handedness*, a habit of treating the views and arguments of our dissenters no less favorably than we treat our own. Failures of even-handedness cause many intellectual harms, including all manner of misrepresentation and harmfully skewed assessment. Conversely, even-handedness helps us prevent such harms.

The 20th-century philosopher G. E. Moore was well known for the even-handed fairness he displayed in the classroom. His student Alice Ambrose explains:

> Moore in his lectures was self-effacing. Criticisms he put forward of claims he himself had made, say, in a previous lecture, could as well have been directed to an anonymous philosopher whose mistakes called for correction.[6]

In this way, Moore observed a critical distinction between two ways of reading the same sentence:

- It is important that *my* beliefs be true.
- It is important that my beliefs be *true*.

Moore would've adopted the second reading. He sought to bend his beliefs toward the truth and the evidence rather than the other way round. When forced to choose, he preferred truth to the preservation of his own opinions. He avoided intellectual double-standards—a habit that helped make discussion partners, including his students, safe from intellectual harm while in his classroom.

So far, so good. But some will want to tap the brakes here. If intellectual double-standards are "out of bounds" for even-handed thinkers, we might worry: does even-handedness (and thus fair-mindedness) require thinking that all views are equally good, true, or reasonable?[7] And wouldn't that be bad news? After all, it seems obvious that some views are better, closer to the truth, and more reasonable than others. Does embracing fair-mindedness require us to think otherwise?

Happily, it does not. It requires not giving views a leg up just because they're ours. But it doesn't follow that even-handedness places all views on par. To suggest that it does is to assume that the relevant evidence, when fairly assessed, always comes out as neutral between competing views. It's to assume that the evidence always points everywhere and thus nowhere in particular. But why think this? Don't some views at least *sometimes* come out as winners or losers when the evidence is assessed fair and square? Most of us think they do. That's why we don't believe the Earth is flat, or that alchemy works, or that Poseidon is real. We don't think the evidence, handled fairly, supports these beliefs. It supports their denials instead. Even-handed thinking requires not that all views be treated equally at all times. Instead, it requires that we maintain a belief due to the reasons that support it, rather than because it's ours, or because we want it to be true, or because it aids our political agenda or keeps our group on top.

Here's a further point, one that parallels a point we made earlier about moral fairness. Fair-minded thinkers don't just enact fairness at the level of behavior. For, like moral virtues, intellectual virtues involve a person's thoughts and motivations. In addition to acting fairly, a fair-minded thinker will also *believe* that others deserve intellectually fair treatment. Further, she'll think they deserve this not on account of sharing (say) her race, her class, or her views—but because they are thinkers. And she'll be *motivated* to treat them fairly because she will care about them *as* thinkers. That is, she will care that they gain truth, knowledge, and understanding, and that they are enabled to keep and share the same.

Intellectual Fairness (and Unfairness) in Action

Let's consider some ways fair and unfair thinking unfold in everyday life. What follow are some realistic scenes in which unfair thinking spoils a discussion. After observing each scene, we'll diagnose where it goes wrong, and consider what it teaches us about fair-mindedness. This will enable us to formulate a series of guidelines for putting the intellectual Silver Rule into practice.

These guidelines will help us understand how the fair-minded person thinks and acts. (You will find our exercise most helpful if you pause after reading each scene before going on to read the diagnosis and prescription. Ask yourself: what went wrong here? And how could things have gone better? Then proceed to the ensuing discussion.)

Scene 1: Bob is a conservative blogger. He is fed up with what he perceives as a trend toward political correctness on college campuses. In his most recent post, "The Day College Committed Suicide," he argues that the university system as we know it is kaput. It's not worth trying to save, he says, and very little good is ever accomplished on campus. The whole racket should be "blown up." To support his view, he cites several high-profile incidents during which conservative speakers have been protested or shouted down at prestigious schools. To him, these incidents show that "the system" is anti-conservative and anti-free speech—and irredeemably so. He casts college presidents and professors as liberal conspirators on behalf of the "deep state." However, as Bob knows, for every publicized protest of a conservative speaker, there are events where such speakers give their talks without incident, and even have productive discussions with progressive students. And he knows that many university presidents work hard to foster free speech on their campuses. However, because these cases don't fit his narrative, he gives them little weight.

Bob's unfairness is apparent. On the one hand, he fixates only on the few incidents that support his position. To his own view, he applies quite a low standard of evidence. (Contrary to what Bob thinks, the few negative incidents don't justify belief in a grand conspiracy theory.) On the other hand, he's aware of evidence against his view, but he doesn't give this evidence the weight it deserves. To contrary views, he applies a high standard of evidence. This is a clear failure to be even-handed, and thus a failure to be fair. If we agree that such thinking is intellectually unfair not only in this case, but in any similar case, we can generalize to the following rule:

> *Guideline 1*: Be even-handed in assessing evidence. When assessing views and arguments that differ from your own, don't favor the evidence that supports your side *because* it supports your side. Don't use different standards of evidence to assess others' views than you use to assess your own.

Unfairness has a way of spreading. Often, one person's lack of fairness prompts another to respond in kind, or prompts others to enter the fray, with predictably bad results. To illustrate, here's a sequel to Bob's blogging adventures:

> *Scene 2*: Jane is an English professor at a public university. She reads Bob's "College Suicide" piece and finds it alarming. In her view, the article overlooks a lot of good things that are happening on campus. With her vocation under fire, Jane musters the courage to write her own op-ed, "College Isn't Dead Yet." Jane identifies herself as a conservative, and opens her first paragraph by emphasizing that she shares Bob's concerns about overreaching political correctness. She then provides several reasons why Bob's original piece was too pessimistic (she includes the evidence that Bob willfully ignored). Jane concludes that, on the whole, college campuses are imperfect, but better off than Bob thinks they are. When her piece is published online, Jane reads the comments section. She is dismayed to find that readers haven't paid attention to her arguments. Instead, they have questioned her *motives*. Trolls litter the feed with remarks like these: "This author is just trying to establish her liberal credentials"; "She doesn't care about the truth"; "This lady is obviously shilling for a leftist think-tank"; "What a farce—Jane is only trying to keep her paychecks coming."

Jane has written her article because she does not want a justified concern about political correctness to turn into an unjustified condemnation of the whole university system. She says that's her reason for writing and, like most of us, she expects readers to take her at her word. As far as her argument goes, it could have been written by either a liberal or a conservative. After all, both liberals and conservatives can be worried about political correctness run amok. And both liberals and conservatives can notice that a few outbursts of political correctness aren't enough to justify chucking the whole university system. But whether out of bias, blindness, or meanness, the trolls shift the attention from Jane's substantial arguments to her motives. They try to discredit her as a person while conveniently ignoring her evidence. In doing so, Jane's critics fail to follow the intellectual Silver Rule. No one wants to be treated in these ways. Instead, we want our views to be assessed on the basis of the evidence we offer for them.

If we agree that the kind of behavior the trolls display toward Jane would be bad not just in Jane's case, but in any case, we can generalize to the following guideline:

Guideline 2: Emphasize substance over motives. Do not explain away or ignore others' arguments by attributing intellectually bad motives to them. Instead, focus on the substance of the disputed views and the evidence offered on their behalf.

Motive-questioning and the embrace of double standards aren't the only practices that spoil our discourse. Another practice concerns the inferences we make from others' stated beliefs. We sometimes think that others' beliefs have unsavory implications, and on the basis of these (alleged) implications, we accuse others of believing awful things. Here's an example:

Scene 3: Mike and Ike are baristas at a downtown coffee shop. One day while on a break, the two of them begin discussing the relationship between God and morality. Mike, a theist, believes that all moral truths are grounded in God's nature: "I believe that God is the source of all goodness, including moral goodness," he says. Ike disagrees: "I think it is virtuous to help the vulnerable even if there is no God; likewise, it is wrong to commit rape and murder even if there's no God who forbids these things. And I'm not just expressing my preferences. I think moral norms are objective. They don't depend on what we humans think or how we feel." "Further," Ike continues, "I'm glad that morality doesn't depend on God—because there is no such being." Flummoxed and feeling defensive, Mike fires back: "If there is no God, all things are permitted. You've denied the existence of God, the very source of morality. So you have denied that morality is real. That's really an endorsement of rape and murder. And only a bad person would endorse such acts."

Mike's reasoning is unfair in a couple of ways. First, he says that Ike denies that morality is real even though Ike explicitly affirms this idea. Ike clearly believes in a real, objective morality. But Mike sums up Ike's view by saying that Ike denies the existence of both God and morality. Mike misrepresents Ike's view.

Second, Mike attributes to Ike a view that is—by both Mike's and Ike's lights—unpalatable. Good, sane people don't tend to endorse rape or murder. By saying that Ike believes such horrors are OK, Mike makes Ike's view out to be much less credible than it really is. To do this is to commit what logicians call the *Straw Man Fallacy*: the error of building a weak version of an opponent's view so that this view is, like a straw dummy, easy to knock down.[8]

If we agree that these practices are unfair whenever they occur, we can formulate the following guidelines:

Guideline 3a: When others explicitly deny a view, be slow to attribute this view to them.

Guideline 3b: Be slow to attribute to others views that are clearly false or implausible.

As a means to following these rules, we might add:

Guideline 3c: When possible, summarize a dissenter's views and arguments to the dissenter's satisfaction, and do this *before* raising objections.

To follow these rules is to act in line with fair-mindedness.

It's also practically wise. If we criticize only weak versions of others' views, we invite our dissenters to reply, "That's a very nice criticism. But it doesn't touch *my* view. In fact, you have not even *addressed* the view I actually hold." When we hear these words, we'll realize that our criticisms are intellectually worthless. Unfairly criticizing others' views might, for a moment, make us feel good. But it does nothing to advance the discussion. And it does a lot to ensure that others won't take us seriously in future discussions.

Here's another scene, one just as painful to observe as the others are:

Scene 4: American comedian Steve Harvey believes in God. British comedian Kate Smurthwaite does not. In separate interviews, the two of them let the world know how they feel about the opposition. When presented with the prospect of someone who does not believe in God, Harvey remarked, "Well then to me, you're an idiot." Smurthwaite was similarly straightforward: "Faith, by definition, is believing in things without evidence. And personally, I don't do that because I'm not an idiot."[9]

Textbooks on critical thinking often discuss the *ad hominem* fallacy—the strategy of trying to discredit someone's view by first questioning the person's intellectual credentials. For example: "Don't believe what Smith says about auto parts; that guy is a moron." "Jones is stupid, so you shouldn't believe a word he says." Here, the move is from a generally negative thought about a person's intelligence or intellectual character to the conclusion that the person's view is false. This is obviously a bad inference, and an unfair one. But notice: there's an equally bad kind of unfair thinking that moves in the opposite direction: from the fact that someone holds such-and-such a view to the conclusion that this person is a "moron," an "idiot," a "dope," or some other such term of abuse. That's what is going on with Harvey and Smurthwaite. Take Harvey, for instance. He endorses the following kind of thinking:

1. Kate is an atheist.

So,

2. Kate is an idiot.

This is not just a bad inference—(1) is weak support for (2)—it's an unfair one. Harvey is treating atheists in a way he would not want to be treated himself. The problem is not that Harvey believes in God, or that he thinks atheists are wrong not to believe. It's that instead of stopping at thinking that the atheist is mistaken, he goes on to explain the atheist's unbelief in terms of a lack of intelligence.

But why should we accept Harvey's explanation? Just having a false belief does not make a person unintelligent; nor does it mean that the person has a poor intellectual character. I'm sure I have a false belief lying around here or there. I bet you do, too. But you and I are not fools, or idiots, or anything of the sort. Further, we may reasonably suppose that Harvey harbors a falsehood or two somewhere in his belief structure. This does not make him a stupid person, nor would he want anyone to think it does. After all, there are many reasons why smart people form false beliefs. Sometimes, people are unaware of relevant evidence. Sometimes their evidence is misleading. Other times, people just make mistakes in assessing their evidence. But mere mistakes do not make someone unintelligent. Fallibility implies *humánness*, not foolishness. To think otherwise, to move straight from the claim

So-and-so's belief is false (by my lights),

to

So-and-so is unintelligent and/or has poor intellectual character

is to exercise a pernicious kind of unfairness. It's like watching a baseball player strike out once and assuming he's a bad hitter; or like reading a single sentence of an author's novel and concluding that she's a bad writer. Accordingly, and by contrast, we may suggest the following rule:

Guideline 4: Be slow to disparage another person's intelligence or character. Try to avoid explaining what you see as others' false or irrational beliefs in terms of a lack of intelligence or a lack of intellectual virtue.

Let's camp for a moment on guideline 4. It's easy to nod along with this rule. Following it may be another story. According to psychologists Lee Ross and Richard Nisbett, while we are disposed to explain away our own mistakes by appealing to our circumstances, we are inclined to attribute others' mistakes to their permanent traits. For example, if I trip while walking down the street, I'll try to save face by blaming the curb or my sticky shoe. But if I see *you* trip while walking down the same street, I'll think it's because you are a clumsy person. Chances are, you'll do the same to me. Psychologists call this pattern of thinking the Fundamental Attribution Error. It involves a quick-and-dirty inference from a single performance (so-and-so took a clumsy step) to a character attribution (so-and-so is a clumsy person). Of course, this is a *bad* inference. However, if psychologists like Ross and Nisbett are right, it's an inference we're prone to make. In their view, we humans so often make the error that it deserves the label "Fundamental."

(And even if Ross and Nisbett overstate the prevalence of the error, shouldn't we be on guard against it anyway?) At any rate, the application of this idea to the intellectual realm is straightforward. We may be tempted to dismiss as fools those who (by our lights) hold a single false or irrational belief. Guideline 4 reminds us that we should do better.[10]

If we follow the guidelines that have been set out above, we'll be well on our way toward treating others fair-mindedly. But we won't quite have arrived. That's because we could follow all the guidelines from the wrong motives. Consider:

> *Scene 5*: Sam is scrupulously fair in his discussions with others, even when others disagree with him. He follows all of the guidelines we have sketched. He doesn't call others' motives into question. He sticks to substantive issues. He doesn't attribute to others views that they don't hold. He considers only the strongest versions of his opponents' views. He upholds no double standards of evidence, and he always seeks the best evidence on all sides of an issue. However, Sam cares little about discovering the truth for himself, and cares even less about helping others find it. His chief goal is to treat others and their views "fairly" so that he can crush them with clever objections. He is only mildly pleased when he stumbles into the truth, or helps someone out of falsehood. By contrast, he is elated whenever he "scores points" by embarrassing his less gifted dissenters.[11]

Much of Sam's outward behavior is just what we'd expect from a fair-minded thinker. However, Sam's motives are not intellectually virtuous. He mostly cares about winning debates while making himself look good. His case underscores the point that intellectual virtue is more than a pattern of behavior. The virtuously fair thinker is motivated by a desire for truth, knowledge, and understanding. And because intellectual fairness is a virtue that centrally concerns *others'* intellectual well-being, a virtuously fair thinker will want to treat others fairly in order that they may get, keep, or share know-ledge. To sum up:

> *Guideline 5*: Foster intellectually good motives—related to your-self and others—while following guidelines 1–4.

If we stick to these guidelines as a matter of habit, we'll be on the path toward intellectual fairness.

Beyond Fairness: Intellectual Charity

Astute readers will have noticed that we have not located fair-mindedness as a virtue lying between vices of excess and de-ficiency. This is with good reason: going beyond fairness need not bespeak vice. What would it mean, for instance, to too often avoid doing intellectual harm to others? Or to go overboard in *not* attributing bad motives to our dissenters? Or to exceed what is wise in avoiding the Straw Man Fallacy—as if we should commit this fallacy some of the time, but not too frequently? In short, it is not clear that we automatically fall out of virtue by exceeding fairness. For one thing, we often compliment others when they do so: "You've been more than fair." For another, there's a virtue—intellectual charity—that lies beyond fair-mindedness, beyond the intellectual Silver Rule.

Let us therefore consider a distinctively intellectual kind of charity. As with intellectual fairness, we can start by laying down a familiar-sounding rule:

> *Intellectual Golden Rule*: In intellectual activities, do to others as you would have done to you.

If we follow this rule, we won't just avoid committing intellectual harms against others. We will go out of our way to foster others' intellectual flourishing. Instead of merely avoiding unfair intellectual practices, we'll do things like these:

- work actively to ensure that everyone has access to high-quality information and education;
- go out of our way to construct the best versions of others' views and arguments—even when these differ from our own;
- attribute as much intelligence and intellectual virtue to others as we reasonably can;
- interpret others' views as being as plausible as we reasonably can;
- go out of our way to paint others' intellectual mistakes in a positive light (e.g., construct a plausible story about how a smart, earnest person could make such a mistake); and
- when we don't have reason to believe our dissenters are smart and intellectually virtuous, actively *imagine* that they are and entertain such possibilities.

If we think and act in these ways reliably, and do so with intellectually good motives, we'll display intellectual charity not just as an isolated action, but as a character trait.

I once heard a story about intellectual charity from a friend who had just completed his PhD in philosophy. Like many students, he had chosen a world-renowned figure in the field as his dissertation advisor. However, unlike any other student I know, my friend devoted his dissertation to *attacking* his advisor's views. Now, many high-profile scholars would have bristled at such a decision. At some institutions, to question the views of an advisor might destroy one's career. In my friend's case, what happened was exactly the opposite. The advisor listened patiently through countless office meetings while my friend criticized his views. When my friend completed chapter drafts, his advisor offered generous feedback aimed at improving the arguments (and in this way making trouble for his own views). The advisor did not just respond to my friend's arguments with fairness. He did not merely assess them as they stood without stooping to sleazy debate tactics. Instead, he sought to correct mistakes in the arguments in order to make them even stronger! In so doing, the advisor was deliberately strengthening a position that countered his own. Why did he do all this? For two reasons: in order to seek the truth himself, and in order to help my friend seek it.

When I recount the story about my friend and his advisor, most hearers seem to find it inspiring. But a few worry that all this business about intellectual charity might take things too far. Moving stories about PhD advisors are one thing. And it's nice if people try to make others' views seem credible, or if they try to cast dissenters as intellectually respectable thinkers. But are there no limits to this? If we're charitable, will we end up attributing good motives to bad people? Will we attribute plausibility to clearly false and harmful ideas? For instance, will intellectual charity lead us to think that the cult leader down the street (the guy who thinks he's the Messiah) is a reasonable man? Will it require us to attribute good motives to a white supremacist? Might intellectual charity devolve into mere niceness? And won't this hinder the pursuit of truth, both for ourselves and for others?

Such questions deserve our attention. Let's start with the ones about what intellectual charity requires us to think about others and their views.

Frankly, I rarely worry that our society is vulnerable to an epidemic of blindness toward others' faults. Aren't many of us, if anything, a bit too quick to see our disagreements with others in terms of *their* liabilities, especially their character flaws? If there were such a thing as an intellectual confessional, wouldn't a lot of us need to confess sins of this sort? I certainly would. If you're like me in this respect, then perhaps practicing intellectual charity can be a part of our penance.

More to the point, it's important to see that charity only requires that we think as well of others' views, intelligence, and intellectual character as we *reasonably* can. It does not require that we think as well of others as we *possibly* can. Nothing about intellectual charity prevents an honest assessment of others' strengths and weaknesses. In fact, because charity is an intellectual virtue, it actually demands that any assessment of others' views, intelligence, and intellectual character be undertaken with an aim toward discovering the truth about these matters. So if others really do have false views, bad motives, or intellectual vices, there's nothing about intellectual charity that need blind us to this fact. (Indeed, if others do have false views or harmful vices, we should consider kindly alerting them to these. It can be profoundly uncharitable to let others languish in falsehood or vice.)

. This last point makes it clear that intellectual charity differs from mere niceness. Niceness is, if anything, a social virtue—a trait that helps us get along with others. Of course, it's important to get along with others, to do what we can to keep social relations from getting unnecessarily difficult, to avoid giving needless offense, and so on. But *niceness* is neither a moral nor an intellectual virtue. Whereas niceness might sacrifice another's intellectual flourishing out of laziness, or to avoid an awkward moment, intellectual charity won't make such a trade. A charitable thinker will want what is intellectually good for others. She will want them to enjoy the goods of knowledge and true belief, and will be willing to shake them out of harmful delusions. Charitable thinkers will see it as tragic, or at best unfortunate, if they see others clinging to inaccurate views. Accordingly, they won't avoid discussing important topics just because this is uncomfortable. Perhaps we shouldn't, either.

Toward Virtuous Thinking (and Thinkers)

Fairness and charity are the last virtues on our list. They're certainly not the least. Our public discourse is riddled with vulgarity, meanness, and willful ignorance. It is filled to the lid with trolling and name-calling and stereotyping. It is, in a word, *diseased*. And some of the discussions that take place in our own living rooms, classrooms, and coffee shops aren't much healthier. If this diagnosis is right, part of the cure lies in intellectual virtues like fair-mindedness and charity. To see what a difference these would make, revisit the scenes discussed in this chapter, or visit a website where the trolls live. Imagine if every instance of intellectual meanness were replaced with an act of intellectual fairness or charity. Then imagine how this would transform the rest of the discussion. A sudden outbreak of these virtues would make our discourse unrecognizable, and in the best way possible.

Of course, such a scenario is a pipe dream. If anything, our discourse seems to be getting worse, not better—and our technologies often make the illness more virulent. To be sure, in the days before the internet, there were nasty newspaper editorials, inflammatory talk show hosts, and mean-spirited conversations. However, in those days, people had to own their remarks, along with the social consequences thereof. Today's internet, with its anonymous posting policies, has largely removed this social safeguard. A fresh invitation to foul discourse appears with every new online forum, which means that every day spawns new opportunities for intellectual vice.

It is unrealistic to think that any individual, or small group of individuals, can stop this trend. No one is pulling the plug on the internet; nor will TV and radio pundits start behaving themselves anytime soon (that would be bad for ratings). What are we to do?

We could choose anger or despair, and both options are tempting. But here is an alternative: we can take responsibility—first for ourselves, and then for the small circles where we can make a difference. In the scenes discussed earlier, people from different political, ethical, and religious perspectives are depicted as committing acts of unfair thinking. This reflects reality. Concerning almost every disputed issue, there are fair and unfair people on both sides.

Perhaps this should be unsurprising. In reflecting on humanity's moral condition, Alexander Solzhenitsyn remarks,

> If only it were all so simple! If only there were evil people somewhere insidiously committing evil deeds, and it were necessary only to separate them from the rest of us and destroy them. But the line dividing good and evil cuts through the heart of every human being.[12]

Similarly, I suggest, the line between intellectual virtue and vice does not run between us and our dissenters. It does not divide (say) conservatives from progressives, or theists from atheists. It runs right down the middle of each of us. Once we admit this, we can take steps to ensure that our own words and thoughts exhibit fair-mindedness, charity, and other virtues. In time, we may find that our friends do the same. With wisely planned efforts, we can help our own coffee shops and classrooms and online chatrooms become places where people pursue the intellectual virtues together. This is largely up to us. No internet troll or cultural trend can keep us from doing it. In the last chapter of this book, we will consider how it might be done.

For Reflection and Discussion

1. The author draws an analogy between moral justice or fairness, on the one hand, and intellectual fairness (fair-mindedness), on the other. Explain this analogy.
2. This chapter considers several cases in which people think unfairly. Have you observed similar cases in the real world? Read some news articles or listen to talk radio with the aim of finding such cases. Then describe the cases in detail and note which guidelines for intellectual fairness are violated. (This exercise will be most effective if you seek cases in which people on your own "side" commit failures of fairness.)

3. Suppose we interpret others' views charitably—so that they don't involve any obvious error. Might we risk *twisting* the views into something others don't recognize as their own? What might be wrong with doing so?

4. Reflect on the quotation from Solzhenitsyn, as applied to intellectual virtue. Does the line between intellectual virtue and vice divide people along political or religious lines? Or does it run "right down the middle of each of us"?

Further Reading

For more on trolling, see Adrienne LaFrance, "Trolls Are Winning the Internet, Technologists Say," *The Atlantic*, March 29, 2017. See also Joel Stein, "Why We're Losing the Internet to the Culture of Hate," *Time*, August 29, 2016. Our discussion of intellectual fairness and justice has merely scratched the surface. For an important treatment of intellectual justice and injustice, see Miranda Fricker, *Epistemic Injustice: Power & the Ethics of Knowing* (Oxford: Oxford University Press, 2007). See also *The Routledge Handbook of Epistemic Injustice*, ed. Ian James Kidd, José Medina, and Gaile Pohlhaus Jr. (New York: Routledge, 2017). For a discussion of intellectual fairness and public discourse see Robert K. Garcia and Nathan L. King, "Toward Intellectually Virtuous Discourse: Two Vicious Fallacies and the Virtues that Inhibit Them," in *Intellectual Virtues and Education*, ed. Jason Baehr (New York: Routledge, 2016), 202–20. For discussions of how to improve civil discourse see Arthur Brooks, *Love Your Enemies: How Decent People Can Save America from the Culture of Contempt* (New York: Broadside, 2019); also John Inazu, *Confident Pluralism: Surviving and Thriving through Deep Difference* (Chicago: University of Chicago Press, 2016); and Justin Tosi and Brandon Warmke, *Grandstanding: The Use and Abuse of Moral Talk* (New York: Oxford University Press, 2020).

Notes

1. October 11, 2017, retrieved from https://www.theonion.com/online-activists-unsure-about-offensiveness-of-article-1819580390.

2. See Adrienne LaFrance, "Trolls Are Winning the Internet, Technologists Say," *The Atlantic*, March 29, 2017, retrieved from https://www.theatlantic.

com/technology/archive/2017/03/guys-its-time-for-some-troll-theory/
521046/. See also Joel Stein, "Why We're Losing the Internet to the Culture
of Hate," *Time*, August 29, 2016, retrieved from http://time.com/4457110/
internet-trolls/.

3. Stein, "Why We're Losing."

4. Miranda Fricker, *Epistemic Injustice: Power & the Ethics of Knowing*
(Oxford: Oxford University Press, 2007).

5. This characterization of fair-mindedness specifies what fair and just
thinkers won't *do*. They won't harm others in their capacities as knowers.
Given considerations of space, I haven't said anything about what harms
these thinkers will *allow*. I do not hereby imply that there is a major distinction to be drawn between doing harm and allowing harm. For discussion of the distinction between doing and allowing harm, see Fiona
Woollard and Frances Howard-Snyder, "Doing vs. Allowing Harm,"
Stanford Encyclopedia of Philosophy, ed. Edward N. Zalta, Winter 2016 ed.,
retrieved from https://plato.stanford.edu/entries/doing-allowing/.

6. Alice Ambrose, "Moore and Wittgenstein as Teachers," *Teaching
Philosophy* 12, no. 2 (1989), 107. I first learned of Ambrose's article in
Robert C. Roberts and W. Jay Wood, *Intellectual Virtues: An Essay in
Regulative Epistemology* (Oxford: Oxford University Press, 2007).

7. One reviewer suggested that the account of fairness developed here
may be insufficient. It allows that we could avoid double standards (and
thereby be fair) by treating our own views in an irrational way, so long
as we apply the same irrational standard to others. But that seems like a
bad result. I suggest that what this objection shows is that fairness needs
to be supplemented by other virtues (e.g., carefulness) that help ensure
that one's intellectual standards are rational in the first place. Fairness then
ensures that those standards are applied evenly to other thinkers.

8. Philosophically serious theists have argued that atheism entails that there
are no objective moral values or duties. But that kind of argument is different from what Mike argues here. Mike is saying that all atheists *believe*
there are no objective moral values or duties. But even if atheism entails
that there's no "real" morality, this doesn't mean that atheists *believe* there's
no such thing. For more on the kind of fallacy Mike commits here, see
Robert K. Garcia and Nathan L. King, "Toward Intellectually Virtuous
Discourse: Two Vicious Fallacies and the Virtues That Inhibit Them," in
Intellectual Virtues and Education, ed. Jason Baehr (New York: Routledge,
2016), 202–20. For more on the topic of God and morality, see *Is Goodness
without God Good Enough? A Debate on Faith, Secularism, and Ethics,*

ed. Robert K. Garcia and Nathan L. King (Lanham, MD: Rowman & Littlefield, 2009).

9. This example is borrowed from Garcia and King, "Toward Intellectually Virtuous Discourse," 212.

10. For discussion of the Fundamental Attribution Error see Lee Ross and Richard Nisbett, *The Person and the Situation: Perspectives of Social Psychology*, 2nd ed. (London: Pinter & Martin, 2011). For more on the Fundamental Attribution Error in relation to intellectual fairness, see Garcia and King, "Toward Intellectually Virtuous Discourse."

11. I owe the point of this case to the discussion of charity in Roberts and Wood, *Intellectual Virtues*, 74ff.

12. Alexander Solzhenitsyn, *The Gulag Archipelago Abridged: An Experiment in Literary Investigation* (New York: Harper Perennial Modern Classics, 2007), 75.

PART III
PUTTING ON VIRTUE

12

How We Grow in Intellectual Virtue

For any well-planned expedition, we need three things: a clear destination, a sense of our current location, and a plan for getting from where we are to where we want to go. Similarly, any good plan for growing in intellectual virtue involves (1) a clear understanding of intellectual virtue, (2) an accurate assessment of our current intellectual character, and (3) a plan for moving from our current state in the direction we want to go.

To this point in the book, we have focused mainly on the first part of the plan. In this final chapter, we'll consider parts 2 and 3, and examine how the three parts fit together.

Our Destination

Our ultimate goal—our destination—should be clear. We want to have excellent minds. By now, we know what that means. Excellent thinkers are curious and intellectually careful. They are autonomous. They are intellectually humble yet self-confident. They are intellectually honest, persevering, and courageous. They are open-minded, firm, fair, and charitable. They exercise this character in order to get, keep, and share knowledge. As we've seen, each intellectual virtue has its own distinctive profile. By way of review:

- *Curious* thinkers cultivate a healthy appetite for truth, knowledge, and understanding. They ask good questions and are disposed to seek good answers.

The Excellent Mind. Nathan L. King, Oxford University Press (2021). © Oxford University Press.
DOI: 10.1093/oso/9780190096250.003.0012

- *Careful* thinkers make serious efforts to avoid falsehood and irrationality. As a means to this, they seek to base their beliefs on good evidence. They attend to the proper rules for assessing evidence.
- *Autonomous* thinkers think independently. They do not overly rely on others; they strike out boldly in new directions. They take responsibility for their intellectual projects.
- *Humble* thinkers are aware of their intellectual limitations, and own these by trying to correct them, correct *for* them, or accept them.
- *Self-confident* thinkers are aware of their intellectual strengths, and own these by exercising and building on them.
- *Honest* thinkers tell the truth, or at least the truth as they see it. They avoid lying, bluffing, bullshitting, and other distortions.
- *Perseverant* thinkers overcome obstacles to their getting, keeping, or sharing knowledge. They do not give up easily. They persist in their intellectual projects.
- *Courageous* thinkers persist despite threats that get in the way of their intellectual projects. They continue in these pursuits even when this is dangerous or painful.
- *Open-minded* thinkers transcend their own perspectives by taking the merits of other views seriously.
- *Firm* thinkers maintain their own perspectives. They hold onto their well-supported beliefs unless given good reasons for revising them.
- *Fair-minded thinkers* assess competing views even-handedly, and avoid giving extra weight to their own opinions. They don't deliberately misrepresent others' views in order to make these views seem weak. They don't easily attribute bad motives or a lack of intelligence or character to others.
- *Charitable* thinkers go beyond fairness. They go out of their way to help others formulate the best versions of their views and arguments. They think as well of others' intelligence and intellectual character as they reasonably can.

A central theme of this book is that intellectual virtues can't be reduced to intellectual behaviors. They aren't just *actions*. They're not even just *intellectual* actions. In addition, intellectually virtuous thinkers have certain *beliefs* and *motivations* when it comes to truth and knowledge. They believe things like this:

- Truth, knowledge, and understanding are valuable.
- Truth, knowledge, and understanding are valuable independent of their tendency to "get us goodies" like wealth, credentials, good grades, or prestige.
- It is bad for a person to hold false beliefs or be ignorant about important topics.
- The pursuit of knowledge is an important part of a good life.

As for motivations, excellent thinkers desire truth and knowledge. They want to avoid falsehood and ignorance. They crave deep understanding. They feel excited when they make a discovery. They are disappointed when they learn that they have reasoned incorrectly. When they find out they have a false belief, they feel a need to correct it.

Finally, virtuous thinkers don't display these patterns of action, thought, and motivation in an inconsistent or haphazard way. Rather, in such thinkers, these patterns are stable and consistent. They appear across time and across situations. Most of the time, in appropriate circumstances, we can count on virtuous thinkers to display their excellence.

All of this goes a long way toward describing what it means to be intellectually virtuous—that is, toward identifying our destination. Another way to pinpoint that goal would be to retell the stories of the intellectual exemplars we've studied in this book—people like Aristotle, Isaac Newton, Albert Einstein, the monks at Skellig Michael, Mary Putnam Jacobi, Jöns Jacob Berzelius, Elizabeth Cady Stanton, Susan B. Anthony, Sojourner Truth, Nicolaus Copernicus, Johannes Kepler, Galileo Galilei, Will Rahn,

Michael Inzlicht, Gottlob Frege, Helen Taussig, Helen Keller, Guy Montag, J. K. Rowling, Ruby Bridges, Winston Smith, Alfred Blalock, Barry Corey, Evan Low, G. E. Moore, and others. When it comes to indicating how it looks for a person to display intellectual virtue, we do well to point at these people and say, "It looks like *that*." Narratives about these people add depth and richness to our conceptual understanding of intellectual virtue. By doing this, they help us to home in on our desired destination.

One more point about our destination: we should speak of it in the plural. As we set out toward the peak of intellectual virtue, we should note the many worthwhile stopping points along the ascent. Our ideal destination—complete maturity of intellectual character—is hard to reach. Depending on where we begin, the realm of full intellectual virtue may be extremely remote. In light of this, we should be mindful of any significant progress markers we encounter along the way. We should pause and be glad when we catch ourselves courageously defending a view when we would previously have backed down. Or when we notice that we are asking more good questions than we used to. Or when we find ourselves listening carefully to a dissenter we formerly ignored. If we experience things like this, we will have undergone *meaningful growth* in intellectual virtue—a worthwhile accomplishment in itself.[1]

Our Current Location

Imagine being lost in the woods. Even if you can locate your precise destination on a map, the map won't help unless you can also find your current location. You won't know what your next step should be, because you won't know the direction it should take. Likewise, even if we have a fully specified ideal "destination" for our intellectual character, this won't help much unless we have some idea of where we stand with respect to it. Unless we know our current location, we can't sensibly plan a route from where we are to where we want to go.

Here's a sensible if rough proposal for finding ourselves on the "map" of intellectual character: the great majority of us are probably located somewhere between intellectual virtue and vice. Now, the best way to show this would be to develop empirically rigorous measures of the various intellectual virtues and vices, and to test ourselves on those measures. Short of this, we might simply ask ourselves: how similar are we, in our intellectual character, to exemplars like Isaac Newton, or the suffragists, or the monks at Skellig Michael? And how similar are we to exemplars of intellectual vice—like Donald Trump, or arrogant leftist reporters, or internet trolls? For most of us, the correct answer is probably "not very." And if we answer that way, we thereby agree that our intellectual character is neither fully virtuous nor fully vicious. Perhaps instead we stand somewhere between virtue and vice.

A common way of discussing intellectual virtue and vice—one we have often followed in this book—obscures this possibility. For the sake of simplicity, we have often presented intellectual virtues as lying between vices and have depicted their relationship as in table 12.1.

This sort of chart is a helpful tool for showing that many virtues lie between extremes. But taken too seriously, it could mislead us into thinking that everyone falls into a tidy category like *arrogant thinker*, *humble thinker*, or *self-deprecating* thinker.

Table 12.1 is, as it were, a high-altitude image. If we fly a bit lower, we'll find that there is a lot of space between virtues and their

Table 12.1 Humility as a Mean between Extremes

Sphere of activity	Vice (deficiency)	Virtue (mean)	Vice (excess)
Assessing our weaknesses	Arrogance	Humility	Self-deprecation

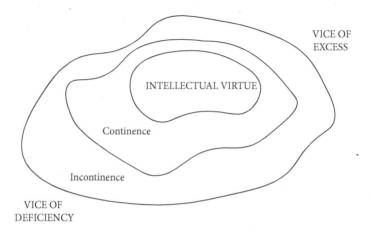

Figure 12.1 A Map of Intellectual Character Traits

corresponding vices, and that the space between categories is not always clear-cut. A better map would provide more detail. Between the valleys of vice and the peaks of virtue, there is vast territory— territory that represents neither virtue nor vice, but other traits, including what philosophers call *continence* and *incontinence*.[2] A more precise survey of the territory surrounding intellectual virtue might look like a topographical map, with the vices lying in the valleys, virtue lying at the summit, and other traits lying in between (figure 12.1).[3]

An intellectually incontinent person understands what is intellectually good. He desires and values truth, knowledge, and understanding. These desires and values would normally produce a tendency to act with intellectual virtue. However, the incontinent person also has contrary desires—desires that compete with his desires for truth and knowledge—and regularly acts on these. For example:

> *Incontinent Ian* is a college student who just finished taking a seminar on intellectual virtues. The class gave him a good grasp of what intellectual virtues are, and inspired him to seek more

knowledge about several topics, including politics, geography, and brain science. He genuinely wants to learn more about these things. He's not intellectually indifferent, though he doesn't care as much about learning as the virtuous person does. Ian *loves* video games, and wants to play them even more than he wants knowledge. As a result, he spends most of his free time playing his Xbox, and hardly any of it reading, or even watching educational films. He feels conflicted about these decisions.

An *intellectually continent* person is in many ways like an incontinent one. She has a good understanding of what is intellectually good. She values and desires truth and knowledge. Like the incontinent person, the continent person also has desires that compete with the desires for truth and knowledge. But whereas the incontinent person gives in to such contrary desires, the continent person fends them off. She acts as the virtuous person would act, even though she is not yet fully virtuous. Consider:

Continent Cathy is a classmate of Ian's. She took the same seminar on intellectual virtues, and as a result, she understands what the virtues are. Like Ian, she is motivated to learn more about the world around her. Indeed, her interests overlap with his—she wants to learn more about politics, geography, and brain science. She also shares Ian's love of video games. She wants to play her Xbox during her free time. But whereas Ian gives in to this desire, Cathy resists it. She unplugs her console, pours a cup of coffee, and starts reading. When she's too tired to read, she turns on her TV and selects a documentary from CuriosityStream. On some days, when her learning is done, Cathy indulges in some gaming, but this is a minor part of her routine.

Do you see the difference between Ian and Cathy? Both of them understand and desire what is intellectually good for them, and both struggle to act well. But in Cathy, the desire for knowledge wins out. In this way, Cathy is closer to virtue than Ian is. But both Ian and Cathy contrast with an intellectually virtuous person, whose intellect and will are unified. Such a person does not have strong desires that pull against the desires for truth and knowledge. Ian and Cathy also differ from the intellectually vicious person, who not only has intellectually inappropriate desires, but also lacks a correct view of what is intellectually good (e.g., he thinks that knowledge is not as valuable as wealth or pleasure).

If we know that we stand somewhere between virtue and vice, some further surveying might help us further pinpoint our location. Do we have a correct view of what is intellectually good? Do we value and desire truth and knowledge? If so, do these desires regularly have to compete with strong desires that run contrary to the pursuit of truth and knowledge? How good are we at fending off those contrary desires? And are we doing what we can to weaken them? Honest self-reflection on such questions can alert us to the direction in which progress lies.

Paths toward Progress

We now have both an idea of our general destination and a sense of how to find our current location. What should we do next? There's no single, fully specified, correct answer to this question. But if we're trying to climb a mountain, it is best at least to follow trails that we know lead upward. Fortunately, there are a number of well-trodden paths that lead up toward intellectual virtue. At one time or another, we'll need to travel each of them.

Seeking Direct Instruction

One important path toward growth in intellectual virtue is to gain direct instruction—to learn more about the nature of intellectual character—virtue, vice, and otherwise. Instruction *about* the intellectual virtues can give us a kind of vocabulary or conceptual framework that will inform our quest. For if we want to pursue the intellectual virtues intentionally, the notion of such virtues must be part of our mental toolbox. As Ludwig Wittgenstein said, "The limits of my language mean the limits of my world."[4] We can apply Wittgenstein's remark as follows: if we understand what intellectual virtues and vices *are*, we will be well positioned to recognize them when we see them. And this can be a great help as we pursue them, because it clarifies our goal. Such clarification has been the focus of chapters 1–11 of this book. So, if you've made it this far, you've already taken an important step toward intellectual virtue!

Managing Our Motives

Imagine a professor world renowned for his philosophical work on the virtue of love. In the course of his research, he learns as much about love as anyone ever has. His writings earn rave reviews. His lectures enlighten and inspire all who attend. However, by all accounts, this professor is a first-class jerk, famous for berating students and colleagues whose acumen fall short of his. He studies love, but does not practice it. The point: knowledge about virtue is not enough, by itself, to make us virtuous. This does not make knowledge unimportant. But it should lead us to ask *what else*, in addition to knowledge, is needed to cultivate virtue.

Part of the correct answer is that we need to foster good motives: if we want to become intellectually virtuous, we must cultivate a desire for and delight in truth, knowledge, and understanding.

To do this, we can start by thinking about the practical benefits of having true beliefs instead of false ones, knowledge rather than ignorance, or a deep understanding of a subject instead of a cursory one. Consider a few scenarios. Imagine trying to get through a day without knowing your email password, your schedule, or directions from your home to your school or workplace. If this sounds hard, then you must agree that knowledge is valuable. Alternatively, imagine being lost in the woods without knowing the way to safety. In those circumstances, how much would you pay for such knowledge? Or picture your boss asking how to understand a company expense report. Knowing the answer might just make the difference between your getting promoted and your getting fired. Or imagine packing your bags for a vacation to somewhere you have always wanted to go. How might knowledge (or ignorance) of local culture and history impact your trip? Finally, imagine a world just like ours, minus the knowledge bequeathed to us by modern science. It's a world with no rapid travel, no computers, no antibiotics, and only rudimentary anesthetics. It's a world where surgery is likely to kill you, and where a visit to the dentist is excruciating. Would you want to live in such a world? If you wouldn't, you thereby grasp the practical value of knowledge—and this should help you desire knowledge in greater measure.[5]

Reflection of this sort can be helpful. It can remind us that knowledge isn't merely academic. As Francis Bacon is said to have put it, "Knowledge is power." But in fostering our desire for knowledge, we shouldn't stop here. To do so would leave our desire for knowledge truncated. Among the downsides of the world just imagined (the one without modern science) is that we would understand that world so poorly. We'd know much less than we do about planets and plankton, molecules and mollusks, quarks and quasars, and all the rest. This would be bad in itself. A view of knowledge as purely practical can't do justice to this insight. (Perhaps paradoxically, too much reflection on the practical benefits of learning can actually *reduce* our desire for knowledge. Some studies suggest that extrinsic motivators—gold stars, best student awards, money, and so on—actually undermine our desire to learn.)[6]

To see another way to foster our desire for knowledge, recall a point from our discussion of curiosity (chapter 3): we *naturally* desire knowledge. Just because we are human, we want to know more about the world around us. We have, as the philosophers put it, a desire for knowledge as an *intrinsic* good. And because that desire is already within us, we don't have to conjure up anything new in order to get it. We already have an intellectual appetite. We just need to feed and refine it.

We might start by making a habit of asking questions that reveal our ignorance. Normally, these questions should concern topics we already care about, and want to probe further. Just as walking past a bakery can remind us that we are hungry, asking such questions can awaken our appetite for knowledge. (While we're talking about this, why not jot down two or three questions of your own, just to get the cognitive cookies baking?)

Of course, if we stop at asking questions, we don't actually feed our desire for knowledge. To do that, we must seek answers. If we get in the habit of pursuing knowledge, of trying to get our questions answered, we'll find that at least some of these efforts are rewarded. Sometimes, we'll discover the truth we were initially seeking. Other times, we may miss the answer we're seeking, but gain some unexpected knowledge in the process. Either way, the satisfaction of gaining knowledge can lead us to want more of it. (As a follow-up to the exercise suggested in the last paragraph, consider seeking a book or article that addresses one of your questions. This should serve up an intellectual appetizer.)

Finding Friends and Mentors

The virtuous search for knowledge is not a solitary one. As we saw in chapter 5 (on autonomy) even the most independent inquirers, if they are virtuous, rely on others. Something similar applies to our quest for the intellectual virtues themselves. If we want to scale the mountain, we need help. We need friends who can prod and encourage us to continue in our ascent. And we need guides—people who have reached the mountain's peak and know how to lead us toward it. It's unwise to climb alone.

This kind of point holds in other areas. Any fitness coach will tell you that if you want to stick with a workout regimen, you should get a friend to come along. Likewise if you want to eat less sugar or quit smoking. Having friends with similar goals improves our odds of success. There are at least two reasons for this. First, friends provide *accountability*. If we fail to "stick with it"—whatever "it" is—we let our friends down. Knowing this tends to keep us going. It tends to push us farther and faster than we could push ourselves. Second, friends provide *feedback*. A friend provides another set of eyes, another way of determining whether we are continuing on course. If we are, friendly feedback can encourage us to keep going. If we're not, it can help us to turn back toward our destination.

Despite its benefits, however, friendly accountability may not ensure that we reach our goals. Imagine two friends starting a novice fitness program. They decide to lift weights, jog, and stretch regularly. These friends will probably make more progress together than they would alone. The trouble is, because they are novices, they may not know what they're doing. Left on their own, they might lift weights that are heavier (or lighter) than is good for them. They might run too slowly, or too quickly, too seldom, or too often. They might pull a muscle on the yoga mat. Working together might raise their chances of success. But it might also raise their odds of injury. In order to ensure that their regimen is appropriate, they should consult a trained coach.

Similarly, when it comes to our pursuit of intellectual virtue, we ought to consider intellectual *mentors* and the role they play in character development. These are people who have the kind of intellectual character we would like to have. They are exemplars of intellectual virtue. As such, they can help us develop our intellectual character.

This point is both important and tricky, so let's consider it in more detail.

Because our exemplars are the kinds of people we want to *be*, it's tempting to think that the best way to become like them is simply to *do* what they do. Thus, we might seek to follow this precept:

Precept A: If you want to become intellectually virtuous, do what intellectually virtuous people do.

At first blush, this seems like good advice. After all, it is hard to see how we could become intellectually virtuous except by doing what virtuous people do. Surely there's something right about this. However, further reflection shows that precept A is incomplete— and potentially harmful. First, it does not specify *how* we should imitate intellectually virtuous people. Second, it is not sensitive to the differences in abilities, vocation, and circumstances that separate intellectual exemplars from "the rest of us."

To see why all this matters, imagine that we want to summit not the mountain of intellectual virtue, but an *actual* mountain. Indeed, suppose we want to become expert mountain climbers. To pursue this goal, it will help to find a paragon of climbing excellence. We can do no better than Alex Honold, the first person to ascend Yosemite's El Capitan without ropes.[7] "El Cap," as climbers call it, is a sheer vertical rock face higher than the world's tallest building—a towering 3,000 feet from base to summit. Only elite climbers attempt El Cap. For most, ascending the peak with safety ropes would be a career-defining moment. So when Honold ascended it ropeless, expert climber Tommy Caldwell labeled the effort "a generation defining climb."[8] Now, if we want to become good climbers, we should somehow emulate Honold. But we could do this in different ways. We could buy all the same climbing gear he uses, or listen to the music he likes, or grow a light mustache. Or we could decide to spend much of our time climbing, improving our hand strength, and working on problem-solving skills. Clearly, the latter group of habits is more likely than the first to help us become good climbers. Likewise, when it comes to intellectual virtue, we could undertake to emulate our mentors in all kinds of ways, some of them quite silly. We could try to be like Newton by wearing a wig, like Susan B. Anthony by riding in horse-drawn carriages, or like the Skellig monks by living in a remote location. Though some of these methods might be amusing or interesting, they would not make us like our mentors in the right ways. For that, we need advice that looks more like this:

> *Precept B*: If you want to become intellectually virtuous, do what intellectually virtuous people do *in their pursuit of truth, knowledge,* and *understanding.*

Precept B is better than A because it specifies the ways in which we'd like to resemble our mentors.

But it's still not quite right. Suppose we tried to emulate Honold by following advice that parallels precept B. In that case, we would end up following advice that says: if you want to become like Honold, try to ascend El Capitan without ropes. But if we followed such advice, we would not end up atop El Cap. Nor would we become expert climbers like Honold. We would become dead. Almost all of us are incapable of accomplishing Honold's feats. We lack the necessary experience, skill, fitness, and so on. For most of us, no amount of training will suffice to overcome these limitations. If we want advice for exemplar emulation that is helpful, then that advice must be specified to *us*—to our life circumstances, our abilities, our vocations, and so on. Such advice will likely tell us to become a bit *more* like Honold in our training and planning habits. But it will tell us to do these things in ways that befit our current constraints.

Similarly, if we want to become intellectually courageous, we would be unwise to start by staring down violent crowds like Susan B. Anthony did, or by piloting dangerous rocket sleds like John Paul Stapp did. If we want to become intellectually autonomous, we shouldn't start by trying to overturn all of astronomy like

Copernicus and Kepler did. If we attempted such feats, we would fail. And even if we succeeded, the activities might not make sense in light of the rest of our lives. Thus, a more reliable guideline for following our exemplars in the pursuit of intellectual virtue is this:

> *Precept C*: If you want to become intellectually virtuous, do what intellectually virtuous people do in their pursuit of truth, knowledge, and understanding, *and do so in ways that befit your current training, abilities, circumstances, and vocation.*

In short, do what the intellectually virtuous person would do *if that person were you.* Precept C is much better than its predecessors. It allows us to learn from our mentors without carrying the burden of unwise or unrealistic expectations. It thereby provides guidance that should aid our quest for intellectual virtue.[9]

Practicing the Virtues

We have just specified the kind of exemplar emulation that should foster growth in intellectual virtue. Crucially, all such emulation involves practice. Growing in virtue is a lot like learning a skill. Suppose you want to become a better golfer, painter, or pianist. If you want to improve at these activities, you must practice. You need to visit the driving range to work on your swing, or spend several afternoons sketching flowers, or playing scales. If you practice intelligently, you're bound to get better. Granted, you might never make the PGA Tour, or the ArtPrize show, or play at Carnegie Hall. But you'll improve. You'll shoot lower scores, or paint something you're proud of, or play a piece of music that seemed out of reach just weeks before. That will be satisfying in its own right. There is nothing mysterious about any of this. If we want to get better at something, we must do it—for we learn by doing. As Aristotle says in connection with the moral virtues,

The virtues we do acquire by first exercising them, just as happens in the arts. Anything that we have to learn to do we learn by the actual doing of it: people become builders by building and instrumentalists by playing instruments. Similarly we become just by performing just acts, temperate by performing temperate acts, brave by performing brave ones.[10]

For our purposes, the take-home point is this: if we want to grow in intellectual virtue, we should start doing intellectually virtuous acts. The possibilities are endless, but here are some examples:

- To foster curiosity, we might pick a topic about which we're curious, then formulate a question and seek an answer.
- To grow in intellectual perseverance, we might select a task that's moderately daunting (say, writing an op-ed for the local paper, or reviewing our knowledge of geometry) and see that task through to completion.
- To become more intellectually careful, we might identify one logical fallacy to which humans are prone—say, the *ad hominem* fallacy—and watch ourselves closely for a week to see if we commit it.
- To develop open-mindedness, we might read an article written from a perspective with which we disagree, and commit to taking its merits seriously.

This sort of practice in the intellectual virtues helps us to become more virtuous than we currently are. And meaningful growth in this area is something to celebrate. As we've seen throughout this book, the benefits of just one act of intellectual virtue can be immense; and the ill effects of just one failure of virtue can be devastating. In light of this, the wise choice is clear: in the company of supportive others, we must follow our mentors by practicing the intellectual virtues. This well-trodden path leads upward toward the peak. And even if we never make the summit, we'll be able to see more clearly for being higher up. We'll find ourselves a step closer to achieving the goal that this book is all about: having an excellent mind.

For Reflection and Discussion

1. What three elements are essential to any good plan for growing in intellectual virtue?
2. Explain how intellectual continence and incontinence differ from both intellectual virtue and intellectual vice. How might these categories inform our understanding of our own intellectual character?
3. The author describes several "paths" of progress toward intellectual virtue. Explain each of these.
4. Consider taking some time to plan your own growth in intellectual virtue. Identify a virtue toward which you would like to progress. Then, using the tools provided in this chapter, chart a path toward growth in this virtue.
5. Explore the idea that there are traits of intellectual character that lie between virtue and vice, but that are neither continence nor incontinence? Might there be traits that don't have names? What would these be like?
6. Select your own exemplar of intellectual virtue, either from this book or from your own knowledge or experience. What would it look like for you, given your current abilities, vocation, and character, to emulate this person?

Further Reading

The framework discussing the territory between virtue and vice in this chapter is a very simple one. For a more sophisticated picture see Christian B. Miller, "Categorizing Character: Moving beyond the Aristotelian Framework," in *Varieties of Virtue Ethics*, ed. David Carr (New York: Palgrave-Macmillan,

2017), 143–62. (Miller's paper focuses on moral virtues, but its insights may carry over to a discussion of intellectual virtues.) See Heather Battaly, *Virtue* (Malden, MA: Polity, 2015), chapter 4 for a helpful introduction to vices and other failures of virtue. Interventions designed to foster growth in intellectual character are still in early stages of development, and await further conceptual and empirical research. Even so, there is much to be gained from the following works: Ron Ritchhart, *Intellectual Character: What It Is, Why It Matters, and How to Get It* (San Francisco: Jossey-Bass, 2002); *Intellectual Virtues and Education: Essays in Applied Virtue Epistemology*, ed. Jason Baehr (New York: Routledge, 2016); Jason Baehr, *Cultivating Good Minds*, chapters 20–34 (available at https://intellectualvirtues.org/cultivating-good-minds/); and Alan Wilson and Christian B. Miller, "Virtue Epistemology and Developing Intellectual Virtue," in *The Routledge Handbook of Virtue Epistemology*, ed. Heather Battaly (New York: Routledge, 2019), 483–95.

Notes

1. In identifying meaningful growth as a central goal, I follow Jason Baehr, "Is Intellectual Character Growth a Realistic Educational Aim?," *Journal of Moral Education* 45, no. 2 (2016), 117–31.

2. For a helpful introduction to the territory between virtue and vice, see Heather Battaly, *Virtue* (Malden, MA: Polity, 2015), chapter 4.

3. Thanks to Josh Orozco for suggesting to me the picture of virtue as a mountain peak, with the corresponding valleys representing vices.

4. Ludwig Wittgenstein, *Tractatus Logico-Philosophicus*, trans. D. F. Pears and B. F. McGuinness (London: Routledge, 1974), 68 (5.6).

5. For more on the practical value of knowledge, see Philip Dow, *Virtuous Minds: Intellectual Character Development* (Downers Grove, IL: InterVarsity Press, 2013), chapter 8. Dow's volume is aimed at the religious reader, but all can profit from it.

6. For discussion see Edward L. Deci, Richard Koestner, and Richard M. Ryan, "Extrinsic Rewards and Intrinsic Motivation in Education: Reconsidered Once Again," *Review of Educational Research* 71, no. 1 (Spring 2001), 1–27.

7. Joseph Serna, "Meet the First Person Ever to Climb Yosemite's El Capitan without Ropes," *Los Angeles Times*, June 5, 2017, retrieved from http://www.latimes.com/local/lanow/la-me-ln-el-capitan-free-solo-alex-honnold-20170605-htmlstory.html.

8. Serna, "Meet the First Person."

9. In constructing the main argument of this section, I benefited from conversation with Steve Porter, and from Daniel Russell's paper "Putting Ideals in Their Place," in *The Oxford Handbook of Virtue*, ed. Nancy Snow (New York: Oxford University Press, 2018), 432–52.

10. Aristotle, *Nicomachean Ethics*, trans. J. A. K. Thomson (New York: Penguin, 1976), 91–92 (Book II, section i).

Acknowledgments

This book was a team effort. As Goethe remarks, "Every one of my writings has been furnished to me by a thousand different persons." And while I alone am responsible for any defects that remain, I am happy to have a long list of people to thank.

For insight, inspiration, correction, and encouragement, I'm grateful to Susan Arellano, Alex Arnold, Robert Audi, Mike Austin, Bryce Bagley, Forrest Baird, Heather Battaly, Keith Beebe, Patricia Blanchette, David Brooks, Ryan Byerly, Tony Clark, Anne Colby, Andy Crouch, Terence Cuneo, Marian David, Mike DePaul, Garry DeWeese, Sam Director, Phil Dow, Philip Eaton, Jim and Janie Edwards, Brent Edstrom, Charles Epton, Doug Geivett, Phil Goggans, Dale Hammond, Kathy Helmers, Robin Henager, Gordon Jackson, Alan Jacob, Eranda Jayawickreme, Larry and Carol Johnson, Tom Kelly, Jonathan Kim, Rebecca Korf, Will Kynes, Emily and Aaron Lane, Charles Lassiter, Steve Layman, Josh and Keely Leim, Jann Leppien, J. P. Moreland, Tom Morris, Mike Murray, Leonard Oakland, Ken Pecka, Adam Pelser, Tim Pickavance, Al Plantinga, Steve Porter, Scott Rae, Tyler Rich, Ron Ritchhart, Robert Roberts, Scott Roseberry, Kamesh Sankaran, Meredith Shimizu, Jerry Sittser, Nancy Snow, Jeff Speaks, Sarah Streyder, Matt Stichter, Kathy Storm, Leopold Stubenberg, Diana Trotter, Fritz Warfield, Ross Watts, T. J. Westre, Jay Wood, and Linda Zagzebski. Patty Bruininks and Melissa Rogers helped me with several issues related to empirical psychology. Kathy Lee directed me to helpful sources on the suffrage movement. Rob Fifield kindly taught me the basic elements of Adobe Illustrator, which enabled me to draw the figures that appear in the book. Leonard Mlodinow and Martha Gady provided invaluable advice about the material on the base rate fallacy in chapter 4. Dan Russell guided me toward the archer image for explaining the nature of the virtues. I borrow the title for Part III from Jennifer Herdt's book *Putting on Virtue.*

For extensive comments on earlier drafts, I am grateful to Nathan Ballantyne, Aaron Cobb, Robert Garcia, Larry Johnson, Christian Miller, and Josh Orozco. Kristie King, Adam Neder, Anne Wilcox, and Keith Wyma provided generous comments on the whole manuscript. Jason Baehr, Daniel Howard-Snyder, Brennan Neal, and Walker Page were kind enough to test-drive the manuscript in their classes, and to provide countless helpful suggestions. Jason Baehr assigned the manuscript multiple times, and was a crucial source of insight and encouragement from start to finish. His help made this book much better than it would have been otherwise. Daniel Howard-Snyder drove across Washington State to discuss the manuscript, line by line, over two full days. For his generous feedback, I owe him a debt of gratitude—and a lot of gas money.

Thanks to Scott McQuilkin and President Beck Taylor of Whitworth University for their support of this project, and to Lynn Noland, Carol Simon, Dale Soden, and Noelle Wiersma for helping me secure the research leave needed to write the book. Thanks also to Christian Miller, Angela Knobel, William Fleeson, and Michael Furr. Their organization of the Character Project and the Beacon Project (both through Wake Forest University) provided research funding and fostered professional conversations that vastly improved my thinking about the intellectual virtues. Both of these projects were generously funded by the John Templeton Foundation. The views expressed in this book are not necessarily endorsed by that foundation.

Peter Ohlin, my editor at Oxford University Press, provided a wealth of wisdom and encouragement. Thanks, Peter, for believing in this project. My project managers, Emily Bang and Aishwarya Krishnamoorthy, sure-handedly carried this book through its production phase. Thanks also to Walter Sinnott-Armstrong, who read an early proposal for the book that helped shape its subsequent development. Two anonymous referees for OUP saved me from several mistakes and encouraged many additional improvements. Amanda Clark kindly and expertly prepared the index.

This project began as a joint effort with my dear friend Robert Garcia. Various shifts in research interests and scheduling led to our decision for me to write the book on my own. Despite this, I would be remiss if I failed to mention that conversations with Robert had an incalculable impact on this book. Thanks, Robert, for letting me tackle this project. No doubt it would have been better as a joint effort.

Anyone who has helped with this project and whose name is not mentioned above is hereby entitled to my sincere apology, and a beverage of choice, on me.

Thanks to my parents, Jim and Dede King, for teaching me the importance of character, and for modeling the virtues discussed in this book. (And thanks, Dad, for painting the cover art!) Thanks to my daughters, Lily and Adele King, for their patience, encouragement, and writing advice. I've tried repeatedly to find words that do justice to the emotional and intellectual support my wife, Kristie King, has provided as I've worked on this project. Alas, there are no such words.

Index

For the benefit of digital users, indexed terms that span two pages (e.g., 52–53) may, on occasion, appear on only one of those pages.

Tables and figures are indicated by *t* and *f* following the page number